Redefining Success in America

Redefining Success
in America

A NEW THEORY OF HAPPINESS
AND HUMAN DEVELOPMENT

Michael B. Kaufman

Dear Deb —
I am so excited
to share this with
you. You were there at
the beginning.
With warmest wishes
Mike

The University of Chicago Press
CHICAGO AND LONDON

The University of Chicago Press, Chicago 60637

The University of Chicago Press, Ltd., London

© 2018 by Michael B. Kaufman

Published 2018

Printed in the United States of America

27 26 25 24 23 22 21 20 19 18   1 2 3 4 5

ISBN-13: 978-0-226-55001-5 (cloth)

ISBN-13: 978-0-226-55015-2 (paper)

ISBN-13: 978-0-226-55029-9 (e-book)

DOI: https://doi.org/10.7208/chicago/9780226550299.001.0001

Library of Congress Cataloging-in-Publication Data

Names: Kaufman, Michael B., 1964– author.

Title: Redefining success in America : a new theory of happiness and human development / Michael B. Kaufman.

Description: Chicago : The University of Chicago Press, 2018. | Includes bibliographical references and index.

Identifiers: LCCN 2017035754 | ISBN 9780226550015 (cloth : alk. paper) | ISBN 9780226550152 (pbk : alk. paper) | ISBN 9780226550299 (e-book)

Subjects: LCSH: Success—United States—Longitudinal studies. | Well-being—United States—Longitudinal studies. | Harvard University—Alumni and alumnae—Longitudinal studies.

Classification: LCC BF637.S8 K3787 2018 | DDC 158—dc23

LC record available at https://lccn.loc.gov/2017035754

♾ This paper meets the requirements of ANSI/NISO Z39.48-1992 (Permanence of Paper).

In Memory of Bert Cohler (1938–2012), Beloved Mentor and Friend

CONTENTS

It was July 2000 when I first encountered the people whose lives would change mine. I sat in the secure reading room at the Henry A. Murray Research Center at Harvard, one of the leading archives in the country for longitudinal research in the field of human development. It houses seminal studies conducted in the twentieth and twenty-first centuries that have shaped our basic knowledge about how people behave, think, and feel as they traverse the course of life. I was on an exploratory visit looking for a baseline data set that I might use in a follow-up study of how the most successful members of our society experience their lives, particularly their well-being. I wanted to know whether going to the best schools and having the most recognized and remunerated careers delivered the prize widely believed in America to result, namely, a good life. I needed longitudinal perspective to know whether competitive success results in a core feature of its promise: a significantly changed emotional experience.

A dumbwaiter raised from the temperature-controlled basement three archival boxes of folders labeled "King and McArthur" (McArthur & King, 1992). I opened the lid to one of the boxes and pulled out a file stamped with a four-digit participant ID. Fingering its pages with care, I was carried back to the early 1960s and the life of William Young as a freshman at Harvard College.

Young came from a rural part of the country, his family was poor, his father was a tradesman, and William had graduated near the top of his high school class. Making it to Harvard was not merely an achievement; it also served as an escape from his father's explosive tantrums, suggestive of mental illness, and his family's stifling Christian rigidity. A gifted artist and an accomplished intellectual, Young seemed determined to make his mark in the world as an artist, though he also betrayed deep concern about the prospect of failure. As I skimmed, Young struck me as a Horatio Alger story in the making with a complex psychology. William Young's file, by the time of his graduation, was several inches thick and contained 493 pages of verbatim transcription of 20 in-person interviews and test sessions from the time he was seventeen until he was twenty-one. Young was in his late fifties as I was skimming his file.

It took me only a few moments to realize that Young's file and the files of forty-eight other Harvard undergraduates much like it—packed with manually typed, crisp pages full of correction marks and faded-ribbon ink—constituted rare gems, only a few of their kind likely to exist anywhere in the world. Here before me was a record of a living man's psychological past, more extensive and revealing than any I had encountered in the field of human development. Young and his classmates who had been exhaustively studied as undergraduates were now approaching sixty years old, their retirements, and the transition out of the middle adult period of life. As this central period of their adult lives was coming to a close, I wondered how things looked on the other side. The jury on their lives as successful competitors in the US world of education and careers would now largely be in. Did they still have the same goals? Had they changed as people? How did they feel about the way things had turned out?

I wondered: Had William Young realized his ambitions as an artist? Was his father still living and had their relationship changed? Did he have a family? Curiosity overtook me. I wanted to meet him.

And so it was that the fifteen-year investigation reported in this book was launched. I tracked down William Young, flew to his city, and spent more than ten hours with him during four interviews discussing his life. Forty other participants also granted me in-person interviews of similar depth and intensity. In all, I traveled to twenty-five cities in the United States to meet these men and find out how their lives had turned out. Along the way, I would serendipitously gain access to—and follow up—207 participants in a larger paper-and-pencil study from which Young and his classmates had been selected for intensive interviewing. This effort would result in a longitudinal study of human development spanning almost half a century.

I don't think it would have deterred me at the time to know the vast time, devotion, and resources required to complete the undertaking. I was propelled by central questions that had arisen in my own life, which cut to the heart of fundamental American beliefs. I was in my thirties and was unclear why I was pursuing the competitive strivings at the heart of my career. I had gone from Amherst College to investment banking to high-tech start-ups and had also earned an MBA at Harvard. I made the decision to change course, first training as a clinician and then entering the academy, in pursuit of answers. The men whose lives I encountered at the Murray Center resonated with me and at the same time stood for something much larger. A generation older, many seemed propelled by strivings similar to those driving my own educational and professional trajectory. Graduates of an elite university and members of an elite professional class, these men were icons of an American ideal. I knew that their experiences in the competitive journey, now largely played out, had the potential to unravel a central unanswered question: Does the pursuit and realization of competitive success deliver on its promise of a good life? The question in my life was no less about a fundamental belief in America.

Most people assume that the social and economic opportunities afforded by competitive success translate into clear psychological benefits. In fact, a surprising number of people do not even consider the two notions separate; for them, competitive success is the *equivalent* of the psychological experience of well-being. For others, who perceive a cause-and-effect relationship, psychological benefits are seen to accrue from advantages in rearing and educating children, getting good health care, and pursuing rewarding work. Competitive success also affords pleasure and ease from material conveniences and luxuries such as comfortable homes, vacations, and transportation. And it often confers dignity, pride, and self-respect from realizing the American Dream.

But do these benefits translate into psychological benefits? What are the costs of competitive success, and what effect do they have? Is careerism in fact an American scourge, robbing people of their spirit and reducing opportunities: for relationships, creativity, self-expression, and self-realization? Might the endless anxiety of the pursuit define the experience, outweighing the benefits?

Men like my research participants devote decades of their lives to pursuing professional success. It is a deeply organizing commitment over the course of adulthood whose roots begin well before adulthood. These men, and women like them, are adherents of an intensifying form of American individualism. More now than when my participants grew up in the 1940s and 1950s, getting into a competitive college is seen as a necessary stepping-stone to professional success. Getting a son or daughter past the looming college admissions choke hold is treated by many parents as a critical race whose outcome will determine the professional and general success and well-being of the future adult.

No small number of parents are already concerned about their child's future admission to a selective college well before the child enters school. It is not uncommon for kindergarten to be seen, especially in competitive urban centers, as a gateway to adult privilege. By the time high school hits, the frenzy of the race is in full swing.

Competition for admission to Harvard began to intensify almost a decade before my research participants matriculated. Other competitive institutions have, of course, moved in parallel. The *U.S. News & World Report* rankings of colleges and universities, established in the 1980s, have come to embody competitive success as a kind of tyrannical force drawing both colleges and universities and aspiring students into its orbit. Whether graduate or aspirant—or parent, partner, child, or sibling of graduate or aspirant—most of us will readily recognize the pressures of keeping up or getting ahead as our own.

It would seem imperative to know whether winning the competitive game translates into winning in the game of life, where happiness is the outcome and the stakes of succeeding could not be higher. Do the prizewinners' advantages translate into a better life? If so, does someone need to go to a selective undergraduate institution, excel in a competitive professional career, and be worth at least millions to be fully happy?

If we don't obtain a resounding answer in the affirmative that this quintessentially American credo of competitive success delivers on its promise, the revelation has the potential to open up a tremendous fault line in a foundation of American life. If it is not benefiting the individuals who "benefit" most, or if its benefits are modest, or its costs too high, the logic of living by such a credo would be fundamentally misinformed. This book, based on a longitudinal study of Harvard men, is dedicated to reevaluating this American promise. Its findings, I will argue, are applicable well beyond this cohort of men and graduates of an elite undergraduate institution.

When I first considered the research question, I assumed that the correlation between competitive success and well-being had been established by previous research. Many in my profession—academics studying human development and, more generally, social scientists—do. If the pursuit of competitive success is such an important part of the American way of life, then its salutary effects on individual well-being must have been thoroughly examined and established. Cause and effect along the success–well-being continuum must have been documented via close studies of the lives of people embodying this ideal. I was surprised not to find a cache of studies definitively answering this question.

Prior scholarship provides only a partial and insufficient answer. It comes from the field known as the scientific study of happiness and is a version of a common maxim: that money and success do not buy happiness, once basic needs are met. The income required to meet basic needs is well below that of privileged earners. Policy research in economics about the relation between material prosperity and national well-being adds a twist to this summary, but its findings remain relatively unimportant to individuals. The answer provided by the scientific study of happiness offers little insight into people and their experiences. It focuses on broad concepts of happiness and their correlates, which are hard to interpret.

To answer the question, one would need to conduct a psychological study of the life experiences of such individuals that would go beyond survey questionnaires or other summary methods of capturing internal states. Such a study would not only examine the role of educational and career success in the well-being of such individuals but would take a broader view of their lives. It would give a rich sense of how they had come to experience their lives and how centrally and in what ways competitive success versus other factors had figured in. It would reveal what mechanisms are at work in their well-being and what, if any, are the trade-offs of succeeding in the competitive journey. It would use a method of observation capable of explaining the *nature* and the *origins* of a person's apprehension of his life and well-being.

Such an approach is centrally featured in this book, namely, a life history approach to the study of individual lives. The book applies this approach to an entire sample longitudinally. It describes the meaning and well-being of lives, seen from where subjects stand, gleaned from their life histories. It does this at different points in time, and it provides explanations for outcomes. The book shows its findings in particular and general forms. It profiles several protagonists in short biographical sketches over the course of the study and identifies statistical patterns in the sample, placing them in relation to other research on the US population. It presents a story of privileged lives and—drawing on other published research—shows how their patterns appear broadly in the lives of other groups of Americans. Given the novelty of its approach, the book also attends to how its story is generated.

While it reaches nominally a similar conclusion as happiness research—that success beyond the meeting of basic needs does not deliver happiness—the book delivers a substantively different explanation of what does shape happiness. It accounts for well-being by looking at what it is in the lives of individual people rather than the averages and abstract generalizations of survey-based research. Its paradigm—holistic, specific, and context-sensitive—is applicable to individual lives in a way that clinicians think about individuals. It explains the experiences of competitive prizewinners by locating them in a larger set of forces shaping the course of their lives. This account replaces an American myth of success and happiness with a carefully researched theory of human development. Readers who pick this book up out of scholarly interest may find its conclusion about the competitive journey resonant personally—in their own lives.

Core variable relationships observed in general research on demographically varied populations by class, sex, race, generation cohort, and so on resonate strongly with the central insights of this book. But the book deepens understanding of how these relationships solidify—not only in the Harvard sample but in other groups—into a unified picture of happiness, long-term development, and the experiencing human subject. I address how this paradigm translates to the experience of groups whose lives differ from those of the Harvard sample in the opportunities, resources, and norms shaping the social landscape on which their lives unfold.

As it turned out, it was not a single mystery but many in how lives unfold that the research reported in this book would unravel. The privileged view my participants afforded me of their lives over almost fifty years has revised my understanding of people and reshaped the view I have of my own life. It has also brought into sharper relief prior research weighing in on the success-happiness relationship and the opportunity for a more integrated, developmental, and humanistic understanding of how lives unfold.

Knowing what I know now, I would readily take this journey of discovery again. Whether you are a general social science reader, a clinician, or a researcher engaged with happiness, personality, study of lives, or human development, this book will, I hope, be a journey of discovery for you, as well. I invite you to join me as I retrace the steps, sharing the main findings and their far-reaching implications.

Chapter 1 surveys how the basic question of the book—How does competitive success affect well-being?—has been previously asked and answered. It also describes the origins of the study of Harvard graduates upon which the book's answer is based. From there the book proceeds in three parts. Part 1 portrays participants' lives from college to late midlife in psychobiographical sketches that illustrate a spectrum of well-being in the sample and trajectories of stability and change in well-being over time.

Part 2 presents the study's innovations in well-being research: a qualitative method for capturing well-being, two models explaining well-being—one of stability and one of change—and key new understandings of the human subject's experience of well-being linked to development. They lead to a novel, integrated, and rich paradigm of adult life grounded in qualitative evidence and retested using quantitative techniques. The qualitative method captures well-being in expansive clinical life history interviews carried out in college and then in late midlife. The longitudinal models—developed qualitatively, retested quantitatively—are sharpened and extended by mixed-methods integration. End-of-book and online (press.uchicago.edu/sites/kaufman/) appendixes document evidence and research tools supporting the book's conclusions.

Participants come to college with a worldview and a central tendency of well-being or ill-being already formed in family, school, and community growing up. In the most common trajectory, stability, that worldview functions as a prism through which new experiences are understood, and it also leads participants to seek out similar experiences of validation or invalidation, particularly in adult family and relationships. In the second trajectory, applicable to a sizable minority of participants, fundamental change in worldview and well-being comes about due to internal and external disruptions to the processes in stability. Part 2 concludes with a decisive broadening of the book's argument that becomes clear from the book's new paradigm: not only is socioeconomic attainment unrelated to participant well-being, but even for these professionally successful men, family life is more important than career experience to well-being.

Part 3 significantly alters conventional understandings and explanations of well-being in lives beyond the Harvard sample. It shows personality and cultural influences that distort respondent reports of experience detected in this study's method but undetected in a widely used survey approach. These distortions lead to the omission of key factors in explanations of well-being. Despite these differences, a surprising convergence exists between core variable patterns observed in this book and those found in happiness and personality research on general samples. Using the book's understanding of well-being and development linked to the experiencing human subject, a decidedly different and richer paradigm of adult life grounded in qualitative evidence, part 3 helps to illumine lives in other groups. The book's rare empirical underpinnings attest to a picture of adult life distinct from those offered by established theories in adult development and narrative personality psychology.

After the journey of steps developing a new approach to the study of happiness and a new paradigm for understanding adult life, the book spells out the implications for the cultural belief that a good life is rooted in competitive educational or career success. This careerist value system and its saturated discourse in American society are misinforming the public about what truly matters: the developmental forces shaping our well-being.

CHAPTER 1

The Study of Success and Happiness

Not the first in his family to graduate from Harvard or work as an elite financier, Spencer Livingston* is responsible for managing billions of dollars of assets. He belongs to a private country club, owns a yacht, and vacations in an exclusive resort town. He gives generously to local charities.

Whipsawed up and down by movements in asset values, Livingston's emotional well-being is tethered to the market. Highs are infused with the knowledge that he has lived up to his father's example—to be honorable, intelligent, and respected for his acumen—and lows reproach him with a sickening feeling that he has harmed clients who count on him to protect and grow their assets. What is worse, he is tormented by the persistent belief that he has failed to be a good enough provider for his family, a role that his own father, who died when Spencer was young, was unable to fill.

Spencer Livingston is one of the 207 men in the Harvard Student Study whose lives I investigate in this book. As described in the preface, my discovery in the year 2000—when these men were in their late fifties and early sixties—of participants' interview files from their college years led me to recognize an empirical treasure that could serve as a baseline for a follow-up study. The original study's unusually rich examination of participant lives until the end of college, extended in an equally rich reexamination of their lives in late midlife, held the potential to reveal new insight into the relationship between competitive success and happiness. Livingston, along with most participants in the Harvard study, is a luminary on two parallel stages in American life: he

---

* All study participants appear in this book under a pseudonym.

holds the most elite undergraduate education available, and he stands at the pinnacle of the American occupational world in wealth and professional status. Livingston reports his household net worth in the top three-tenths of 1% of the US population. The group as a whole are multimillionaires with a household net worth ten to twenty times the national median. Whether lionized as American icons or scorned as the "1 percent," these business executives, doctors, lawyers, academics, and other successful professionals have what so many Americans regard as the good life.

But have these men truly won the ticket to the good life? If so, why has Spencer Livingston felt a grating and chronic sense of failure after the highest educational and occupational achievements? Why have other participants experienced their own kinds of long-term dissatisfaction? Urgently needed in our public reexamination of elite undergraduate admissions and wealth disparities in America, answers to these questions promise to shed new light on core assumptions we hold about the good life.

The Harvard Student Study's meticulous examination of participant lives over half a century offered the prospect of answering these questions. It could identify how their lives unfolded, the meaningful experiences they had, and how competitive success figured into their journeys. Importantly, it could observe their happiness and its trajectory across the period of their education and career. It could identify the experiences in these areas and others that shape happiness.

Most prior scholarship examining the relationship between success and happiness has focused on discrete variable correlations gleaned from survey instruments rather than on lives. What this means practically is that, in pursuit of a general theory of happiness, this research has sought to map out what variables correlate with happiness in cross-sectional samples. It has not been concerned with what this book focuses on: a fuller understanding of how individuals experience their lives and an account of human development that explains it. The conventional approach yields a picture that is hard to relate to. What is really being tapped by survey questions asking respondents about an abstract concept of happiness? What does it mean that happiness correlates with a certain personality trait or behavior? Variable correlates describe samples and populations but do not tell us what happiness is or how variables interact with it in any single life and its trajectory.

HAPPINESS RESEARCH

The hedonic tradition of happiness research has focused on the outcome of interest in my investigation, a life *experienced* well rather than a life that is good or virtuous for its enactment of certain values deemed important. Its flagship construct, subjective well-being, conceptualizes psychological experience as a hybrid structure made up of life satisfaction judgments and positive and negative affect (Diener, 1984; Haybron, 2011). By contrast, I do not make such prior assumptions about the components of a life experienced well; I rely heavily on clinical life history interviews to reveal the contours of well-being (and ill-being). While the concept of well-being that emerges in this approach shares features with conventional concepts such as subjective well-being, it is more integrative and it contextualizes a life experienced well within a rich understanding of the individual's world and circumstances. In this book I use the terms *well-being* and *happiness* interchangeably to denote this fundamentally different concept of a life experienced well.

The scientific study of happiness, including the field known as positive psychology, has been principally concerned with determining the causes of and contributors to happiness and how happiness might be affected by interventions at both the individual and national policy level (Diener et al., 2017; Seligman, 2011; Lyubomirsky, 2007; Diener, 2009a; Lucas, 2008). While there are competing claims as to how best to define and observe happiness, my prior summary of this research—that money and success don't buy happiness once basic needs are met—captures prior scholarship focused on a life experienced well.

My summary is a simplification of three lines of research salient to the questions I am asking about competitive success and happiness. These lines of research address the roles of (1) hedonic adaptation, (2) wealth and privilege, and (3) goals and values in happiness. Each has something to say about how competitive success affects happiness. A chart by Lyubomirsky (2007) (see figure 1.1) classifies three broad categories of factors in chronic happiness into which main factors relevant to this book's inquiry can be located, and it depicts the relative importance of these categories to chronic happiness:

- Fifty percent of our chronic happiness is determined by genetic factors explaining hedonic adaptation (described by Set Point Theory);
- Ten percent of our chronic happiness is determined by life circumstances, defined as "whether we are rich or poor, healthy or unhealthy, beautiful or plain, married or divorced, etc." (Lyubomirsky, 2007, p. 21);

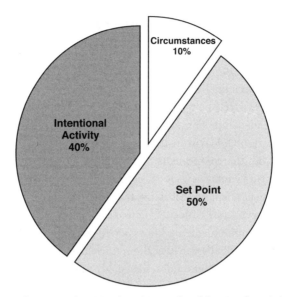

FIGURE 1.1. What Determines Happiness? Reproduced from Lyubormirsky (2007), p. 20.

- Forty percent of our chronic happiness entails the effortful, intentional action of the individual—thoughts and actions such as practicing gratitude and positive thinking, investing in social connections, and managing stress and hardship.

The first category refers to an influential concept in happiness research called Set Point Theory, the observation that people's chronic levels of happiness remain relatively stable because of a powerful process of adaptation to life's circumstances (Brickman & Campbell, 1971; Brickman et al., 1978; Diener et al., 1999; Lyubomirsky, 2007; Frederick & Lowenstein, 1999). Lottery winners and people who have suffered a spinal cord injury are often held out as exemplars; they were found to return to close to their previous homeostatic setpoint of happiness within a few months of the monumental change in their objective circumstances (Brickman et al., 1978). This theory helps to account for evidence of a strong genetic influence on happiness (Tellegen et al., 1988; Lykken & Tellegen, 1996; Lykken, 1999; Røysamb et al., 2002; Stubbe et al., 2005). At one time some scholars argued that genes determined 80% of chronic happiness levels (Lykken & Tellegen, 1996), but this strong version has been rejected recently in favor of a weaker version allowing for more change in an individual's happiness (Diener et al., 2006; Lucas et al., 2003; Yap et al., 2014;

Lucas & Diener, 2015). Lyubomirsky's chart and work (2007) are part of recent efforts to allow for and facilitate more individual agency in well-being.

Set Point Theory has also been linked to the finding that traits in the five-factor model of personality (McCrae & Costa, 1987, 1997), particularly neuroticism and extraversion, are substantially related to subjective well-being (Pavot & Diener, 2011; Steel et al., 2008; Diener et al., 2003; Libran, 2006) and that these traits are relatively enduring in adulthood (Caspi & Roberts, 1999; Roberts, 2003). Traits are assumed to be associated with genetic factors in happiness (Diener et al., 1999; McCrae & Costa, 1999).

Whatever its degree of influence, Set Point Theory is the main answer to this book's research question offered by prior research. According to this theory, happiness inheres in something other than educational and occupational attainment. Specifically, it inheres in the person. We would conclude from this research that Spencer Livingston's happiness is determined largely by his genetic setpoint rather than by the career he has chosen, the degree of success he has realized or—from his point of view—at times has not realized, or even other personal circumstances, such as the early loss of his father.

A second relevant line of happiness research addresses the association of wealth and privilege with happiness. Lyubomirsky's chart would classify these variables as life circumstances, a category that accounts for approximately 10% of chronic happiness. Most scholars summarize the effect on happiness of wealth and privilege, the subset of variables that interest me, as both relatively weak and mixed, once basic needs are met (Diener, 2009a; Diener et al., 2006; Pavot & Diener, 2013). They observe that advantaged groups, such as the wealthy, are slightly happier than others (Diener, 2009a) and yet that some advantaged groups, such as men and the highly educated, do not always report higher levels of well-being (Diener, 2009a). More than one-third of better-off individuals report below-average happiness (Pavot & Diener, 2013). Recent research focused specifically on undergraduate education moves in the same direction as these scholars' synopses in finding no association between attending a selective undergraduate institution and adult happiness (Brown, 2014; Ray & Kafka, 2014). In general, resources such as income and educational privilege show surprisingly small correlates with happiness, whereas personality variables are much stronger predictors (Diener, 2009a; Diener et al., 2006; Pavot & Diener, 2013; Lucas & Diener, 2015).

Research in economics suggests a $75,000 annual household income as the threshold above which material circumstances recede in influencing happiness in the United States, even in more expensive urban centers (Kahneman &

Deaton, 2010), yet it adds a new twist to the established finding that money and success don't buy happiness. It finds that above this threshold increasing income is positively correlated with some measures of happiness and not others (Kahneman & Deaton, 2010; Diener et al., 2009). While this finding might usefully inform policy, it has little bearing at the level of the individual. The gains in happiness for affected variables above the threshold show diminishing marginal returns (Kahneman & Deaton, 2010) and, importantly, show a relatively small effect when compared with personality variables (Lucas & Diener, 2015). Lyubomirsky's chart suggests a similar relatively small effect for life circumstances, the category to which these influences belong.

These findings suggest that competitive success is not a principal factor in happiness. Spencer Livingston's household net worth, his prestige as a successful financier, and his Harvard education do not decisively contribute to or detract from his happiness. Classified as life circumstances in Lyubomirsky's chart, wealth, occupational prestige, and educational attainment are relatively uninfluential factors.

Goals and values belong to the category of intentional activities in Lyubomirsky's chart—"what we do and how we think" (Lyubomirsky, 2007, p. 64)—accounting for 40% of our chronic levels of happiness. This third line of happiness research suggests that people who value money or materialism above other values are less happy (Diener & Seligman, 2004; Kasser, 2002). So are those who pursue the goal of financial success (Nickerson et al., 2003) or those who pursue career success and material gains rather than goals that reflect a commitment to family, friends, and social and political involvement (Headey, 2008). From this perspective, Spencer Livingston's concern for material success in the world of finance may be having a deleterious effect on his happiness.

Many kinds of goals, values, and intentional activities discussed by Lyubomirsky and other scholars—beyond material, financial, and career goals—may account for this category's effect on happiness. While Livingston's pursuit of material success may be having a deleterious effect on his happiness, the size of its influence is unclear. Its impact could be very small or it could account for fully 40% of his chronic happiness.

In summary, happiness research recognizes hedonic adaptation as establishing an outer limit of influence that competitive success has on happiness. It restricts the portion of happiness that might be affected by the pursuit and realization of competitive success to 50% or less. This is because wealth and privilege seem to have little benefit to well-being, and the pursuit of material success, while found to be detrimental, is bounded in its effect by the forces of adaptation. Applied to Livingston, this synthesis of the field's findings suggests that his happiness is mainly determined by genetic factors; that wealth may (or may not) have a small positive effect; and that financial and professional goals may have an adverse effect—to some indeterminate degree.

Happiness research findings relevant to questions about success and happiness, like other research in the field, provide general parameters without specificity. It is difficult to interpret its findings for any individual or the general population and to weigh the relative importance of individual factors in happiness. Divergent and changing assessments of the importance of genetic factors exemplify these challenges; some scholars assign more weight to genetic factors than Lyubomirsky, whereas others suggest even less (Lucas & Diener, 2015). Further, the universe of variables within Lyubomirsky's chart categories are neither well defined nor well bounded. Fragmented variable correlations comprise a vague and imprecise picture of the effect of competitive success on happiness; the effect may be deleterious, in small or large measure, or the effect of goals may be offset by a small salutary effect of income or wealth. We cannot tell from this research.

The challenge of using the field's findings to address my research questions is compounded by contentious debates over definitions and the right way to view and measure happiness (Haybron, 2011). The field's heavy reliance on the survey self-report method is no small part of the problem. Questions such as "Taken all together, how would you say things are these days—would you say that you are very happy, pretty happy, or not too happy?" (Smith et al., 1972–2016) are typical of this self-report method. It is hard to know what experiences respondents are considering and how they are weighing them in selecting answers and how they understand the vaguely worded answer choices. The method distills experience into abstract and poorly defined summaries without understanding the respondent's assumptions.

The field's reliance on survey self-reports also fails to expose whether cultural assumptions are skewing responses. Forbes 100 Billionaires, who report slightly higher levels of happiness than other Americans (Diener, Horowitz, & Emmons, 1985), may be acknowledging their status and the cultural belief that it *should* make them somewhat happier than other people, not reflecting on how they feel about their lives. Cultural beliefs alone could account for much of the positive association found between income and certain happiness measures (specifically, reports of life satisfaction) at higher levels of income. Lacking sensitivity to this issue, happiness research cannot answer the question that interests me; it may be picking up cultural beliefs offered as substitutes for experienced well-being or ill-being. This book makes clear how cultural beliefs influence survey responses—at least the responses of my sample.

Finally, influential factors in the unfolding of lives seem to be largely left out of happiness research. Lacking person-centered and longitudinal perspective, the field's cross-sectional correlational designs impede fuller understanding of how competitive success affects happiness and the larger set of forces shaping long-term happiness.

The field of happiness research has burgeoned in the past forty years and today has a public presence as an evidence-based science offering self-help advice and happiness interventions. The field's advances and contributions notwithstanding, the popularity of the field should not obscure the limits of its evidence. Ed Diener, a founding figure of this field, has expressed concerns similar to my own (Diener, 2009a; Diener et al., 1999). Calling for innovation to ensure the field's continued progress, he wrote, "There are more powerful designs to determine the causes of subjective well-being than simple cross-sectional correlations, and these designs should be used more frequently" (Diener, 2009a, pp. 34–35). The research reported in this book leverages a design that has not been used previously in happiness research.

The Harvard Student Study files, I recognized in my first encounter, offered the possibility of extending into a long-term longitudinal study that could examine both the effects of competitive success and broader forces of human development contributing to happiness. Such a study would be able to circumvent many of the challenges facing conventional happiness research, which limit its ability to address my questions.

THE HARVARD STUDENT STUDY

In the summers of 1960 and 1961 the names of 667 rising Harvard freshmen were drawn from incoming class lists.[1] These young men were sent a letter asking them to report to the University Health Services shortly after their arrival to campus. Coming from all corners of the United States as well as abroad, these young men could not have imagined what was in store for them. Not in the first meeting to which they had been invited, and not in the next four years—nor, for that matter, in the next half century. A team of Harvard psychologists and sociologists wanted to study them and their psychological development while they were in college. As it turned out, the Harvard research team members could not have imagined the long-term consequences of their study. They had shot an arrow into the future.

At the heart of the Harvard Student Study were 50 men,[2] drawn from the 667, who were going to be studied intensively. They would be interviewed and would undergo in-person psychological tests multiple times during each year of college while also participating in the paper-and-pencil study of the larger group. One of the fifty men never showed up to that first meeting, but the other forty-nine did. For the next four years, these men met frequently with two members of the research team. Stanley King, the avuncular son of a minister, a lecturer in the Department of Social Relations at Harvard, and the director of the study, met often with members of the intensively studied group. At times smoking a pipe, King turned on a tape recorder at the beginning of his meetings and plotted a course from academics to fathers to friends to dating to career plans to drinking to study habits to an assortment of topics of interest to him and the National Institute of Mental Health, the study's primary sponsor. The other member of the team who most often met with the participants was Charles McArthur. Known as a skilled interpreter of personality using the Rorschach inkblot and other specialized psychological techniques, he was also the director of an earlier and still ongoing longitudinal study of a pre–World War II cohort of Harvard men, the Grant Study, which would gain notoriety under a later director, George Vaillant.[3]

The goal of the Harvard Student Study was to determine whether the years from late adolescence to early adulthood—the college years—were marked by the kind of disturbance and crisis (Erikson, 1959, 1968) that filled popular novels and shaped psychological theory of the day. The study found that crisis was the exception, not the norm, and that most participants exhibited "evolutionary change and continuity" (King, 1973, p. 190) in their coping styles and in their personality development across the college years (King, 1973).[4]

Though the study had been one of the most extensive studies of human development during the college years ever undertaken, its findings were not received with notable distinction (Whiteley, 1976; Heath, 1974).[5] Further, Stanley King had intended that the study files be burned; he felt their contents were too sensitive to risk their falling into the wrong hands, according to Elizabeth Keul, his former secretary (Keul, 2004). But after completing the college research with publication in 1973 of *Five Lives at Harvard* (King, 1973), King gave the files to another Harvard researcher, Samuel Osherson, who conducted a study on a different subsample of the original participants in the late 1970s and early 1980s, when participants were in their late thirties.[6] When he completed this research, Osherson turned the files of the original forty-nine interview participants and the files of those he studied over to the Murray Center for safekeeping and for use by future scholars, where I subsequently found them.

In 2004, four years into my research, I met at the University of Michigan with David Winter, a social and personality psychologist whose past involvement with the Harvard Student Study I had recently learned of. The arrow shot by Stanley King and his colleagues—its arc at one point redirected by Samuel Osherson—met with another inflection point. Winter had recovered the surviving magnetic IBM mainframe computer tape that contained the coded responses of the paper-and-pencil participants during college. If these data had not been discovered and preserved, they would have been lost to history. If Winter had not provided these data to me for the follow-up, the study described in this book would have been much narrower, would not have been able to address certain central questions, and would have excluded members of the larger survey sample. With Winter's help, I was able to repeat, in the follow-up study, the mixed-methods design of the original study.

STUDY OF LIVES RESEARCH TRADITION

That the Harvard Student Study might provide insights needed to answer questions about the relationship between success and happiness was not entirely due to the fortuitousness of its survival and my discovery of it in the year 2000. The study began under the influence of scholars who pioneered a research tradition called the *study of lives*. In addition to Henry A. Murray (the namesake of the archive where the Harvard Student Study was housed), two of the best-known scholars who helped found this field are Robert White and Erik Erikson.[7]

The study of lives has its roots in personality psychology (a subfield of psychology examining individual differences in thoughts, feelings, behavior, and total personality), but its modern form, called the *narrative study of lives*, is located in multiple disciplines in the social sciences (Josselson, 1993). It goes beyond the variable or the single construct as the unit of analysis and seeks to understand the whole person and his or her development in explaining how lives turn out. One of its hallmarks is that it brings rigorous empirical evidence, especially narrative evidence, to the study of humanistic concerns (McAdams, 2008a).

It was in this tradition that King was operating when he and his colleagues gathered the extensive interviews whose files I encountered at the Murray Center. King was a student and protégé of Robert White. White (1952) approached the study of personality through exhaustive case history analysis, relying to a great extent on clinical interviews. King incorporated this approach into the study's design, placing life histories, obtained through clinical interviews, at the heart of the study. Rather than noticing and explaining problems, the interviews focus on normal development and capture the lives of participants in a way that seems to jump off the page. Their scope and depth offer the basis of a biography for each participant.

My interest in a person-centered rather than variable-centered approach, and in understanding lives across time as context for examining the competitive journey, led me to recognize the value of the data that King and his team had assembled. It also led me to preserve the original mixed-methods design of the study in the follow-up I would undertake. I continued King's clinical interviewing and case-study approach as well as the larger survey study of which it was a part. But I used these data for more narrow aims than King, and I placed the Harvard Student Study in conversation with more recent developments in the field. At the time I assumed direction of the study, there was a renewed interest in life history as a form of personal narrative in personality psychology and the social sciences, contrasting with the earlier zeitgeist in which King was operating, when personality psychology had been concerned with the totality of the individual's functioning.

The renewed and refocused interest in personal narratives emerged in the 1980s, as scholars in the social sciences began to rediscover the power of stories at the heart of human experience. Life stories came to be understood as personal narratives that lend order, meaning, and purpose to human lives (Cohler, 1982; McAdams, 1985; Sarbin, 1986; Bruner, 1990). Today the interest in life stories and other personal narratives of lived experience (Van Manen, 1990) as units of study represent a significant commitment within personality psychology and the social sciences more generally. The Harvard Student Study belongs to this renewed commitment.

THE FIELD OF HUMAN DEVELOPMENT

The Harvard Student Study is a study of human development, as is a meaningful subset of research conducted in the Murray-White study of lives tradition, because it examines human growth, development, and behavior across the lifespan. Specifically, the Harvard Student Study produces a clinical developmental understanding of lives over time by extending White and King's clinical case history approach in a longitudinal study of a sample. The Harvard Student Study also falls within a more sociologically focused field of life course research concerned with the socially defined sequence of events, roles, and transitions that individuals undertake in their own lives (Giele & Elder, 1998; Elder et al., 2003).[8] This is because of its longitudinal design and its interest in the progression of lives and the experiences shaping them over half a century. While sharing interests with other clinical developmental and life course research, the Harvard Student Study ultimately advances a different research agenda.

Erikson's theory of personality development (Erikson, 1950) and Vaillant's (1977) work empirically testing Erikson's theory using the Grant Study of Harvard students are well-known clinical developmental perspectives. So, too, is Levinson's (1978) psychosocial examination of development. These scholars paint a dynamic picture of adult life made up of stages and transitions patterned by society. As I will show in this book, the Harvard Student Study portrays a different picture of adult life enabled by its expansive clinical life history interviews spanning decades and its analytic approach. Erikson developed his theory from clinical and societal observations rather than in a research context. The Grant Study examined evidence supporting Erikson's theoretical framework to account for a sample's lives rather than building theory in data from the ground up and testing it, as the Harvard Student Study does. (Note 9 describes the Grant Study and how it differs from the Harvard Student Study.)[9] These other clinical developmental theories were based on different empirical resources and did not use, or have access to, the Harvard Student Study's unique data and methods for understanding lives. (I discuss these theories in chapter 10.)

The perspective developed in this book differs also from other life course research. Even landmark studies in the field—such as the Institute of Human Development at Berkeley's Intergenerational Studies (Elder, 1998) and the Terman Study of the Gifted (Holahan, Sears, & Cronbach, 1995)—do not include the Harvard Student Study's clinical life history interviews.[10] Along with the Grant Study (Vaillant, 2012), these longitudinal studies began many decades before the Harvard Student Study and with different research questions and goals guiding their collection of data. While providing foundational knowledge about aspects of human development and the life course, these studies are not principally concerned, as am I, with a reexamination of the American competitive journey.

This book approaches the question of success and happiness by first delving exhaustively into lives and their trajectories, then aggregating their patterns for a sample, and, finally, considering their application to other groups of Americans. Critically, it starts by teasing out what happiness is and the trajectory of influences shaping it for each participant. This personal and longitudinal perspective, which is missing from conventional happiness research, not only leads to a fundamental rethinking of the success-happiness relationship but also exposes formative influences on happiness in the context of human development.

* 1 *

Patterns in Lives

CHAPTER 2

Brightness and Darkness

William Hovanec and David Martin are participants in the study whose lives illustrate patterns that became a central focus of my work. Placing their lives side by side reveals forces shaping their well-being that are much broader and earlier than their competitive careers and elite undergraduate educations. Understanding these forces and how they influenced how these men experience their lives is part of the broad inquiry of this book.

I present Hovanec and Martin for a first time in college and then a second time roughly four decades later, when the men have reached late midlife. My portrayal restricts its focus to what was known about a participant in a given era. The college sketch does not draw on what later became known about him in adulthood, and the adult sketch does not incorporate material acquired by the study during the college era. The entire sample was studied in this way—interviewed and then analyzed in each era in isolation, as its own research project—to allow longitudinal patterns to be identified with greater clarity and confidence. The themes I incorporate into these sketches were identified by a team of independent observers, using a procedure for assessing clinical life history interviews described in chapter 4. My first encounter with participants occurred as their adult interviewer. To ensure the independence of the adult data, I intentionally remained ignorant of their lives in college by not reading the archival data.[1] This approach had the effect of placing me in an elevated state of suspense not only at our first meeting but also again when reading the college interviews, as I wondered what secrets would be revealed about individuals I had come to know decades later, on the cusp of their old age. Unlike me, the reader will discover the participants' lives unfolding in the chronology in which they were lived. Many participants show longitudinal stability in how they view their lives; this insight provides direction for the remainder of the book, which seeks to understand the nature and origin of forces shaping well-being in a context broader than competitive success.

HOVANEC IN COLLEGE

William Hovanec was a nontraditional student recruited by Harvard as part of its effort to redefine its student body in the early 1960s. He was in the top 5% of his high school class and an athletic star. Hovanec and his family lived in a rural area just outside a small town of several thousand people. His father worked in middle management for one of the town's biggest employers. Hovanec's family, especially Hovanec and his father, spent considerable time outdoors.

Going to Harvard had not even occurred to Hovanec. Cambridge was a remote, urban setting unfamiliar to him. He had imagined going to a regional college to study engineering or business. He intended to live a life not very different from the life he was accustomed to: a life centered in a nuclear family in a rural environment with hunting and fishing nearby. Hovanec knew the rules of this world and felt confident he could be successful in it.

But Hovanec did not know the rules at Harvard, where he was surrounded by strangers. He quickly found it difficult to operate with the pressure of various demands. Hours of practice during sports seasons left little time to study. Early in his Harvard career he did poorly in some of his classes and had to withdraw for a time from the sport he most enjoyed playing. Hovanec felt unprepared intellectually and culturally for this new environment.

Hovanec strove to adhere to the dictates of his conscience early and consistently throughout his Harvard career. He aspired to maintain the personal standards of conduct and high performance that he had learned in his family and that had served him well prior to Harvard. His concern that at Harvard he would lose faith or lose his determination to maintain his standards showed up in his romantic relationships, in athletics, and in planning his future career. He was afraid he might succumb to having premarital sex, in spite of parietal rules and sexual prohibitions of the era. Hovanec felt driven not to be outperformed by other athletes but was not sure his abilities would allow him to excel. In making career plans, although he thought about entering a professional field such as business, he wasn't confident he would be accepted into a corporate training program or business school.

Hovanec experienced his internal world shifting by the end of his sophomore year. He began to see people he grew up with as narrow-minded. At the same time, when he was at Harvard, he couldn't assume that he would be able to win an argument or be accepted for his point of view. Everything was dissected. At home he was a big fish in a small pond, and at Harvard it was the reverse. His beliefs and his ability to maintain them were being drawn into question.

By junior year Hovanec felt his situation at Harvard begin to turn around. He was less distracted and less homesick. He began to study more selectively and productively in his courses. His grades rose. He met a girl at a mixer who, like him, was an outsider in this Ivy collegiate world. They appeared to share similar values.

By Hovanec's senior year his career plans began to crystallize. An advisor gave him advice on how to find a corporate training position or go to graduate school.

Hovanec finished Harvard with respectable grades. He believed that he had performed up to his potential as an athlete, and he knew that his teammates and coaches respected him. Hovanec was also warming up to the idea of marrying his girlfriend. In his past relationships he had felt the need to distance himself, but not with her.

Hovanec hoped to move to a rural part of the country and work his way up the ranks of a company. He wanted a career that offered him a social outlet, something concrete, a chance to win in a game. He wanted time for outdoor recreation. But he also wanted to live his life by a philosophy that was still in the making. He wanted to be remembered by others for living this philosophy rather than for adhering to some social requirements or standard. Money was not as important to him as other things were, he said.

Hovanec came to Harvard with a vision for his life, and Harvard challenged that vision. That vision was to get his stamp validated at a university so he could enter business, form a family, and live the kind of life that he was accustomed to. The scholastic and cultural demands of Harvard threatened his clarity. Hovanec hadn't been sure he was going to return to Harvard after his freshman year. As his senior year came to an end, Hovanec took pride in having surmounted the challenges. Harvard went from a trial to a win. It was a turbulent period of his life that could have gone otherwise.

HOVANEC AS AN ADULT

Hovanec graduated from college and not long after married a woman he had known in college. They had several children together. He entered a large conglomerate and worked his way up the managerial ranks. He encountered difficulty gaining as much responsibility as he wanted, and he felt out of place in the culture. In time he became dissatisfied and left for a position at another large company. This pattern repeated itself several times: becoming dissatisfied, leaving for another large company.

When in his forties Hovanec decided to make a major life move. He took his family to an area of the country with outdoor recreation and bought a small business there. He relied on his prior industry experience in running this company. A priority for him was creating a responsible and hospitable company culture. After a number of years the business was not doing well. The pressures spilled over into his marriage. Hovanec had already begun to feel some loss of connection with his wife as their children left the house, but he was committed to his marriage and was grateful to his wife for being a good mother to their children. She had been instrumental in raising them during the years he was building his career.

Hovanec spent a great deal of time participating in outdoor activities with friends and his children. This helped temper difficulties in other areas of his life.

Eventually Hovanec resolved the problems affecting his business but lost some motivation. He wanted to sell his company and find a more exciting role in another company, hoping to resume the intense pace of his business career once again. Hovanec was in discussions to carry out this plan. He hoped to work for ten or so more years and retire when he was seventy.

Hovanec experienced his life, including its challenging aspects, in terms of a superordinate frame as a father. He had not compromised his contributions to the lives of his children. They were a potent and fundamental satisfaction in his life. They turned out well, he had good relationships with them, and their futures seemed promising. They had come to appreciate and share Hovanec's values centered on nuclear family, the outdoors, and personal responsibility. He was extraordinarily proud.

MARTIN IN COLLEGE

David Martin came to Harvard after boarding school. He had done well academically and gotten into Harvard but now worried that his luck might run out. He planned to go to graduate school after Harvard. If his trajectory of success were thwarted, he said shortly after arriving at Harvard, it "would break me."

Martin's father was a successful corporate executive, exceeding his own father's career success. The family moved several times before settling in a suburb of a large city while Martin was in grade school.

Martin felt estranged from both his parents. He admired his father's intelligence but didn't understand why he and his father were not closer. Martin's mother seemed to him poorly informed and overly attentive to the needs of others. Martin had an older sibling whom he respected but with whom he did not spend much time. Martin seemed to want a closer relationship with his father but not with his mother. He also strongly disliked a relative who spent time with his family. Martin observed of himself that even when he was younger he had not been much of "a family man."

Martin's significant experiences at Harvard were in the areas of academics and dating and clarifying plans for a future career. An emotional crisis his junior year overshadowed his Harvard career.

Martin got high grades his freshman year. He found Harvard easier than high school. He still felt flooded with anxiety when he didn't do well on tests, but the worry he felt in high school about faltering academically was beginning to recede.

Martin considered majoring in one of the humanities but wanted a career that would afford him a certain lifestyle. Martin's family had wealth for many years, and his father provided him with an allowance during college. Martin did not want to pursue a course that would involve a drop in social status or material resources.

One of Martin's roommates freshman year became a friend. Sophomore year this friend withdrew from Harvard for personal reasons. Martin joined a social club and spent considerable time there. He enjoyed interacting with other people in its low-stress environment.

Freshman year Martin had a girlfriend whose cultural sophistication he respected and with whom he had fun. He could confide in her and she was his closest friend. By sophomore year Martin had become excited about the prospect of marrying her after college or maybe earlier. He came to feel that he had been overly focused on his studies as a freshman.

But junior year she expressed misgivings about continuing the relationship because of Martin's social isolation. Martin entered a period of soul searching and began talking with a psychiatrist. He came to see that his deepest motivation did not come from a desire to please his girlfriend; instead, he was often reacting to his parents. His high academic achievement was an effort to earn his father's respect.

His junior year Martin's uncertainty about his major and career took on greater urgency and weight. The closer he got to his graduation, the more pressure he felt.

Senior year Martin and his girlfriend broke up. Martin dated other women, but these interactions ended badly. Martin fell into crisis. He felt that he had been overly dependent on his girlfriend. His freshman-year loneliness reappeared and he felt it acutely. He was angry and vulnerable. His parents tried to offer emotional support with limited success.

Martin managed to graduate with honors. He was offered an entry-level position after graduation in a nonprofit organization but declined it because of geography. He thought he might pursue a graduate degree in the humanities, but this idea was not well developed. Uncertainty about his future and ongoing fallout from his recent crisis set the tone as Martin left Harvard.

Martin's college career had the bleak overtones of struggle and instability. His academic achievements offered some validation, and so did his relationship with his girlfriend until it ended. His socially isolated college years and the breakup led up to the fall that Martin experienced.

As Martin was leaving Harvard, he was asked his thoughts about what he'd like to make of his life ten or fifteen years into the future. He wasn't very enthusiastic, he said. "I'm not actively looking forward to it at all . . . which is kind of sad."

MARTIN AS AN ADULT

After graduating from Harvard, Martin took an entry-level job in a corporation. He earned a graduate degree part time as he rose up the ranks to a relatively senior manager. The company experienced financial difficulties and laid off a portion of its workforce, including Martin. Deciding to act on a longstanding desire to own and run his own business, Martin took a major risk launching a business that marketed creative products in a field he was familiar with. The business was a small player and Martin felt constantly threatened by larger, better-financed competitors. He forged strong relationships with some customers, but he was sober about the possibility that at any time he could be put out of business by his competitors or could suffer a cash-flow crisis. Martin worried about many aspects of the business and what he would do if he went bankrupt. Despite his estimated net worth of $7 million, he was terrified about the prospect of being out on the street with a cup in his hand. Martin exercised daily to help him relieve intense anxiety.

In his twenties Martin grew tired of being single. He met a woman with whom he was smitten and eventually married her. After roughly thirty-five years together, Martin and his wife appeared to be in a steady, if somewhat fragile, holding pattern. She stayed at home and didn't work. Martin seemed to harbor a general disrespect for her. He described frequent conflicts and estrangement. To avoid disturbing the fragile peace and stability of their relationship they decided not to have children. Both Martin and his wife struggled with the legacies of painful childhoods and felt it better not to re-create a similar experience by having children. Martin had met other women with whom he thought he could have had children.

Martin recognized his efforts to succeed in business as an attempt to earn his father's respect. He felt his father's career accomplishments set a high standard for him, and during most of his adult life he had felt inferior and devalued by his father. For a period in his father's older years Martin's father became more vulnerable, and this afforded the two of them the chance to become closer. Martin was grateful for that time but said it did not alter his feeling that he had never measured up to his father.

Martin had been in psychoanalysis for a period when he was younger. He recalled having a crisis in college. His family life growing up had had a lot of conflict and he was resentful toward both his parents.

More so than with many other participants, Martin's statements about himself and his life, as conveyed through anecdotes and other means, did not articulate the full import and range of his feelings. (The study later would use the word *leakage* to describe unacknowledged feelings when assessing and recounting experiences, as described in following chapters.) Martin was available to meet for only one interview. He cited work demands but may also have wanted to limit the discussion of painful experiences.

Martin deeply missed his father and the security he felt when his father was alive. His mother had died long ago, and he now felt very much alone.

Martin planned to keep working into the foreseeable future, barring any catastrophe with his business or his health. He thought he and his wife would most likely remain together. He saw value in the longevity of their relationship, in spite of its significant problems. Martin's mental world and social life appeared restricted to a narrow radius and he seemed resigned to a general sense of failure about his life.

REFINING THE STUDY'S FOCUS

When I encountered Hovanec and Martin and other participants and tried to make sense of their lives, my objective was to address the study's research question: What effect does competitive success have on the happiness of adult participants? Since competitive success includes both educational and career components, I decided to examine them separately, taking participant career experiences as my initial analytic focus. I would use the college data as a baseline and tease out career-related changes in well-being in the adult data. Specifically, I would observe how career success—conceptualized *objectively* as the attainment of wealth and status—affected participants' subjective experience of their careers and, in turn, their overall sense of well-being. After conducting the interviews, and coming to know participants' lives longitudinally, I thought that I would be able to home in on an answer.

But my progress toward an answer required a sequence of steps of discovery and verification that involved multiple kinds of analyses that I had not foreseen. (See appendix 4 for a description of the analytic procedures and the sequencing of their deployment in this research.) And it required a further refinement of my focus, one that would redirect the course of the study.

What became clear was that although a participant's career followed a clear trajectory of roles and showed an overall emotional valence, a broader and more encompassing trajectory of roles, situations, and circumstances existed as well, along with the participant's feelings about them, himself, and his entire life in this life history. This overall pattern emerged, unexpectedly, as the central factor characterizing the quality of a participant's life and to a large degree subsuming the experience he had of his career. It also underscored the value of the study's broad net of discovery: a narrow view of the career and its history—without observing it in the context of the participant's life history—would have obscured the connection between the career experience and the overall life experience.

Martin's life overall seemed to be colored by negative feelings, as did his career, in spite of the exceptional accomplishment of starting his own business, making more money than he expected, and remaining solvent against difficult odds for many years. Similarly, Hovanec conveyed a sense of satisfaction with and acceptance of his career, even though he was not as successful as he wanted to be. His overall satisfaction in his career appeared to resonate with the overall satisfaction he seemingly conveyed about his life.

Further, for both Hovanec and Martin, the overarching pattern of how the participant felt about himself and his life appeared consistent between the college era and the adult era of the study. This is particularly striking given the divergent life situations and circumstances of the college-age and adult participants.

In college Hovanec emerged from his senior year feeling that he had overcome the challenges of college and realized a personal victory. The same was true for Hovanec in adulthood; his children were a mark of his life as well lived. The challenges and scenes of college and adulthood, however, were quite different: he was grappling with his grades and academics, sports, his career decisions, and the cultural challenge of the Harvard setting during the earlier period, whereas in adulthood he grappled with decades of a career, marriage, and parenting and realizing a lifestyle. In the college era he was embarking on adult life, and in the adult era he was looking back on the middle adult years and contemplating the transition to retirement and older age.

Martin, too, showed a stable apprehension of himself and his life across starkly contrasting circumstances and periods of his life. At the end of college he felt pessimistic about his future and viewed college as a bleak period of struggle and instability. He had felt in the shadow of his crisis with a lack of life direction and a sense of invalidation by others, including his parents. As an adult he felt deeply anxious in his business, estranged and lonely in his marriage and in his social isolation, and inadequate in relation to his departed father. Martin's dominant themes across time paint a darker emotional experience than Hovanec's, but both men show a remarkable consistency to themselves across time.

A large portion of the interview sample follows the pattern illustrated by Hovanec and Martin. (Chapters that follow characterize the pattern in detail.) Identifying this pattern led me to proceed with my inquiry by pursuing two new aims. This kind of revision and redirection of analytic focus is central to the discovery process intended by grounded theory (Glaser & Strauss, 1967; Charmaz, 2003) and is a hallmark of much research.

First, I sought to characterize the essence of each participant's feelings about himself and his life in each era of the study. I wanted a construct that captured the overarching pattern of these feelings and would allow me to compare a given participant to himself at different times and to other participants in each era of the study and longitudinally. The conceptualization of the construct could not be preconceived or conceptually detached from the data. It needed to tap the richness and breadth of the life histories; it needed to link with the psychobiographical perspective on participants' lives. Even to know whether the overarching patterns in adulthood diverged from those in college and were the result of objectively measured career success, the study would need to capture them systematically for all participants.

Second, I reformulated my research question because I now doubted that for most participants objectively measured career success explained their happiness as adults. If career experience seemed to be subsumed into an overall life experience, and the pattern of this overall life experience preceded the career, then it seemed to follow that (at least for Hovanec and Martin and others like them) there had to be a set of forces other than objectively measured career success that significantly explained how happy participants were. Indeed, Hovanec and Martin shared the objective circumstance of owning and running their own businesses, but how they felt about themselves and their lives seemed to have only a limited connection to this circumstance. Further, Hovanec and Martin shared an elite Harvard education, but this too seemed to have little connection to the quality of their experiences. My new research focus therefore became the question: If it wasn't objectively measured career success or even an elite undergraduate education that seemed to explain the happiness of an adult participant or the adult sample, what else did? What would be a better explanation?

I therefore incorporated into the focus of the study these two research aims: (1) systematically capturing a participant's feelings about himself and his life in each era of the study and (2) explaining the adult sample's happiness (or unhappiness). I would consider the question of how competitive success affects the happiness of research participants, but it became clear that these two new aims would speak to the central patterns in the data. I devote a large portion of this book to these aims before returning to the questions of how career success and educational success affect the well-being of participants.

METAPHOR OF INTRAPSYCHIC BRIGHTNESS AND DARKNESS

A great deal of what distinguishes Hovanec from Martin (and any participant from another) can be seen within the psychologies of the two men. Patterns in each man's life are not simply characterized by a series of roles, events, circumstances, or situations—or good or bad luck. Rather, there is a patterning of affect across the broad range of situations: those in the distant past, those in the not-too-distant past, and those in the present. A deep and abiding quality in each man's life experiences transcended specific situations. It was this observation that led me to use a metaphor to describe this essential feature of a life history, that of *brightness and darkness* in the internal world of a participant. Brightness and darkness, common dimensions of visual perception, conjure the quality of a person's subjective world in a recognizable way.[2]

Here the similar demographics of Hovanec and Martin (and other participants) helped to show the utility of this metaphor. Both men went to Harvard and both owned their own business (though some factors in their lives growing up and in adulthood were different). It is noteworthy, then, that in Hovanec's life history many of his experiences and many aspects of his life are bright. The light is dominant; negative (dark) experiences ultimately seem to be subsumed within it. By contrast, there is little light or the light is clearly muted within a generally dark set of experiences in Martin's life.

After identifying this metaphor, I explored the possibility of using constructs or assessment frameworks developed by other scholars that might capture a similar phenomenon, but I found none that could be applied to interview data to characterize the participant's perspective on himself and his life. The only candidate, Neugarten and colleagues' life satisfaction rating scales (Neugarten et al., 1961), failed to detect key dimensions of the study's rich interview data. It also introduced a theorized concept of well-being that was not visible in the data.

I also considered using survey measures to capture how participants felt about themselves and their lives. I administered to the adult sample a widely used survey measure of the construct of subjective well-being, the Satisfaction with Life Scale (Diener, Emmons, Larsen, & Griffin, 1985). This measure was not available in the college data set, which made it difficult to recognize change and continuity across time. But even without this problem, there were numerous others. The measured construct, a global judgment of life satisfaction, was detached from the psychobiographical perspective (discussed in online appendix 3). It spoke to a different paradigm working with large samples and survey data. The measure was insensitive to certain affective and cognitive processes in reviewing and evaluating one's life that participants displayed in interviews. Critically, this measure introduced a significant set of assumptions not supported by the qualitative data. It discriminated among members of this sample in unexpected and problematic ways. (Chapter 9 describes these findings with the study's use of the Satisfaction with Life Scale.)

I therefore concluded that if the study was to capture how a participant felt about himself and his life in each era of the study, an approach would need to be derived within the data set. Intrapsychic brightness and darkness stood out clearly in this study's voluminous life histories side by side and over time. It tapped the range of the study's data. I decided to use a grounded theoretical approach (Glaser & Strauss, 1967; Charmaz, 2003) to derive the analytic framework for capturing this construct. Once defined and captured for participants, the construct could tie directly to psychobiographical evidence.

MARTIN AND HOVANEC AS EXEMPLARS

Based on the results of observer assessments (and the grounded theoretical analysis that preceded it),[3] Martin and Hovanec illustrate two patterns of overall affect in a life history in the sample—loosely speaking, two ends of what I will show is a spectrum of intrapsychic brightness and darkness. They also represent a longitudinal pattern of overall affective stability when viewed in

TABLE 2.1. Intrapsychic Brightness and Darkness at Two Ends of a Spectrum

Characteristics of the Intrapsychically Bright	Characteristics of the Intrapsychically Dark
· Hovanec has more intrapsychic brightness than Martin, and overall he has intrapsychic brightness as a central tendency	· Martin is darker than Hovanec and overall negative, suffering a kind of despair or anguish
· Hovanec is more secure with himself	· Martin feels he is damaged and has goals that involve repairing himself
· Hovanec is more open to other people and to new experiences than Martin	· Martin is on guard and self-protective against further injury and (concomitantly) the stimulation of other people and new experiences
· Hovanec is more invested in other people	· Martin is less invested in other people and more isolated
· Hovanec is trying to accomplish positive things for himself and others in the world	· Martin is trying to protect himself from further loss of value
· Hovanec perceives and is involved in a broader social radius beyond his marriage and work	· Martin is secluded from a broader social radius
· Hovanec experiences a sublime or spiritual sense and seeks to cultivate this sense	· Martin does not have a sublime sense, nor a sense of life meaning beyond the immediate life he is leading
· Hovanec enjoys a sense of play and spirituality—enjoys doing things—beyond life course pressures (in his case work and family demands)	· Martin is struggling to meet life course pressures (work and marriage / intimacy in his case) without available resources for doing things beyond these requirements
· Hovanec internalizes successes and minimizes the internalization of failures; he externalizes many problems	· Martin internalizes failure. He is dominated by problems residing within himself and does not locate many outside of himself or recognize or internalize successes
· Hovanec is hopeful	· Martin is pessimistic
· Hovanec feels in control	· Martin feels controlled and buffeted by external forces; he does not feel his efforts affect the direction of his life
· Hovanec has a broader range of emotions	· Martin is affectively constricted and unaware of the limited range of his emotions
· Hovanec is less incongruous between statements about his experiences and the conveyance of emotion (positive or negative) in those experiences	· Martin leaks out negative emotion, which he does not recognize or include in the evaluations he makes of his major experiences, such as his marriage
· Mental illness seems at odds with the central tendency of Hovanec's life	· Mental illness seems to be an extension of the central tendency of Martin's life

relation to this spectrum.[4] The number of other participants who share the descriptive pattern with Hovanec and Martin in part or in whole at a single time, and across time, is striking and a dominant feature of the sample as a whole.

Table 2.1 presents the descriptive characterization of Hovanec and Martin and other similar participants. It shows what intrapsychic brightness and darkness looks like at ends of the spectrum after a careful review of the entire sample in each era of the study.

This chapter has provided some sense of Hovanec and Martin and their lives across time. For this book, Hovanec and Martin's lives serve to illustrate a conceptual cornerstone. Their lives help show how the study came to discover intrapsychic brightness and darkness and to illustrate what the construct is. The variation in this construct in the sample, its varying trajectories over time in the lives of participants, and the explanation for these trajectories guided the study and helped determine the direction it would take.

CHAPTER 3

The Varieties of Experience

Hovanec's and Martin's lives illustrate a conceptual cornerstone in the study's discovery about its participants' lives, two ends of the sample's spectrum of overall brightness and darkness. Their relative stability in their respective locations on this spectrum represents only one longitudinal pattern, however. A sizable contingent of participants migrate along this spectrum from college to late midlife, changing to brighter or darker central affective tendencies to varying degrees. To complete the picture, the sample as a whole changes, undergoing affect elaboration from college to late midlife. This chapter explains what that means. Figure 3.1 depicts the entire array of patterns in the lives of the study participants and identifies pattern exemplars.

A MIDDLE CATEGORY OF PARTICIPANTS: MIXED AFFECT

Participants who do not appear overall bright or overall dark in the central tendency of affect in their life histories instead reveal a strong presence of both positive and negative affect, neither of which represents a dominant affective experience. The study described the central tendency of affect displayed by them as *mixed affect* or *mixed*, falling in a middle category between the overall bright and overall dark.

As an adult Alan Caulder's central tendency was mixed affect. His personal life shows a darker affective tendency and his career a brighter affective tendency, neither of which subsumes the other. Further, his hope in the possibility of a future relationship infuses the darker strand of his story with some offsetting positive affect.

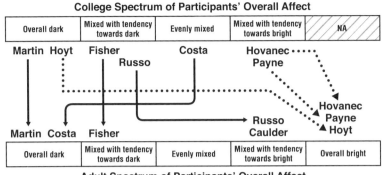

FIGURE 3.1. Spectrum of Brightness and Darkness and Individual-Level Change

Note: This figure displays the patterns and participants presented in this chapter and includes Martin and Hovanec for comparison. The spectrum of overall affect in individual participants' lives appears in the top and bottom rectangles. (The college spectrum does not include overall brightness for reasons explained in the chapter.) Solid lines with arrows denote individual-level change longitudinally. Dashed lines with arrows denote relative stability longitudinally.

Exemplars illustrate patterns as follows:

- Caulder: the overall category of mixed brightness and darkness (presented as an adult only).
- Fisher and Costa: gradations of mixed brightness and darkness (in college and adulthood).
- Costa: longitudinal change to more darkness, contrasted with Fisher's relative stability.
- Hoyt: significant longitudinal change to more brightness.
- Payne: affect elaboration (a form of relative stability) in the sample as a whole rather than individual-level change.
- Russo: the most common pattern of significant change.

Alan Caulder never married, although he had a series of lengthy relationships in which he noticed a pattern: the woman grew close to him and he pushed her away, at which point she would leave the relationship. Caulder came to realize that a deeper motive laid claim to his energies. He had a serious financial insecurity that he had to overcome before he could feel comfortable committing to a relationship.

Caulder got a graduate degree after college that prepared him to enter a relatively small company at the ground level. The company grew and was increasingly profitable, in no small part due to Caulder's contribution. A senior manager recognized his potential and promoted him repeatedly, entrusting him eventually with a senior executive role. In the year before I met Caulder, his business acumen produced a remarkable gain for the company, and he was rewarded with a bonus in the tens of millions of dollars.

During the years when Caulder was devoted to his business career, he came to see himself as belonging to a family in two regards. First, his success shepherding the business through challenging periods and to ever-improving performance ensured the financial well-being of its employees, whom he cared a great deal about, and who saw him as a sort of protector. When I met him, we went to lunch with several of his employees, who are also his friends. At the same time, Caulder grew closer to members of his family of origin. They regarded each other with a respect and fondness that Caulder as a younger adult had not imagined he might share with them. Caulder was explicit that he nurtured these relationships in the absence of creating a family of his own.

Caulder felt a sense of loss at not marrying and having a family, but he felt enormous pride in his accomplishments as a business executive and in caring for the people who work for him. Caulder looked to the future as a time when he might build on his newfound security and enter into a stable relationship with a woman. His health is good, and although he isn't sure he will overcome his past patterns, he is instilled with motivation and hope that he might.

Caulder's history shows that a participant's stance toward his unrealized central strivings helps to identify his central affective tendency. (*Life goals* is the term used to refer to central strivings in the study's assessment procedure.)[1] This heuristic is particularly important in discerning mixed-affect participants from overall bright and overall dark participants. Mixed participants are actively engaged with their unrealized central strivings, whereas overall bright and overall dark participants seem not to be.

Caulder had realized his career aspirations but not his central strivings to marry and have children. If he had been resigned to failure in these unmet strivings, he would have been overall darker. If he had been content with how his family aspirations had turned out, he would have been overall brighter. Mixed-affect participants are neither resigned nor resolved in how their central life strivings have turned out. They are still trying to realize them.

By contrast, overall bright participants have resolved their central strivings, and overall dark participants are resigned to failure in them. Hovanec found overall peace in his children and in nature, which resolved the unmet strivings in other parts of his life. Martin was less engaged than Caulder with the deficiencies of his life; he was resigned and anguished and not actively trying to realize his strivings.

Three Subgroups in Mixed-Affect Category

Mixed participants engage their unrealized central strivings with the conviction that their efforts matter, but they hold the view that the outcome of their efforts is unclear.

One subgroup of mixed participants is hopeful, believing they are likely to succeed in realizing their central strivings; they have a tendency toward brightness. (Caulder exemplifies a mixed participant tending bright.)[2] A second subgroup is evenly divided between believing their efforts will be successful and believing they will be unsuccessful; they fall in the middle of the mixed category. And a third subgroup is doubtful, believing they are unlikely to succeed, although they are still trying; they are located at the dark end of the mixed category. These three stances toward unrealized life strivings thus delineate three positions within the mixed category of brightness and darkness: tending bright, evenly mixed, and tending dark.

Vincent Costa as a college participant illustrates an evenly mixed central affective tendency. He seems unsure which eventuality he believes is more likely to happen: that he will or will not realize his unmet central strivings. This sketch of him is followed by a sketch of Joseph Fisher, a college participant classified by the study as mixed affect tending dark. Drawing out the subtle differences between two overall mixed participants, these sketches also lay the basis for what later will be shown to be divergent longitudinal trajectories.

Costa and Fisher, like Hovanec and Martin and the rest of the college sample, show differences in brightness and darkness in the early era of the study against a common backdrop of the college environment and the transition to adulthood. The backdrop includes academic, intellectual, extracurricular, and social opportunities and demands and the expectation that one will forge meaningful direction toward a career and a future social and personal life. These concerns are shared by college participants despite differing parental relationships, family background, interests, and abilities. A participant's central affective tendency is linked to how successful he feels himself to be in navigating a path. Costa's mixed tendency, slightly brighter than Fisher's, reflects his being equally hopeful and doubtful of his success, whereas Fisher seems inclined to be more doubtful.

Costa in College

Vincent Costa approached college with a decidedly mixed attitude toward the opportunity it offered. He came from a working-class family and was not sure he wanted to enter the world that Harvard opened to him. At the same time, he sought to escape the suffocation and stagnation that he felt intellectually and socially in his family and ethnic community and to avoid a certain rut he knew would stifle his future as a working-class laborer. These opposing concerns permeated his college career. Early, he appeared to have decided to loosen his ties to his family and community, but later he seemed to retreat from his foray into the new world. He never fully gave up either position. His indeterminate attitude organized his college experience in every area of his engagement: academics, athletics, friendships, dating, and his plans for his career. As a college student, Costa falls into the group of mixed participants inclined to give equal weight to faith and doubt that they will surmount their challenges and realize their unmet central strivings.

Costa grew up in a tight-knit community in which his family was known and well respected. He and his friends played sports and palled around with other kids in the neighborhood. He would be the first one in his family to go to college. Costa knew he didn't want to end up with a dead-end factory job supporting a family. He excelled academically and as an athlete in high school but was surprised when he got into Harvard. An adult in Costa's community had contacts at Harvard and recommended him.

Costa found the intellectual conversations at Harvard unfamiliar and refreshing. He was used to discussing sports and politics with his friends back home. His freshman year Costa spent hours studying, training for sports teams, and avoiding getting sidetracked by "over-involvement" with other people and frivolous concerns. He spent time with teammates but didn't drink or smoke and was resolutely determined to learn as much as possible and to take advantage of this opportunity.

But life at Harvard posed problems. Freshman year Costa got a sports injury that interfered with his practice. He found the academic work demanding. It took him longer to read and write, he estimated, than it took other students. Even though he was working extremely hard and long hours, he was unable to get Bs. Even when he was not injured, he was not performing athletically at his pre-Harvard levels. He knew he had the potential to do better. He was choking at Harvard.

Even with his scholarship, money was a problem. To save money, Costa lived with relatives in Boston rather than on campus. This made him somewhat of an outsider, as Harvard was overwhelmingly a residential college. Costa's parents and relatives were supportive of his being at Harvard but uninvolved in his academic experiences and in decisions about his future.

Costa's discipline and engagement freshman year receded some by his sophomore year. He determined that he did not want to end up living in a Waspy suburb any more than he wanted to follow the prescribed course of life for young men from his hometown.

Junior year Costa continued to struggle to get respectable grades and carve out time for sports practice.

Costa realized that life after Harvard did not offer the prospect of being easier. Financially, graduate school was out of reach; it would be a long shot at best. Costa's ideas about his future had germinated all four years but remained general by the time he graduated. He was interested in the arts but had no specific plans to pursue them. The one thing he was sure of was that he didn't want to fall into a rut.

Costa wrote a thesis and graduated with honors, which softened his frustration over his academic performance at Harvard. Time pressure had been constant all four years. He had not had time to participate in extracurricular activities. Although he was active as an athlete all four years, he felt unable to perform to his full potential. He withdrew from one of his teams because he was given limited time to play.

Stimulated and broadened by his Harvard experience, Costa was also conflicted. Reflecting on his college years, he described himself as a loner and an outsider. He did not have any close friends at Harvard. He had not dated during college because he did not feel comfortable with girls in the Harvard world. He also had not dated girls back home because he did not want to tether his future to his home community. Costa still had strong ties to his home community and to his family but felt they had been weakened during college. He was reluctant to weaken them further. It was unclear whether Costa would shift his life trajectory after Harvard through a career or a stronger embrace of the social connections offered by this new world. Costa left Harvard with a decidedly mixed experience and a decidedly uncertain future.

Fisher in College

Joseph Fisher hoped college would allow him to clarify his scholarly interests and forge a career that would satisfy both himself and his parents, who wanted him to pursue a professional career that did not interest him. The pressure he felt from his parents led him to focus on academic achievement at the expense of extracurricular involvements and deeper social connections. He completed Harvard College early, feeling out of control of his life and mourning lost opportunities. Fisher was more doubtful than Costa that he would transcend the prospect of stagnation.[3]

Fisher was near the top of his class in a competitive high school. Fisher's parents had immigrated to the United States before he was born. They had long encouraged his scholastic achievement. They felt Harvard would be a good choice for him because it would prepare him for a successful career and allow him to profit intellectually. Fisher agreed.

Harvard assigned Fisher its highest ranking in its undisclosed formula predicting a student's likely academic performance during college, its Predicted Rank List, weighing high school grades, test scores, and other evidence of scholarly promise. His intelligence and a scholarly ability gained the notice of his instructors immediately when he arrived at Harvard.

As a freshman Fisher declared his major and began completing required courses ahead of schedule. Fisher had been considering a practical career, but his scholarly interests and abilities indicated an academic direction.

Sophomore year, Fisher's academic work claimed nearly all of his time. It was disappointing to him and his parents that his grades were lower than what he had achieved in high school, so he redoubled his efforts and regained his former high average as a sophomore. But this meant that Fisher had little time for much else, including dating.

As a sophomore Fisher considered a career in the academy but worried that college teaching might be a nonlucrative grind. He knew that his parents wanted him to enter an established profession, such as medicine. It would be practical and secure.

As a junior for a brief period Fisher seemed to resolve his career conflict by deciding to keep his intellectual interests an avocation and pursue a more secure career path. Fisher's parents were pleased, but Fisher felt uncertain of how to proceed. He saw no way to gain experience and confirm his interest in a field before having to apply to graduate school.

By senior year Fisher was in a position to graduate early, which brought on a painful sense of loss. Fisher had begun to experience a social renewal. He had time to socialize for the first time since freshman year, as he was now working less hard. He met new people in his house, made new friends, and enjoyed conversations. Fisher also felt that he had not yet had a chance to date, and he was unsure how, after Harvard, he would overcome his inexperience and his sense of isolation; he did not understand why his parents were not more concerned. Fisher wished he could stay at Harvard for the full year but felt pressure from them to press on. He felt they seemed to notice only his academic achievements and not the other aspirations and hopes he had for his life.

Fisher credited Harvard with expanding him intellectually and familiarizing him with important thinkers. He was also pleased by his academic accomplishments. But Fisher did not feel these accomplishments translated into a greater sense of career opportunity.

Fisher left Harvard fighting to claim the direction of his career, to engage interests and activities beyond academic work, and to gain traction socially. He felt himself fighting an uphill battle and doubted he would be successful. He exhibited a central tendency of overall mixed affect tending toward darkness.

CHANGE IN INTRAPSYCHIC BRIGHTNESS AND DARKNESS OVER TIME

The mixed-affect category and its subgroups fill out the sample's spectrum of brightness and darkness in each era of the study, which allows for detection of more granular change in longitudinal trajectories. Costa and Fisher illustrate individual change in brightness and darkness—divergent trajectories—during adulthood. Their adult sketches help to define change.

The stagnation that both Costa and Fisher feared in college asserted itself in their adult lives. But Costa changed to greater darkness, whereas Fisher maintained his mixed-tending-dark central tendency. Family and career strivings are the central concerns of the adult sample. Fisher retained a sense of efficacy in his career, albeit not as strongly as he would have liked, whereas Costa felt thwarted in his career efforts. Fisher was also still trying to achieve greater closeness with others, whereas Costa was defeated and resigned. Despite Costa's brighter presentation in college, Costa became darker than Fisher in late midlife, exhibiting overall darkness and a sense of hopelessness.

Adult Costa

After college Costa held a series of jobs in the arts and in service fields. He relocated several times. Twice he worked for an arts organization, which he found a source of great enjoyment. Costa hoped to gain a foothold as an artist but was not successful.

Some years after college Costa met Susan, a woman he was strongly attracted to. He changed jobs to a new field to work closer to her, hoping to form a relationship. She did not reciprocate, and after several years, he realized all chances had been exhausted. It was a painful period of rejection in his life, which led him to capture the experience in multiple works of art.

Costa took his portfolio of work and relocated across the country to try to sell it. He worked at jobs during these years, but his efforts to sell his art were unsuccessful. Eventually he reached a dead end and decided to move back to his home community.

Costa had been living with relatives for the past fifteen years. He was commuting to a job doing clerical work that was steady employment and steady pay. But it was not nearly as enjoyable as the job he had at the arts organization; that turned out to be the best job he ever had. Costa had pursued other women over the years since Susan, but none of them measured up to her. Now he spent much of his free time alone, reading and doing other solitary activities. He saw his siblings regularly throughout the year, and he provided care to an aging relative. Saturday was the most social day of his week. He spent it at a bar talking with old friends.

Costa had come to see his life as a collection of failed possibilities and his best days behind him. He felt he had gotten into Harvard under the radar without the proper credentials; he conjectured that he had been accepted to round out the class as a token disadvantaged student. The honors his reader gave him on his thesis and the overtime hours he recently received from his boss were similar gestures of compassion. When I asked him how he hoped to be remembered, he refused the question. "Never crossed my mind," he said. He protested the class-based presumptions of my question asking him to focus on himself and his legacy. They weren't how he thought about the world. Costa had not saved up enough to retire and did not think he would be able to do so. He planned to work until he died, he said. Costa had become overall dark in his central affective tendency and was resigned to failure.

Adult Fisher

Joseph Fisher went to graduate school after Harvard and entered the academy. He became a well-respected scholar and teacher. His parents were distraught by his career choice.

Fisher's experience of his career had an overall mixed quality. He was one of the most productive faculty members in his institution and he felt well liked and well respected by colleagues and students. He felt intellectually and socially enriched. He had made some friends among colleagues and students. He took pride in the success that some former students had realized in their careers. Fisher also appreciated his freedom to read, think, and write broadly.

On the other hand, Fisher felt that he had not realized his potential to work at a more prestigious institution. The institution that had been his first choice had not offered him a position. He also felt that his reputation and his scholarly output placed him in the second, rather than the top, tier of scholars in his field. His field was narrow, and he did not feel motivated to write and publish within its restricted focus. He felt that he would have been happier working in another field more aligned with his interests. He saw his career as having stagnated over many years.

Fisher felt that he had chosen his career prematurely. His scholarly abilities had allowed him to enter academia against the wishes of his parents, but he did not realize the demands and expectations that would ensue. In response to the question, "What advice would you give to a Harvard senior on the life ahead of him?" Fisher cautioned against making premature decisions about a life direction. "The danger of Harvard is that a lot of people have precocity. They see themselves as full-fledged adults who know everything they'll ever know in their lives."

Fisher's career was the most active part of his life, and its mixed quality kept him from being overall dark. He felt efficacy in his career that he did not feel in his personal life.

Fisher had not been in a romantic relationship during his life, although he had tried on numerous occasions as an adult. He had discussed with his therapist the possibility that he might be acting in ways not serving his interests. Fisher felt his life was the poorer for not having married or having a family.

Fisher felt that his parents had been negative influences on his life. He thought his mother would now view his life as inadequate because he had not married and was not more successful as an academic, whereas his father would be disinterested in him. The negative quality of Fisher's father, as he described him, took on a more barren tone than it had in college.

Fisher seemed to feel a hidden hand thwarting his conscious desires. He wanted to be closer to others and to address the feeling of "unhappiness" that he experienced, but he was not sure how. He had begun to consider where he might move during retirement but did not feel ready to finalize his career or advance into another phase of life. He was still trying to figure out who he wanted to be when he grew up, he said. Fisher had not realized the possibilities for his life that he had hoped. He was still trying, but he seemed doubtful that his efforts would bring about change. Fisher had become mixed, tending dark, in his central affective tendency.

Costa and Fisher exemplify the concepts of change and stability. Costa in college seemed more open to his life turning out favorably, but following a series of setbacks in adulthood, he retreated to a more self-protective holding pattern and felt his life no longer held promise. Fisher, by comparison, remained engaged with his unmet strivings in adulthood and as doubtful (perhaps more so) as in college that he would realize them. The winds of time exerted great effect on both men, but Costa seemed to lose more ground in the face of them.[4]

THE STUDY'S CONCEPT OF CHANGE

Systemic Change

Costa's change is significant because it reflects a long-term shift in the balance of affect visible in his life history. It is not the product of short-term or periodic variation in affect and mood, the ups and downs we all experience in the course of our lives. Intrapsychic brightness and darkness is a construct capturing the central tendency at a global level of many moving parts. It is akin to average temperatures, which may be a measure of seasonal variations in the weather or of more lasting changes in climate. In the summer some days are hotter than others, but changes in the average temperature over the long term reflect systemic change. The evidence gathered by this study shows clear patterns of systemic change over time among some participants.

Individual versus Sample Change

Systemic change in an individual appears most clearly when viewing the individual against the whole sample, which exhibits another kind of change from college to late midlife, which I call *affect elaboration*. Costa appears to change because he deviates from the patterns of the group, while the group itself is changing.

The adult sample shows more saturated affective tendencies in their life histories than the college sample. The ends of the spectrum of brightness and darkness were further apart in adulthood than in college—that is, study adults on the dark end of the spectrum were darker than college students on the dark end of the spectrum. Adult participants on the bright end of the spectrum were brighter than college participants at the bright end of the spectrum. The sample's affective range seemed to expand from college to late midlife.

Costa shows no clear overriding tendency in college toward darkness or brightness; that is why he was classified by the study as evenly mixed. Yet he crosses into a decidedly dark place in adulthood, changing more than overall dark college participants or mixed-tending-dark college participants, such as Fisher.

A metaphor helps to illustrate this expansion of the sample's affective range over time. Imagine paddling a raft on a river. Even as you might pull your oar in one direction or another striving to move the raft, the current carries you downstream, similarly to how inertia is at work in the central tendency of affect among participants over the life course. At one point the river forks into multiple braids. On the far right—let's say a subjectively overall bright braid—the water pulls you in that direction more and more if you are already on the right side of the river. On the far left—an overall dark braid—the same thing happens if you are traveling on the left side of the river. You will most likely not be drawn into the far left braid of the river if you are on the far right side of the river and vice versa.

Hovanec and Martin travel the braids of the river closest to the banks, following the overall bright or overall dark subjective trajectory over the entire course of the study. Their travel in the outermost currents brackets the trajectories in between taken by other participants and helps show what is happening with the whole sample.

To continue the metaphor, if you are in the middle of the river, the forces at work are more complex and involve competing parts of the current. The forces to go to the far right and far left are working on your raft at the same time. Participants in the middle range of the river are carried by the balance of these two forces acting upon them. They are subject to this mix of forces unless they change, like Vincent Costa. Costa defies the inertia. For the most part, mixed participants don't slide into the extreme braids of the river. Opposing forces hold them in the middle of the river, such as Joseph Fisher, who is relatively stable as a mixed-tending-dark participant across time.

The affective river gains a wider footprint as it cuts through the territory of adult life. From the college to the adult era the river splays out into a broader and more vivid range of affective tendencies. The braids in adulthood draw a large portion of participants out onto a relative floodplain. Bright participants like Hovanec follow the channels that lead far to the right, onto braids of even greater brightness. Dark participants like Martin follow the channels that lead far to the left, onto braids of even greater darkness. Even mixed participants show themselves to be more vividly mixed in adulthood than in college.

The affect elaboration of the sample from college to late midlife seems principally to reflect a change in the sample's perspective on their lives and greater life experience. As young men launching into adulthood, college participants experienced great promise in their futures but also great uncertainty. They had not yet lived the large portion of their lives that they would by the time of late midlife. Further, they had not acquired the experience with themselves and their lives that would later contribute to a more vivid experience of the lives they had led.

Darker participants in college perceived a longer horizon and more opportunity for redemption from the problems overwhelming them than darker adults were able to conjure. Martin's opportunities for realizing career and relational aspirations seem more possible in the long future viewed during college. Similarly, college participants on the brighter end of the spectrum, such as Hovanec, although hopeful about their prospects, entered adulthood with uncertainty and anxiety about how their lives would play out. This tempered enthusiasms. They still had the large share of their lives left to realize their central life strivings; certainty about their eventual success was not clear. These influences on participant perspective placed floor and ceiling effects on brightness and darkness in college.

Further, from their younger vantage point participants were not as aware of themselves and were not inclined to reflect on their lives as a whole, as they later would be in what Erikson (1950, 1982) describes as a phase of adult development, "ego integrity versus despair," entailing reminiscence (Butler, 1963). Even if reminiscence had been a perspective available to college participants, it would not have allowed taking stock of an as-yet unlived future. By contrast, it was not only possible but normative for participants as late-midlife adults to take stock. In this phase individuals size up the merit of the lives that they have lived and reach a more positive or more negative resolution. Participants well past the halfway point in the expected course of life had acquired considerable experience, contributing to more elaborate affect in both experience and display.[5]

Hovanec and Martin: Defining Significant Change

This account of affect elaboration allows a more accurate description of the lives of Hovanec and Martin than that provided in chapter 2. I suggested that Hovanec was overall bright in college, but in fact he was classified in college by the study as a mixed-tending-bright participant. This was the brightest affective classification observed among *any college participant*. Hovanec exemplifies affect elaboration in the sample. He followed the brightest channel in the metaphorical life course river. In adulthood he was classified as overall bright, a classification that, although it had not appeared among the college sample, did appear among the adult sample.

Similarly, although Martin was classified by the study as overall dark in college—the outermost dark classification observed among the college sample—the degree of his central tendency of darkness seemed greater in adulthood. The most extreme form of overall darkness did not appear in the sample until adulthood and required a further degree of classification.

Participants who undergo significant change, as Costa did, do not follow the currents that pull them along in the metaphorical river. They are not exemplars of the sample's affect elaboration over time. Psychological and behavioral factors—which I discuss later in the book—move in tandem, taking participants *across the center of the current*, and from there they are carried along by a new balance of forces. Some move into the extremes of the river but some simply move far enough from where they started so that they stand in a decidedly new position in the current.[6] This kind of shift has major implications for how a participant feels about himself and his life. These are the participants whom I refer to in the remainder of this book when I speak of *change* and *changers*.[7]

CHANGE VERSUS AFFECT ELABORATION

While some participants change to greater darkness, others change to greater brightness. To fill out the patterns in the sample, I now present a psychobiographical sketch of such a positive changer, Lawrence Hoyt, and contrast him with Robert Payne, who follows a brighter channel of the river from college to late midlife. As adults both Hoyt and Payne end up on brighter braids of the current, but they get there from different starting points.

College Hoyt

Hoyt was not the first one in his extended family to go to Harvard but only when his grades improved at boarding school did he think Harvard might be within reach. Hoyt's father was pleased when he got in and decided to go.

Hoyt had lost his mother some years earlier. Hoyt's father had had an accomplished professional career and had often been traveling when Hoyt was growing up. Hoyt and his siblings had caregivers after their mother died, but Hoyt missed his mother. She was a beloved figure.

Hoyt's emotion in talking about his mother exposed by contrast the muted emotion he conveyed at other times in his college interviews. One interviewer noted that Hoyt seemed withdrawn in general. Throughout his Harvard career Hoyt would have difficulty forming lasting connections with others.

When he first arrived at Harvard, Hoyt enjoyed meeting people from backgrounds different from his own but soon found he had little time to explore.

His classes were too demanding. Time management was a central concern (as it was for most other participants, as indicated in the sketches of Hovanec, Costa, and Fisher).

By sophomore year Hoyt was concerned that his grades were not adequate. He felt he was not using his time well, as he spent considerable time in two extracurricular activities (one more artistic, the other more social) and other involvements. Hoyt's father advised him to pursue extracurricular activities to gain useful skills for a professional career like the one his father had. But Hoyt was considering careers in public service, education, and other areas. Extracurricular involvements diverted time from studying.

Hoyt's junior year started well. He enjoyed his roommates and had begun dating someone he liked. He told his interviewer he had fallen in love, an experience he had not known before. Hoyt felt his roommates and girlfriend respected him.

But Hoyt's positive start to junior year did not continue. His relationship with his girlfriend cooled. He found himself overcommitted extracurricularly, which left no time for other things. His grades suffered. He had little in common with others in his main extracurricular involvement and felt none were his friends. Hoyt became unsettled about his future, because he equated his immediate difficulty managing his life at Harvard with his being unable to forge a satisfying future career. He was feeling the pressure of his father's expectations.

When Hoyt came back to college senior year he was less on edge. He had decided to apply to graduate school and now saw his extracurricular experiences as helpful. But this reprieve dissipated. Hoyt was disappointed by the grade his thesis received, although he felt intellectually enriched by having written it. He regretted that his academics had suffered at Harvard because he had diverted too much time to extracurricular involvements. Hoyt experienced conflict with roommates. And he felt that he lacked definite goals for his future. He had come to decide that he would enter his father's professional field but hoped it would not be permanent. He did not want it to become a "trap."

As a freshman Hoyt, when asked, said he could form no picture of a future with a family. He now said he planned to push back marriage until he was thirty-five and settled in other areas.

Early in his junior year Hoyt experienced more promising connections with his girlfriend and roommates but they did not last. Hoyt left Harvard without close relationships or confidence in his ability to form them. He seemed only dimly to perceive that he might transcend his social disconnection and the life that had been imagined for him. Hoyt left Harvard carried along by forces to which he seemed resigned.

Adult Hoyt

Hoyt worked in his father's professional field for many years after graduating from Harvard. He also got a graduate degree. But Hoyt felt unfulfilled and unsuccessful. Further, he dated regularly but he kept distance on occasions when the woman expressed an interest in a relationship. Hoyt recalled this as an unhappy time in his life. He felt a general distance from people.

The pattern broke when a relative died, a loss that deeply impacted him. Although Hoyt's life proceeded outwardly as before, he came to feel that he was spinning his wheels and not doing what he wanted with his life.

A few years later Hoyt undertook a major reorientation. He changed his work to a service role that was more personally fulfilling and that he felt made a more valuable contribution to others. He began receiving positive feedback from those he was helping.

Part of what compelled Hoyt to make a change in his career is that he sensed a change would provide stability for having a family. He found a therapist helpful in forging a new direction. Hoyt married and had children. He was an active parent.

The marriage did not last, and Hoyt became even more active as a parent, scaling back his work commitments. Hoyt recognized that his children needed his help and that his efforts were having a positive impact on them and on his relationship with them. Eventually Hoyt met another woman with whom he formed a strong, long-term relationship and who had a knack for parenting. He felt deeply gratified by his family life.

Hoyt felt that superficial relationships had given way to deeper connections than he experienced when he was younger. The closeness he felt with others was incongruous with the professional life he had pursued when younger. Hoyt enjoyed his work and knew he was making a contribution. Hoyt felt that he had become the father to his children that his father had never been to him. Hoyt realized that his father, who had passed away some years earlier, would not have related to his current life. Hoyt had traveled a great distance emotionally. Having started out overall dark in college, he had become one of the brightest participants in the sample.

Hoyt Compared with Payne

Lawrence Hoyt came to his overall brightness by way of significant change, whereas Robert Payne reached an even brighter position in the life course river by way of affect elaboration. Hoyt struggled with the legacy of an unsuccessful first marriage and its effect on his children, and with problems even earlier, in the family that introduced him to the world. Payne did not.

The contrast between Payne's and Hoyt's trajectories is more striking in light of common aspects of their family backgrounds, private secondary educations, and careers. Payne grew up in privileged circumstances in an established family and went to a private boarding school, as did Hoyt. He felt a calling to serve and entered an occupation serving others similar to the one that Hoyt eventually moved into. (Payne had to work to provide for himself and his family, in contrast with Hoyt.)

Despite these common characteristics, Payne's trajectory began differently from Hoyt's. He came to Harvard with a positive start to his life. His parents were alive, his family was intact, and he felt supported by his parents and both sets of grandparents. He showed a solid foundation of earlier well-being across the board in other ways as well—in sibling relationships, friendships, most school and community experiences, and in his religious background. These were all infused with positive affect.

Consequently, as Payne negotiated the demands of college and the clarification of his future life direction, he seemed better endowed with emotional resources than Hoyt. This point of contrast with Hoyt is especially highlighted by Payne's situation upon graduation from Harvard. He had no specific direction or even general plan for his future education or career. Payne had explored career possibilities during college but by the time he graduated, he determined that his earlier ideas would not suit him. Rather than being despondent or demoralized, he accepted the situation as a reasonable development. He felt some anxiety about graduating without clarity or a plan, but he believed that he had experimented profitably and would do so with other possibilities. He expected to work out his career direction satisfactorily. He did not know the specifics yet, but he did not need to.

Payne also dated during college, formed friendships, participated in extra-curricular activities, and applied himself in his course work. He did not personalize setbacks in these areas any more than he did in his career exploration.

As he left college, in contrast with Hoyt, he was neither resigned nor fighting an uphill battle against social disconnection and a future predetermined for him. Payne explored career options for several years after college, earned an advanced degree, married, and fathered children. He felt successful and satisfied in his career. He felt that he made a meaningful contribution to those he served, that he was well respected by his colleagues and his community, and that his work was intellectually and spiritually enriching. For a time Payne's wife needed to relocate for her career, and Payne took leave to support her and their family life.

By the time of late midlife Payne glowed in nearly every realm of his life. His relationship with his wife was a profound connection. His young adult children struggled with forming careers and relationships but he was proud of their ethical compass and their character and felt that he had parented them well. He wished he had made more money, but he determined it was a worthwhile tradeoff to have been enriched by his work rather than depleted by it.

Payne's adult life was not all a cakewalk. He had a general parental concern about his (now-grown) children's futures. Payne struggled with an extended period of depression, and his wife struggled with a different illness. And, most significantly, he had lost a close relative, who died unexpectedly.

Payne's affect about his life was not as bright or glowing when he left Harvard as it was in late midlife; when he left Harvard, his life consisted of untapped possibilities carrying uncertainty about the future. Further, the life experiences that he would acquire would vividly fill in for him the picture of his life. Still, despite the more muted tone, in college Payne's central affective tendency was mixed bright and it seemed to point him to the destination of overall brightness that he eventually reached. Payne did not cross the center of the current of the life course river. He followed a channel of the current that splayed out and became brighter in adulthood.

Payne's path carried him to the furthest reaches of the sample's brightness. Hoyt came to within a stone's throw of him, also in the further reaches of the sample's brightness, but he began nearly the entire width of the river away.

MODEST SIGNIFICANT CHANGE TOWARD MORE BRIGHTNESS

A brief sketch of Louis Russo illustrates the most common pattern of significant change in the sample: significant change in modest degree and positive direction. Russo's change is less dramatic than Hoyt's but shares the same direction, positive change. Russo's change both is smaller in degree than Costa's and moves in the opposite direction. (The frequencies of the sample's trajectories are displayed at the end of this chapter.) Russo went from a darker mixed tendency in college to a brighter mixed tendency in late midlife, owing to emotional gains he made through work and family life.

Russo, like Costa, grew up in working-class circumstances. He made it to Harvard on the basis of academic merit alone without the benefit of an advocate with connections to Harvard, as Costa had. He knew in college that he wanted to enter the academy and, like Costa, he experienced deep ambivalence about the implications of upward mobility. He did not want to lose his connection with his family and community. Also like Costa, his background deprived him of knowledge of and access to graduate education and career opportunities available to most classmates. Russo focused on academics during college but was unable to apply himself fully. He was frustrated by his lack of discipline. His grades were mostly Bs with few As and occasional Cs. He left college uncertain about pursuing his chosen career and doubting that he could do so. He seemed less poised than Costa to find his way.

By late midlife Russo had overcome his reticence and lack of resolve. He held a senior appointment at a well-respected academic institution and enjoyed a relatively satisfying family life as husband and father. However, he had not reached an overall bright position on the life course river.

Russo suffered years of relative career stagnation on the way to his current position. At one point, frustrated by his lack of advancement, he left a stable job in a gamble for another one of lesser status in the hope that it would lead to a desirable appointment. The gamble paid off but not as Russo had anticipated it would. He was grateful that it had worked out but the capriciousness of his career trajectory left him deeply unsettled.

Russo discovered a fuller life with his wife and children than he imagined; he was grateful to his wife for helping him overcome his resistance to having children and teaching him to parent. But things had not always been easy with her. She had health problems, and they had faced parenting challenges. Russo and his wife obtained professional help to deal with these difficulties.

Finally, even though Russo had acted decisively to advance his career and class standing, he was still coming to terms with the distance his success placed between him and his community of origin. He felt a deep sense of loss and longing for what he had left behind.

Russo had not become overall intrapsychically bright, although not far away, and he was significantly brighter than he appeared in college.

INSIGNIFICANT CHANGE

In contrast with Costa, Hoyt, and Russo, for some participants individual change is insignificant. The study's interview assessment procedure, presented in the next chapter, provides further insight into how participants were classified. There is no meaningful difference in the pattern across time, or in the forces at work, for the participants with insignificant change and the

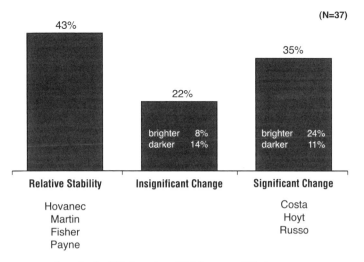

FIGURE 3.2. Longitudinal Trajectories of Brightness and Darkness

Note: The figure displays frequencies of three kinds of trajectories of intrapsychic brightness and darkness from college to late midlife observed in the interview sample. Insignificant change, although presented as distinct to represent the full picture of observed longitudinal patterns, closely resembles relative stability and the forces that explain it. Subsequent chapters account for the two combined trajectories in a single model of stability and significant change in a second model.

participants who follow the same current of the river across the two eras of the study. Still, I identify them separately for completeness of presentation. What distinguishes the former group from participants who follow the same braid of the river longitudinally is that their affect balance moves against the current (although modestly) rather than staying the same or splaying out. This movement could potentially be explained by error in the study's observation method and short-term vagaries influencing the participant's presentation at the time of observation. The pattern, therefore, may not be one of change at all. It seems to have more in common with relatively stable participants than with participants who change significantly. It is for these reasons I regard participants in both trajectories as relatively stable and account for their pattern in chapters 5 and 6 in a single model of stability.

DISTRIBUTIONS OF LONGITUDINAL TRAJECTORIES

The histogram in figure 3.2 shows the frequency of the types of longitudinal trajectories of brightness and darkness in the sample delineated in this chapter.

Participants are positioned along a spectrum of brightness and darkness, and they follow a variety of trajectories down the life course river. After showing how the study systematically captured their happiness across eras of the study, I return to these men's lives as I take up the question of what explains these longitudinal trajectories. (Appendix 1 summarizes the lives explored in depth in this book and can be used as a quick reference.)

* 2 *

Observations and Longitudinal Models

CHAPTER 4

The Qualitative Assessment
of Well-Being:
An Innovation in Happiness Research

This chapter launches the analytic sections of the book by describing how interviews were used to observe the study's fundamental concept of intrapsychic brightness and darkness. It is the answer to the question I am often asked about my research: "How are you measuring happiness?"

Although qualitative approaches have been attempted, happiness has not previously been soundly measured using interview data, much less using the voluminous life history interview data obtained by this study. Existing reliable measures are designed for survey research. This study's development of a procedure for capturing the construct of brightness and darkness first detected in grounded theory (Glaser & Strauss, 1967; Charmaz, 2003) allowed it to identify and explain patterns in lives across time without losing the rich insight offered by the interviews. The procedure addresses a variety of conceptual and empirical issues without imposing a simplifying framework on qualitative data. It is an innovation for studying happiness and well-being in the fields of happiness, clinical, personality, and adult development research.

My research team and I found that survey approaches to capturing happiness did not tap the construct of intrapsychic brightness and darkness. We considered subjective well-being (Diener, 1984, 2009a; Diener, Emmons, Larsen, & Griffin 1985) and psychological well-being (Ryff, 1989; Ryff & Keyes, 1995)—both well known to happiness scholars. While subjective well-being was conceptually useful, neither is measured with interviews. Other constructs and associated measures, such as adjustment, ego strength (Barron, 1953), positive mental health (Jahoda, 1958), morale, and life satisfaction (Lawton, 1972, 1975; Neugarten et al., 1961; Peterson & Mangen, 1982) had not been operationalized for qualitative data either; some, such as the Philadelphia Geriatric Center Morale Scale (Lawton, 1975), are concerned with well-being under conditions and in populations far afield from this study's sample.

The closest prospect for a measure usable with the study's interviews was Neugarten et al.'s framework (1961) for assessing life satisfaction of middle-aged and older adults. The Life Satisfaction Rating Scales, developed for a study in Kansas City in the late 1950s, assess interview data along five dimensions: zest versus apathy, resolution and fortitude, congruence between desired and achieved goals, self-concept, and mood tone. We found the five scales neither conceptually clear nor reliable when applied to our life history interviews.

The lack of suitable extant measures made it necessary to create an assessment procedure capable of capturing numerous component constructs and, eventually, the Scale of Intrapsychic Brightness and Darkness, which is illustrated in table 4.1. Although we succeeded, the effort to develop our own procedure carried the significant risk that independent observers would be unable to reach the same conclusions in assessing a participant's life history.[1] The study's findings would have been the poorer, and the results of the assessments would not have been usable in other analyses (descriptive, correlation, and regression analyses presented later in this book). The lead qualitative coder and I first achieved independent agreement. We then recruited and trained new observers, incorporating their input to refine the procedure. They gained independent demonstrable agreement in their conclusions with us and with one another.

Note that in this chapter I use the words *assessment* and *evaluation* interchangeably. I refer to members of the research team who carried out this work as *coders, raters,* and *observers* interchangeably.

DEVELOPING THE PROCEDURE

Our procedure took as its focal aim the capture of overall *affect* appearing in the transcribed life history interviews, another way of describing intrapsychic brightness and darkness. My use of *affect* has only some overlap with its common meaning in psychiatric and other psychological and social science research, where it means the observable expression or observable experience of emotion and feeling (Kaplan & Sadock, 1998). Each of these fields conceptualizes affect in relation to the concepts of interest and the types of data presumed relevant. For example, the psychiatric interview attends to physical indicators of affect—eye contact, speech, tone of voice, facial expressions—

along with the content of a patient's experiences, and in this way seeks to assess the psychiatric distress of the patient. By contrast, we did not assume that affect in a life history would entail distress or any particular affect. We focused on affect conveyed by the spoken words of the participant, as recorded in writing; a participant's physical presentation was not part of the formal data record for the assessment, although audible features of voice and of audible nonverbals expressing emotion were noted in the transcription.

We winnowed our focus to the most important areas where affect appears in the life history interviews. At a general level, these areas include events, situations, sequences, roles, and role experiences; oneself, other individuals, relationships, groups of people, and society; orientations toward the future, the past, and the present; and more abstract categories of thoughts, perceptions, actions, reactions, and other behaviors. Over time we came to structure the areas, as I will show in the procedure.

Many qualitative coding procedures allow for shortcuts to save time and conserve resources. The assumption is that the patterns in narrative data are redundant or repetitive and that it suffices to analyze a select portion of the interview material. For example, in coding the defenses of participants and their level of maturity, the Grant Study selected vignettes from interviews and did not code complete interviews (Vaillant 1977, 2002, 2012).[2] This was deemed sufficient to capture constructs of interest.

It was neither sound analytically nor expedient for this study to use only a portion of the interview record for its coding procedure. Interviews in both eras of the study had been carried out assiduously to ensure coherence and completeness of understanding; abbreviated inquiry in coding risked leaving central questions unanswered and reframing the participant's life history. In the adult interview record, for example, prior to the point of saturation (where the participant's own conception of his account felt stable and complete to him and to the interviewer, and no further probing for new material was required) neither I as the adult interviewer nor the research team knew enough about a participant to have confidence in our judgments about how he felt about himself and his life. The redundancy in the full record confirmed themes and ruled out false leads, speeding up the analysis and leading to more reliable numeric and thematic conclusions.[3]

The procedure's many steps and considerations require judgment and experience to carry out. In addition to myself, four coders were recruited and hired for pay from doctoral and master's-level clinical and counseling psychology training programs. One was an undergraduate senior. (Coders are listed in the acknowledgments.) After several months of practice to become proficient, a coder spent fifteen hours on average to read and analyze the interview record for one adult participant and slightly longer for a college participant.

CONCEPTUAL INSIGHTS BUILT INTO THE RATING PROCEDURE

Two key conceptual insights are built into the rating procedure. The first recognizes that positive and negative affect in the life history appears from two distinct perspectives—one bottom-up and the other top-down. Used in parallel, they produce the richest and soundest assessment of intrapsychic brightness and darkness.

The top-down perspective takes the life history as a holistic unit of data, focusing on the participant's overarching life goals (introduced in chapter 3 and developed in this chapter) and whether he feels he has realized them. The bottom-up perspective assesses smaller units of experience, affective domains, where participants commonly invest in and speak about experience loaded with affect; for example, in adulthood, domains include career, marriage and romantic relationship, and parenting.

Metaphorically speaking, one process is the equivalent of scouring the beach for the green pebbles, stones, rocks, and boulders, and drawing lines around clusters of these mineral aggregates to carry out a close study of these green pigmented areas; they add up to the totality of the green presence on the beach. The other process is the equivalent of hovering one hundred feet above the beach in a helicopter and discerning the entire pattern, the whole picture of green aggregations on the beach. The first process captures knowledge of the beach that comes from careful consideration of the parts; the second captures knowledge of the beach from an impression of the whole.

The assessment procedure guides the observer to look at the beach both ways in the same evaluation, a key innovation that lends power to the analysis. The two perspectives provide an internal check on each other, because they are two sides of the same coin. Participants carry out life goals in the areas or domains where they experience affect; the affect reflects their experience of success or failure in realizing life goals. The two approaches take different perspectives at the outset of analysis, but if properly carried out, they converge by the end. They lead to the same conclusion about the overall affective tendency in the life history.

The two vantage points on affect in a life history also give a depth and organization to the observer's perspective by encouraging him or her to toggle back and forth. The top-down perspective orders otherwise unrelated parts that are

TABLE 4.1. Scale of Intrapsychic Brightness and Darkness

1	2	3	4	5	6	7
Overall Dark			Mixed Range		Overall Bright	
Most dark	Dark	Tendency toward dark	Evenly mixed	Tendency toward bright	Bright	Most bright

the focus of the bottom-up process. The joint application of both perspectives minimizes the chance that the observer is overlooking key displays of affect in the life history that another observer would notice.

The second insight leveraged by the rating procedure is the synthesis of positive and negative affect. I have already illustrated it in the psychobiographical sketches when concluding by summing up a participant's overall affect. The synthesis employs the concept of "affect balance," in which positive and negative affect are first recognized separately and then weighted in an overall summary. Bradburn (1969) operationalized this concept in the survey measurement of happiness called the Affect Balance Scale. I recognized that this study's procedure shares a solution to synthesis in common with his measure only after the grounded theoretical analyses independently led to the procedure. The synthesis allows the observer to conclude overall how happy or unhappy—how intrapsychically bright or dark—a participant's experiences are, whether overall or within a domain, such as career. Although positive and negative affect in the life histories are distinct and observable, they combine into a range of balances. This range is the spectrum of intrapsychic brightness and darkness illustrated in psychobiographical examples in part 1. The assessment procedure captures the range in a numeric scale, shown in table 4.1 and explained throughout this chapter.[4]

WHAT CONSTITUTES A SOUND ASSESSMENT?

The assessment procedure (reproduced in online appendix 5) guides the coder through a series of steps on a form. Coders could conduct parts of the analysis differently and reach the same conclusion about the participant's overall brightness and darkness.

The Master Ratings Grid on the form holds the coder's numeric ratings of parts of the life history in building up to an overall rating at the bottom of the grid. Lower on the form, text boxes, shaded gray, show where a coder wrote companion thematic descriptions for domains and various other steps. The text box "Explanation and Rating of Overall Adult Affect" holds the thematic conclusion.

I assigned cases randomly to at least two coders for each case, although immaterial factors, such as scheduling considerations, sometimes influenced my assignments.

After observers carried out and documented their evaluation of a life history independently, they met to discuss the case and compare their conclusions. It was rare that a coder produced a sound numeric conclusion without a sound thematic conclusion or vice versa.

The best evaluations were well reasoned, addressed the various considerations embedded in the steps of the rating procedure, and were internally consistent across these steps, synthesizing an overall summary reasonably accurate to the thematic content of the life history. Together, these features of an evaluation made it sound and persuasive to other trained observers. Meetings to discuss a case exposed agreement and disagreement because the guided procedure was clear in the steps and considerations an observer was to take into account. Persuasion was possible, and the texts of the life histories were the ultimate arbiter. In this chapter I first present key conceptual issues in the procedure and then evidence of a high level of agreement between coders and support outside the interview data for the procedure's capture of the intended construct.

Three independent coders evaluated Hovanec and assigned ratings of 5, 6, and 6. They were sound analyses and, despite differences, substantially in agreement overall. The observer who assigned the rating of a 5 was not incorrect. She thought Hovanec's marriage and business relationships weighed him down more than the other observers did; she was carrying out the evaluation procedure correctly. In my own evaluation (not presented here), I wavered between a 5 and a 6 in my overall determination, for the same reasons identified by this observer, and I can see the sound empirical support and judgment in both of these ratings.

The reader similarly might have felt while reading Hovanec's psychobiographical sketch that he was not as bright as other overall bright participants, such as Payne (rated a 7 by coders). One reader of an early draft of this book had a similar reaction to his psychobiographical sketch. Had an observer rated Hovanec overall as a 1, 2, 3, 4, or 7, however, it would have been a mistake.

Steps in the Assessment Procedure

What were these observers noticing in Hovanec's life history? What evidence did they draw upon and how did they weigh it? Text box 4.1 lists the main steps in the assessment procedure. Rather than tracking the layout of the form, the evidence is listed in conceptual order, to illustrate how someone would approach the assessment. The conceptually most important of these steps are explained in this chapter.

DOMAINS ANALYSIS

For illustration I will track two independent assessments of Hovanec's life history, starting with the domains analysis.

Identify Most Important Affective Domains

The important areas of Hovanec's life, those material to his overall brightness and darkness, were identified by the observers to be his career,[5] marriage, parenting, and recreation domains. Sometimes observers differed in the areas of a life history that they thought were most important, but not in Hovanec's case; and in the cases in which they did, differences often did not materially affect the conclusion, because observers might recognize the same themes but locate them in different domains. Similar to the life history interviews, the guided assessment procedure could accommodate the encounter of different individuals with the format, while still retaining a discipline in addressing the main concepts and reaching conclusions.

Notably, our two observers omitted the following areas as less important for Hovanec: community life, social relationships outside nuclear family, spiritual and religious life, mental health or health, and experience in adulthood with family of origin. These areas show up in other participants' lives. Observers tailored the procedure to reflect the commitments of each participant rather than applying universal criteria (something much more difficult to do using survey methods).

Sometimes observers specified additional affective domains if those listed on the form did not capture an important area for a participant. Observers most often used this option for participants deeply invested in, and affected by, a geographic place, such as a region or town where he had lived or currently lived.

Text Box 4.1. Conceptual Steps in Evaluating a Life History

A. DOMAINS ANALYSIS

1. Identify the most important domains in the life history contributing to affect, for example, career, parenting, community life. Mark each on the Master Ratings Grid.
2. Comb experiences in these domains for positive and negative affective themes. Write a description, and cite lines in the interviews supporting the themes, as needed.
3. Synthesize thematic material into an affect balance for each domain. Assign a "raw affect" number. This assignment precedes any consideration of how the participant regulates affect.
4. Consider self-regulating responses to affect, visible in the narrative, if they are salient to the domain's central tendency of observed affect. If applicable, assign an adjusted affect number, and write a description.
5. Consider recency and temporariness of experienced affect, that is, situational effects, which might be distorting the record of the long-term central tendency. If applicable, assign and describe a situationally adjusted rating.
6. Establish your perspective as distinct from the participant's conscious statements about his own affective experience in the domain. If it would be different from your rating, assign a rating that you think the participant would give to himself, and explain this "participant self-rating."

B. LIFE GOALS ANALYSIS

7. Identify central life goals, which are either values or long-term strivings. The participant reveals goals throughout the life history as his internal standards by which he evaluates the quality and success of experiences. In recording life goals, consider and record subordinate goals, if any. For each life goal, verify that you see manifestations of them influencing domain affect. Record your supporting evidence.
   a. Internal check: Verify that the life goals you identify are standards that cut across multiple domains and explain affective themes in those domains.

    b. Internal check: Confirm that central themes in domains are explained by, or linked to, life goals.

8. Determine which life goals are fully and partly achieved and which are not. Record with supporting evidence.

9. Determine the participant's self-regulating responses to unrealized life goals: Is there a mitigation or amplification of negative affect visible in the narrative? Specify the responses and their effect on overall affect, and provide examples in domains.

    a. Internal check: Self-regulating responses to unrealized life goals should correspond to self-regulating responses to negative affect in domains, and vice versa.

    b. Internal check: Reconcile the conscious and unconscious record.

        1) Identify distorted self-understandings or presentations of affect in the form of leakage, over- and under-cognized features of the life history, contradictions, and incongruence between the conscious and unconscious presentation.

        2) Identify other notable features of the affective register, such as restricted range of affect—for example, "cutting off"—which help to interpret the participant's statements about his affective experience.

        3) This step should inform your analysis of self-regulating responses, as well as whether to assign a "participant self-rating" for the overall rating or the domains ratings of affect.

10. Synthesize overall affective material into an affect balance for the life history. Record your numeric summary and specify supporting themes and relevant considerations drawn from each preceding step in the evaluation.

11. If applicable, assign an adjusted rating reflecting the buoying or depressing effect of self-regulating responses to unrealized life goals. Record and explain.

12. If applicable, assign and explain an adjusted rating accounting for situational effects.

13. If applicable, assign and explain a "participant self-rating" for overall affect.

Comb the Domains for Affective Themes and Synthesize into an Overall Affect Balance for Each Domain

The two observers assessed the themes, the positive and negative affect, and the overall affect balance in each domain. For example, the two observers assessed Hovanec's career domain as a 5 and 6, respectively. They focused on the roles, relationships, activities, situations, and involvements in the life history belonging to Hovanec's career domain. To carry out this analysis, the observer determined which experiences were included, following the form's instructions for this step:

> **Career:** List each career, career period (jobs the participant combines as a discrete part of his career), and types of jobs held. For each career segment, list the dates of the segment. For each job, list the job title, organization, and number of years the job was held. Also specify whether the person is currently working full-time, part-time, is retired, about to retire or has no plans to retire soon.

To maintain confidentiality, an example of this completed part of the form for any participant cannot be provided. A generic case might look as follows:

XYZ Law School: 1964–1967
ABC Law Firm: 1967–1977
QRS Law Firm: 1977–1983
FG Partners (partner): 1983–present (full time)

For each domain assessment, the observer created a list of which experiences were included. Experiences included, for relevant domains, each important romantic relationship, each child and stepchild, the religious and social communities to which a participant belonged and his major activities within them, the important social relationships outside of nuclear family, and so on. This step ensured specificity and focus in the analysis of affect within domains.

Just as certain domains were common and important across the sample, so too were there common themes within each domain where affect was loaded. The observer identified these themes, but the form prompts consideration by listing themes that commonly show up in the life histories for a given domain. The list is a product of the grounded theoretical analysis. Table 4.2 lists common themes connected to affect in career.

Themes for five domains—career, marriage / romantic relationships, par-

TABLE 4.2. Aspects of Career: Common Themes

Skills	Relationship Quality	Purpose / Meaning	Status	Goals	Work Preferences	Person's Fit with Role and Culture
- Used - Challenged - Recognized - Sense of mastery	- Colleagues - Clients - Mentors	- Impact people - Impact organization or profession - Intrinsic pleasure in work	- Social - Monetary - Within place of work - Within field	- Close to (perceived) original goals at beginning of career - Achieved professional potential	- Autonomy - Security - Creativity - Financial	- Work-life balance - Types of people - Types of values

TABLE 4.3. Two Ratings of Hovanec's Domain Experiences

	Rater 1	Rater 2
Career	5	6
Marriage	4	4
Parenting	7	6
Recreation	7	7

enting, community life, and relationships outside of nuclear family—appear at the end of the form. The themes are reasonably complete for this sample, and represent a major product of the study. Still, they are not exhaustive, only suggestive, to help coders in analyzing domains.

The observers analyzed and rated each of the domains that they determined were important for Hovanec's overall brightness and darkness. Table 4.3 shows the ratings.

The two observers rated these domains of Hovanec's life similarly, thematically as well as in their numeric ratings. This level of domain agreement was not necessary for raters to agree overall.

These ratings underscore the benefit of saturation in the interviews. In both Hovanec's career and his marriage, the assessment was complicated. There were countervailing affective themes, and some apparent contradictions in how he felt overall. The abundance of material and nuance clarified uncertainties. Hovanec spoke about his marriage and his career from many more perspectives and in many more contexts than would have been possible in a briefer and less exhaustive interview. The burden then shifted to the observation task: it took a long time to weigh the various possible considerations and capture the overall experience faithfully to the complexity that he conveyed. The two observers succeeded and also reached agreement.

The remaining steps of the domains analyses—of self-regulating responses to affect, situational effects, and the participant self-rating—are conducted in the same way and best illustrated later in the chapter in discussing the analysis of life goals.

In summary, the domains provide buckets for the coders to hold the green-pigmented aggregates they find on the beach. They direct the coders to look for green-pigmented aggregates that might fill these buckets; participants commonly reveal affect in their life histories in the domain areas. The coder synthesizes affect into a balance for each of the important domains.

Affect is visible in Hovanec's life history in four important domains. His career and marriage are mixed, and his parenting and recreation appear positive. Both observers' domain assessments (and the details of Hovanec's psychobiographical sketch) suggest that his affect is not overall negative, but we cannot say for sure whether overall it is mixed or bright.

This is as far as the domains analysis can take us. We cannot average or sum or apply any other formulaic algorithm to weigh these domains in reaching an accurate overall synthesis. We need more guidance from the participant on what his priorities are and how he experiences the relative importance of these affective themes. We also need a framework that distinguishes the points on the spectrum of intrapsychic brightness and darkness so that we can know where to locate an eventual synthesis of Hovanec's overall affect.

LIFE GOALS ANALYSIS

The domains capture experiences that contribute to overall affect in the life history, but only the life goals analysis orders them in a coherent and unified picture of overall affect in the life history.

Life goals are the overarching standards that a participant uses throughout his interviews to evaluate the success and quality of his efforts across domains and across time. They are not necessarily explicitly stated or recognized by the participant. They are the superordinate frame of concerns that he brings to his life. Life goals come in two forms—values as well as strivings—both of which end up serving as the participant's personal standards as he views his life.[6]

Determine How Affect Links to Life Goals

Hovanec's life as a parent is glowing because he realized a central striving to have and to rear children, to enjoy good relationships with them, and to impart values to them. Succeeding in these ways as a father comprises a life goal because it serves as a standard for evaluating his experience across multiple domains, not only in parenting. In his career, Hovanec was satisfied by the balance he maintained with his family life. In his marriage, he was satisfied by his wife's leading role in raising their children and being a homemaker. In his recreation, Hovanec was satisfied by having introduced his family to the natural world that he cherished.

Hovanec felt positively because he felt he was successful in his strivings as a parent. This life goal had ramifications for his domain experiences: manifestations of this goal are seen within domains, through affect-laden themes connected to this goal. Hovanec took pleasure in aspects of his life that reflected realization of this goal in career, marriage, and recreation, as well as in parenting. The two perspectives—life goals and domains—mirror each other. (This is the value of undertaking the domains analysis separately from the life goals analysis: it provides a second way of looking for important affective themes, although it cannot yield a synthesis of overall affect by itself.)

Identify Life Goals

Hovanec and other participants usually reveal multiple life goals. For example, in addition to his aspirations as a parent, Hovanec aspired to success in his business career, financially, in the size of the organizations he ran, and in owning his own business. He also sought a hospitable climate. Hovanec's goals for his career were a life goal because their impact and execution encompassed other areas of his life. He married a woman who would support his career aspirations. He relocated his family several times to leave inhospitable business cultures and to acquire and operate a business of his own. He strove to find balance between his career aspirations and his family and recreational life. Hovanec experienced positive and negative affect across multiple domains reflecting this central aspiration.

The assessment form instructs the rater to identify life goals as follows:

Directions: Please list the participant's life goals. The life goals are the participant's own way of organizing his life efforts and/or the criteria he uses in evaluating his experiences. These goals may involve work, family or other roles, but rise to the level of a life goal because the individual organizes his life efforts, not merely his role efforts, around it. Here are some tips for identifying life goals.

- Explicitly stated
- Strong or visible emotion
- Discusses or thinks about at length
- Repeated mention
- Externally or self-directed (e.g., have a good family versus be a good father)
- Avoid a negative or seek out a positive (e.g., maintain security versus be a provider)
- Goals may not be visible, or only some goals may be visible to you, for certain cases
- Conceptualize the life goal at the highest level of abstraction that is still specific

Coders sometimes conceptualized, grouped, or summarized life goals differently, as the two observers do in assessing Hovanec's life history. Both focus on his work and family priorities. One observer delineates a third life goal for Hovanec, to impart his values in both work and family endeavors. The other observer weaves many of these considerations into his description of family and work life goals and does not treat them as a separate goal. Both observers convey a sense of Hovanec's particular vision for the realization of a value system.

Unrealized and Partially Realized Life Goals

The better Hovanec was doing in relation to his life goals, the more positively he seemed to feel about the various areas of his life where they were manifested and vice versa. The converse is also true: unrealized or partially realized life goals reveal some amount of negative affect in Hovanec's domain experiences and life overall. Hovanec revealed negative affect in his wish that he had achieved a higher level of professional success. But there is a second consideration in assessing affect connected to unrealized or partially realized life goals. (I will refer to them simply as "unrealized life goals.")

Capture the Effect of Responses to Unrealized Life Goals

Hovanec demonstrated an obvious secondary process in self-regulating responses to unrealized life goals. Hovanec tempered the unsatisfying aspects of his marriage and career by reframing them. He recognized the positive aspects of these and other areas of his life that were offsetting, particularly experiences with his children, the prized achievement of his life. Hovanec perceived a positive frame overall. Reframing defuses some of the negative affect associated with unrealized goals, helping in Hovanec's life history to locate the overall affect in the bright category (or mostly bright) rather than in the mixed category. Reframing appears in domains as well.

To capture the effect of responses to unrealized life goals, the form asks coders to assess "raw affect" separately from "adjusted affect" in each domain and overall, where such responses are visible. *Raw affect* refers to the unmediated affective display in the life history, whereas *adjusted affect* reflects the adjustments to affect that result from the participant's responses. (The assessment procedure attends only to this visible type of coping rather than using a theory of coping more generally.) Hovanec is an example of a participant whose response to negative affect elevates his overall affect; for many participants, the responses have no effect or exacerbate negative affect.

Several steps of the procedure capture unrealized life goals and the affective impact of self-regulating responses to them. First, coders identify attained and unattained life goals. Both observers of Hovanec note that he did not succeed as fully in his business career as he had hoped. Second, coders describe the participant's response to unrealized life goals. The form prompts coders with examples of common types of participant responses to unrealized life goals, listed below.

- Individual is not overinvolved in one area of life (not all eggs are in one basket)
- Negative experience does not overwhelm individual
- Able to compensate or be buoyed by other areas/experiences
- Able to adapt to new situations
- Able to bound affect, or to distance from affect
- Reframes negative affect to something less negative or positive

- Defensive (overly distances self from negative emotions)
- His reaction intensifies or expands the impact of the negative felt in one area of experience
- Pervasive negative affect or pessimism reduces positive areas or exacerbates negative areas of experience
- Clinical depression
- One area depresses affect felt in another area

- Effort geared at trying to plan-
  fully take action to solve
  unrealized goals
  —developing a new strategy to
   achieve goal
  —continuing old strategy to
   achieve goal

- Clear interference with functioning evidenced in
  —work,
  —relationships,
  —constricted social radius

The two observers described Hovanec's responses to unrealized life goals similarly. They recognized that he largely contains the negative affect he experiences. One observer saw Hovanec as compartmentalizing, and both observers spoke of Hovanec's reframing by focusing on positive aspects of his life.

Coders noted an "adjusted affect" rating if the response to unrealized goals elevated a participant's overall affect. The first observer elevated Hovanec's (raw) rating of 4 to an adjusted rating of 5, whereas the second rater did not adjust, having already determined an overall score of 6.

The same thought process applies to adjusting affect ratings in the domains. In fact, the same effects are visible. The second rater judged Hovanec's career affect elevated by these effects.

The life goals perspective reveals how a participant deals with negative affect—that of unrealized life goals—in the most important commitments of his life and helps to guide the observer's attention to manifestations of these strategies in domains. Hovanec's focus on his children to reframe the unsatisfying aspects of his career would be invisible to an observer focused only on his career experiences. Thus, without the life goals perspective, the observer would be hard pressed to see these psychological (coping) strategies in domains.[7]

The life goals analysis for the participant can be synthesized as follows: Hovanec's mostly realized life goals and his amelioration of the negative affect of unrealized goals suggest that he is on the brighter end of the spectrum. Participants whose lives are darker offer additional insight in reaching this conclusion.

FILTERS: SPECIAL CONCERNS IN EVALUATING THE DARKER LIFE HISTORIES

Martin's life goals have a different quality from Hovanec's, as they have a significant protective and defensive component. A great deal of Martin's strivings seem directed to protecting himself from experiencing further pain.

As a result, the assessment task in Martin's case is different than it is for brighter participants. Life goals and responses to unrealized life goals are blended together. These "responses" have taken over as central strivings, so much so that life goals preceding or underlying them are not even detected. Martin devoted a relatively large share of his energies to self-protection.

The permeating darkness in Martin's life history poses a unique empirical challenge found among darker participants. He did not acknowledge the darkness as fully as it appears to the observer. Martin's conscious record of affective experiences and unconscious record of conveyed affect are at odds with each other more than for the brighter participants. Martin presented his story in a more pat way than Hovanec presented his. The telling by Martin had less variation in affect. It was muted.

Martin and Hovanec have different strategies for responding to the painful feelings of unrealized life goals. Rather than reframing, Martin filtered the affect coming through in his conscious reflection and communication. This is part of a larger strategy of self-protection (which seems to function as a life goal rather than as a response to unrealized life goals). He did not want to experience the pain of his situation (or to report it). But he was not altogether successful in tamping down the negative affect, and it leaked out for the observer to see, resulting in what the study called *leakage*. Martin revealed painful affect in his life, which seemed out of reach to him and more buttoned down than the affective displays—dark and bright—of the brighter participants, such as Hovanec.

The empirical problem is how reliably to recognize the presence of the filter and verify the negative feelings conveyed, but not affirmed, by the participant.

Capture the Filters in Interviews

The first step in recognizing filters occurs in interviews. Consider two participants as further examples of the phenomenon, which I recognized while interviewing them.

One participant was uniformly enthusiastic and reported that everything with his wife was positive. At the same time he had clearly not disclosed difficulties in his career. The painful problems in his marriage and his career were revealed later in the interview, but not explicitly. The participant had had an affair. He had also lost his job and was working in a marginalized position. He kept a stiff upper lip about both these difficulties, but the fuller truth of his experience in these areas spilled out in other ways. His wife found out about the affair and issued an ultimatum that it end, and his employer released him from employment for misconduct. His lack of reliability as a narrator—whether intentional or unconscious—was exposed. He did not acknowledge or reconcile the incongruence. He continued the evasion of the earlier representations.

Consider this second example. The participant wept during multiple interviews. He was extremely labile and often seemed on the verge of tears. He seemed to suffer from traumas that reached as far back as his earliest years. Yet he was unaware of how much pain he struggled with. He reported himself on a survey measure of subjective well-being (Satisfaction with Life Scale) to be the second-happiest participant in the interview sample. This incongruence was jarring. He could not see his pain.

I resolved the incongruence in the interviews by asking these participants multiple times to affirm my understanding. They confirmed their conscious perspective without acknowledging the unacknowledged aspects of these experiences. I concluded that the person was upholding an incongruence but that he didn't see it as such. He saw his conscious story as a perfectly reasonable accounting of how he felt.

Detect Filters in Assessment

The transcribed interviews showed these incongruences, enabling their use in assessment. Interviews exposed incongruences not only in the conscious record but also through their capture of the range and types of emotions comprising the participant's emotional palette. (Online appendix 2 explains the study's approach to clinical interviewing.) For example, Martin's greater closeness with his father at the end of his father's life showed positive affect prominently missing in Martin's other experiences. The depth of Martin's loneliness after both parents had passed away stands at the opposite end of Martin's personal range of affect. The range serves as a legend for interpreting the emotion in any single event, situation, or episode or in key aspects of the life history.

This is where a whole-person perspective becomes critical to understanding Martin's recounted experiences. Without the range, we would lack critical context. Unless they paid attention to this feature of his life history, coders would be working strictly at the conscious level of Martin's report of his experiences. He might appear unhappy about the conditions of his life—his marriage and his career—but it would be easy to downplay how significantly he feels his negative affect. He might seem, like Hovanec, to be containing or ameliorating negative affect. Martin consciously perceived, believed, and conveyed that he was happier than he was, or more accurately, that he was not as unhappy as he was.

Conversely, Hovanec's strategy for ameliorating the sting of unrealized life goals produced a recognizable shift in his affect. It is believable and persuasive because we saw him display a range of emotion.

Identify Affective Restriction Coupled with Leakage

The assessment procedure asks the coder to determine whether two conditions are present in a life history: affective restriction and any incongruence between the conscious recounting of experience and conveyed affect or leakage.

The observer would notice these features already in weighing affect in the domains. The participant's story would leave him wondering whether he had correctly perceived the affect at work in domains. There would be little affective range to go on. And he would perceive mixed messages about what the participant felt.

The major challenge, however, would be in assessing life goals. Consider the two participants discussed above as illustrations of filters. The lack of negative experiences in both men's lives—as they consciously convey them—would sound too good to be true, since even the brightest participants reported some negative experiences or unrealized goals. You can't feel only positive affect and no negative affect if the things you cherish and have striven for over a lifetime are unrealized. Hovanec and other bright participants got to the highest levels of overall affect not strictly by an absence of negative experiences. They attained goals and they metabolized failures.

Further, in assessing life goals, it would become clear that such participants were organized around protecting themselves from experiencing further pain. This would be visible in their strivings over time as well as in their endeavor to avoid pain during the interviews. As in Martin's example, the life goals and the responses to life goals would blend together.

The observer would thus detect a problem in assessing both domains and life goals. He or she would recognize the signals of filtered-out darkness in the form of a restricted emotional range, leakage, the protectiveness of central strivings, and the apparent blending of central strivings with responses to unrealized life goals.

Online appendix 4 reproduces the guide I developed, borrowing from the Adult Attachment Interviewing coding manual (George et al., 1984, 1985, 1996), to train coders in typologies of incongruence. I used this guide in training sessions to sensitize them to these issues.

Identify Affective Restriction without Prominent Leakage

A few participants at first seemed to present with a restricted affective range, either in relation to an earlier baseline or in relation to more vibrant participants. But it later became clear that they showed neither leakage nor incongruence between their conscious and unconscious presentations. These participants lacked the distorting filters described above, displayed by participants with affective restriction coupled with leakage. Their cognitive and emotional style, which the study called "cutting off," appeared with some happier participants who had adapted to early hardship or who, by disposition, perceived in more muted affective colors.

In one case, a participant's response to painful early poverty and traumatic military service may have led him to restrict his emotional range as part of his pursuit of a more contained, stable life. He showed this motive in choices for geographic and occupational stability and in his family life. In contrast with Martin, he felt content within this posture. He did not leak negative feelings. Rather, he conveyed positive experiences as well as negative ones, all using a subdued palette, lending credibility to his reflections.

Another participant spoke of his family relationships from what appeared at first as an emotional remove, using muted language and problem-solving skills borrowed from his managerial career. This remove, however, did not seem to paper over the emotional reality of the love and closeness he felt toward his family, either to him or to the observer. His wife and children complained of his distance, but he was actively grappling with these issues rather than blocking them from view or filtering out how they made him feel. He felt strong positive affect toward his family as well as in his professional accomplishments, which he also expressed in his muted style.

Record the Judgment of a Filter: "The Participant Self-Rating"

Once tipped off to filtering and leakage in the life history, the observer could reconcile evidence in the participant's record—conscious and unconscious— and use the full record in assessing affect in domains and life goals.

The procedure asks the observer, further, explicitly to acknowledge when a participant's record required this kind of integration. The observer recorded how he believed the participant would rate himself in domains and overall if he were to use the procedure. "Participant self-ratings," as the study called them, acknowledged that the participant would uphold his perspective on his life, even with contradictions, as he did with me during interviews.

This step ensured crispness of thinking and provided coders a way to communicate observations with each other. Participant self-ratings did not supersede or alter the observer's ratings. They were simply a tool to track the observer's judgment that a distorting filter was at work in the empirical record.

THE SCALE

My review of important considerations in the study's rating procedure will now serve as groundwork to show how the procedure discriminated among participants and located them on the Scale of Intrapsychic Brightness and Darkness.

Participant's Relationship with Unrealized Life Goals

The first decision locates the participant in one of the broad categories of overall dark, overall mixed, and overall bright. Doing so might be straightforward if the affect balance is unquestionable. The extremes, such as Martin and Payne, are easy to place this way. Sometimes the mixed are easy to identify as well, since they don't clearly fit either of the other two classifications. But this classification is not yet a position on the scale.

A participant's posture in relation to his life goals helps with this broader classification as well as in pinpointing positions on the scale. If the participant was still striving for his unattained goals, he was in the mixed category. If he felt it was a lost cause and was resigned, he was in the overall dark category. If he had realized his life goals, or if he was resolved, fulfilled, and at peace with how they had turned out, he was in the overall bright category. This heuristic helped especially to place those participants potentially on the border between the mixed and the overall bright or overall dark categories. Hovanec was a 6 for observers who saw him as generally fulfilled and at peace with the way things turned out; he was a 5 for the observer who thought that he had not reached resolution with his strivings. Similarly at the other end of the mixed category, whether the participant felt that his strivings were a lost cause or that success still might be feasible determined which category he belonged in, dark or mixed.

The participant's posture toward his life goals discriminated more granularly as well, among the three gradations of mixed participants. How much hope or doubt did the participant have that he would succeed in resolving his issues? The answer to this question suggested an attitude with affective import. Hope tilted mixed participants toward the overall bright end of the mixed

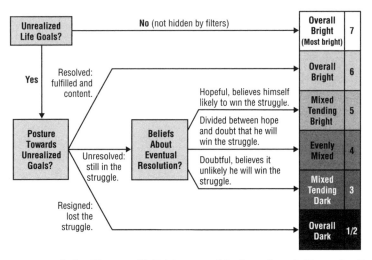

F I G U R E   4 . 1 . Scale of Intrapsychic Brightness and Darkness (1 to 7) Observed as Participant's Relationship with Life Goals

category, a 5 on the scale. Doubt tilted mixed participants toward the overall dark end of the mixed category, a 3 on the scale. If a participant was equally divided between hope and doubt, he was in the middle of the mixed category, a 4. The affective tilt arose not only from the hope and doubt observable in these positions but also from how much control the participant felt in relation to his unrealized life goals. Figure 4.1 shows the positions on the scale in terms of a participant's relationship to his life goals. The procedure incorporates other considerations determining the rating as well.

Leakage

Prominent leakage and affective restriction meant the participant was a 4 or below and probably a 3 or below. Brighter participants did not show these characteristics.

The Struggle for Self-Repair

Participants at the 3 and 4 positions on the scale frequently are marked by their struggle with strong pressure from family expectations or societal demands, which they experience as forces equal to or larger than their own will in directing their lives. Participants experience a gravity-like pull toward a particular life and future. These struggles often become focally organized around pivotal life choices and express an effort to come to terms with—and locate oneself in relation to—values and traditions held by one's parents or socioeconomic, religious, ethnic, or national group. It is not uncommon for participants to grapple with the expectation to follow a specific educational or career path, such as going to Harvard or entering business or law, valued by a parent. This may reflect a class aspiration held by the participant and his family—whether it entails overcoming disadvantage, realizing a middle-class aspiration, or perpetuating a legacy of privilege. It also may reflect parental esteem for a particular profession. It is also not uncommon for struggles to crystallize around the expectation that one will marry someone of the same religious or ethnic group, or more generally that one will marry, have children, and reproduce a nuclear family.

Martin was no longer in the struggle with what he felt were his father's expectations. But some adult participants are still struggling. Because they are in the struggle, they are at least a 3. Those who doubt they can succeed are a 3; those divided between expecting success and failure are a 4. This kind of struggle is not found among participants rated 5 and above. They may have chosen to follow similar expectations, but they are resolved about it. Their choice is not ego-dystonic.

This kind of struggle marks a type of life goal, one the study came to call a *self-repair goal*, found in the bottom half of the scale. The participant seeks to correct or improve what he perceives to be a deficient self or deficient conditions in his present or past life. Something about the participant or the world is not right, or not yet right, in his eyes, and he devotes a great deal of energy to fixing it. The pressure, such as Martin felt, to enter a business career, registered with him strongly because he understood it to offer the chance to bolster his deficient sense of himself. For Martin, a business career might have redeemed him in the eyes of his father. The pursuit of self-repair takes precedence over other enjoyments or gratifications until the problem is fixed. The long-term consequence of a self-repair goal is that it suppresses well-being (unless the goal is attained, which is rare in the sample). It holds the participant in a long-term quest in which he is attuned to the deficiencies in himself and his experiences. It creates strife with other desires the person has.

Participants at the level of a 5 and above don't show a motive for self-repair or the drag on their well-being that comes with it. Their personal sense of value is not deficient or at risk. By contrast, the life goals that mark them are oriented outwardly, toward relationships, activities, roles, and society. They are seeking to enact positive outcomes rather than avoiding negative ones in the future.

The Extremes of the Scale

Experience with the sample helped to determine the extreme positions of 1 and 7 on the scale. The full realization of life goals indicating a 7 was easiest to see in relation to other overall bright participants. The comparison showed the relative lack of disappointment of a 7. The intensity of anguish and hopelessness indicating a 1 stood out in relation to other overall dark participants. These rating considerations are summarized in table 4.4.

Exemplars of Points on the Scale

The differences between Martin and Hovanec, first introduced in their psychobiographical sketches, show what it looks like in the sample to have a happy life and to have an unhappy life. Characteristics of each of their patterns appear—to a greater or lesser degree—at each point on the scale. Armed with the scale and classification criteria, the reader can now notice the configurations of these characteristics for participants sketched in this book. Table 4.5 shows the participant's adult rating, while figure 4.2 shows the adult samples' distribution of brightness and darkness. Nonintegers average multiple coders' ratings.

WHAT DOES THE SCALE OF INTRAPSYCHIC BRIGHTNESS AND DARKNESS REPRESENT?

The scale is a rich description of psychological characteristics in a life that cluster along points on a spectrum. Its positions discriminate among and organize well-being phenomena observed in the grounded analyses. It is a *typology* specifying the terms of happiness or well-being, organized around the construct of intrapsychic brightness and darkness in participants' life histories.

The happiest participants are generally fulfilled, feel their lives to be purposeful, and are not plagued by injured selves or chronic dissatisfaction. They are much less likely to have suffered from mental health issues in the past (or the present). They show a sense of gratification from their efforts at living. These are not merely reported; they are conveyed. By contrast, the unhappy are disengaged from or limiting of their engagements with others, with roles, with society, and with the future, to protect themselves from further injury or loss of value and from being stimulated into awareness of their sense of injury. The unhappy display an emptiness and a malaise, a monochromatic affective display arising from their effort to avoid negative stimulation but without having meaningful positive experiences.

TABLE 4.4. Classification Heuristics

Levels of Overall Positive and Negative Affect Observed in Participants' Narratives			Heuristics for Identifying Different Levels of Overall Positive and Negative Affect			
Rating	Overall Affect	Further Differentiation of Overall Affect	Fulfillment of Life Goals	Response to Unrealized Life Goals	Leakage	Directedness of Life Goals
7	Overall Bright	Strongest overall positive.	Not struggling with issues. Feels content and fulfilled.	No unrealized life goals or significantly troubling issues.	Leakage not a factor.	Goals are oriented outwardly toward relationships, activities, roles, and society and with a view toward enacting positive outcomes in the future.
6		Overall positive with some areas that are exceptions but subsumed into overall positive.		Some unrealized life goals but in control of how they make him feel. Still feels positive.		No visible self-repair goals. Self-acceptance. The self is not a site of struggle or deficiency.
5	Overall Mixed	Strong positive and strong negative but tending toward positive.	Struggling with issues but not overwhelmed by them. Still engaged.	Has hope that he will win the struggle. Believes it likely. Unlike 6, shows some psychological drag from unrealized life goals.	Leakage not a factor.	No visible self-repair goals. Problems do not generalize into problems with the self.
4		Strong positive and strong negative and no clear sense that person is tending in one direction. Evenly mixed.		Divided between believing (hope) and not believing (doubt) he will win the struggle.	Leakage can be a factor.	Some self-repair goals alongside some orientation outwardly and toward the future.

(continued)

TABLE 4.4. (continued)

	Levels of Overall Positive and Negative Affect Observed in Participants' Narratives		Heuristics for Identifying Different Levels of Overall Positive and Negative Affect			
Rating	Overall Affect	Further Differentiation of Overall Affect	Fulfillment of Life Goals	Response to Unrealized Life Goals	Leakage	Directedness of Life Goals
3	Overall Mixed	Strong positive and strong negative but tending toward negative.	Struggling with issues but not overwhelmed by them. Still engaged.	Doing best he can do. Doesn't expect to win the struggle. Unlike 2, still engaged but not engulfed by the struggle. Has areas of positive affect that are separate.	Clear constriction of affect with leakage.	Self-repair goals are prominent but at least one bright area is not subsumed by these goals. A rejecting self-concept, feels he lacks value and is damaged in important ways. Being able to pursue and enjoy externally oriented goals is conditioned on achieving self-repair.
2	Overall Dark	Strong negative that outweighs areas that are positive or absent negative.	Struggling with issues and overwhelmed by them. Resigned.	Engulfed by the problems and the negative feelings and sees no way to fix them. Feels his life is a lost cause.	Constriction of affect with prominent leakage.	Subsumed by self-protective and self-repair goals.
1		Strongest overall negative.		Overcome by unrealized hopes. Lost the struggle; given up hope. Shuts down; learned helplessness. Anguished.		

The basic difference is not best described as one of mental health versus mental illness. Rather, it is best described as the experience of self-injury versus an uninjured self, and positive engagement versus self-protective withdrawal. All participants combine aspects of one or both of these two essential forms. The scale captures variations in them.

T A B L E 4 . 5 . Exemplars of the Adult Scale

Adult Rating	Participant	Chapter Sketched
7	Payne	3
6	Hoyt	3
6	Vaughn	7
5.7	Hovanec	2
4.7	Russo	3
2.5	Fisher	3
2	Costa	3
1.7	Martin	2

THE CONTRIBUTION OF THE ASSESSMENT PROCEDURE

The study's procedure for assessing intrapsychic brightness and darkness captures essential variety in the sample's well-being without oversimplifying or obscuring the richness or uniqueness of each participant's life. It differs from survey self-report methods of assessing happiness because it describes whole and real persons rather than facets of persons hypothesized from averaged respondent scores. It weaves into a coherent understanding the deeply complex motivations, concerns, and mental processes that organize and shape a participant's feelings about himself and his life. In both the life goals perspective and domains perspective a great deal is revealed about the pursuits and reactions that figure into a participant's central tendency of affect.

The procedure captures the individual's experience in a long-term context. It considers his experience of his life over decades rather than the brief period of recent days and weeks targeted by more superficial measures.

A naturalistic approach, the procedure understands happiness in relation to the individual's experiences and central strivings in the contexts that he knows from his life, using his own concepts, categories, language, and far-reaching reflections.

Concerned with transparency, the procedure attends to the considerations and judgments an individual brings to reviewing his life and those the observer makes in assessment. It considers blind spots and weightings, and for some participants it shows filters distorting their perspectives on their emotional experience. The guided assessment is comprehensive and systematic in weighing considerations for each participant. It offers meaningful independence of the psychological processes affecting a participant's conscious reporting.

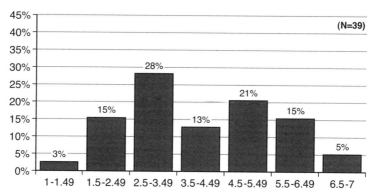

FIGURE 4.2. Intrapsychic Brightness and Darkness of the Adult Participants

The grounded analyses exposed a deeply felt internal construct seen from different angles. The procedure operationalizes this construct, not only revealing long-term trajectories of well-being but also, as I will show in later chapters, helping to explain them as phenomena nested within a larger array of forces shaping human development. Figure 4.2 shows the distribution of the adult sample's brightness and darkness.

WHAT KIND OF MEASURE IS THE SCALE?

In figure 4.2, the intervals of the *x* axis show brightness and darkness along the seven positions on our scale. The scale is ordinal, meaning that the order is a ranking but numerical differences between positions are not meaningful. I have grouped the averaged life history ratings of independent observers into intervals so that their midpoints reflect the conceptual understandings we had of the scale's positions, which are integers.

At the same time that the scale is ordinal, it indexes a typology. It is thus a rank ordering that is composed of two primary forms or factors (intrapsychic brightness and darkness) which are combined in various degrees at each position on the scale. Each of these positions indexes psychological characteristics operationalized by the heuristics used throughout the rating procedure. What this means is that a dual measure—both numeric and thematic—is built into the measure. There is no need to conjecture about the thematic characteristics of the scale positions or to carry out additional correlation analyses to understand the ranked positions of our scale, because they are part of the scale's conception. The meaning of a position along the scale is not left to mystery because of the grounded approach to developing it.

The Meaning of the Scale Distribution

The ratings of the sample are reasonably well distributed, suggesting that the distinct positions on the scale were viable conceptually and visible empirically to observers. But there is also a slight skew toward the darker end of the scale. Thirty-nine percent of participants were evaluated to be in the mixed positive category and higher (4.5 or greater), as opposed to 48.8% who appear in the mixed negative category and lower (less than 3.5). This skew is not the basis for any significant interpretation. Since no comparable data exist to compare this sample to others for this measure, it is not clear whether they are brighter or darker than other groups.

Below I consider evidence that suggests this sample is reasonably representative of the Harvard classes from which it is drawn. Since I have a specialized sample, the reader will already recognize that it is significant for our research question that the distribution is somewhat dispersed; it means that happiness (or unhappiness) doesn't necessarily follow from the competitive educational and career success well represented in the sample.

The Reliability of Observers' Ratings

Agreement between observers was quantified using an intraclass correlation with all available cases ($N = 41$) and the ratings of six observers. For the reader unfamiliar with coding qualitative data, getting agreement between two observers of qualitative phenomena is no small accomplishment. When you introduce hundreds of pages of transcribed interviews to read and a complex evaluation procedure, with many steps to perform, it becomes all the more difficult. The raters are generating their observations blind to each other and independently, following only the rules of the procedure and their acquired experience in applying it. When seeking blind independent agreement for observations made by six raters, the pursuit becomes all the more elusive. It is a major accomplishment of this study, and demonstration of the procedure's soundness, that the novel approach to assessing the life histories reached a high level of agreement. The intraclass correlation, based on a one-way analysis of variance of ratings of the six raters, totaling more than one hundred observations, was 0.80.[8]

Correlations with Other Measures

Although the grounded theoretical approach lends substantial support to the measure's capture of brightness and darkness, the measure also shows significant correlations with conceptually related survey measures completed by the interview sample, presented in table 4.6. It positively correlates with measures of life satisfaction, subjective well-being, and self-esteem, and negatively correlates with symptoms of depression. These measured constructs correlate, as would be expected. They are different from our saturated, multifaceted rating based on life history interviews, but they share some variance with our measure. Our sample size is small and these measures are much less sensitive to our population, so we would not expect a high degree of correlation.

The measure does not associate with recent affect queried by the Affect Balance Scale (ABS).[9] This does not mean that it does not capture affect as intended but that it does so nested within substantial domains of life experience, spanning decades, and may not capture affect that has more recency, given that the ABS focuses on the last few weeks. This is an advantage of our measure, suggesting that it likely captures a construct that is more like a trait than a state and is not heavily influenced by recency effects. Although the ABS

TABLE 4.6. Correlates of the Adult Scale of Intrapsychic Brightness and Darkness

	Pearson coefficient		N
Other General Measures of Well-Being			
Satisfaction with Life Scale	0.49	**	39
Satisfaction with life as a whole	0.34	*	37
Rosenberg Self-Esteem Scale	0.36	*	38
CES-Depression Scale	−0.36	*	38
Recent Affect			
Affect Balance Scale	0.20		36
Disavowal of Negative Affect			
Disavowal of distress, mistrust, social anxiety and emotional dysregulation—factors drawn from MMPI K scale[a]	0.05		37

[a] The measure uses the heaviest-loading items for each factor on a four-factor model of the MMPI K scale.

***p < 0.001; **p < 0.01; *p < 0.05; +p < 0.1

See appendix 5, Variables and Measures.

may be thought of as capturing some quality of a trait, it is unlikely to detect the trait characteristics of our sample as well as our measure does. It poses general, nonspecific, and decontextualized questions in a survey format, which are much less sensitive to the saturated affective experiences of our population.[10]

Finally, the Scale of Intrapsychic Brightness and Darkness appropriately does not associate with a measure of disavowed negative affect, using the K scale (Hathaway & McKinley, 1951)[11] from the Minnesota Multiphasic Personality Inventory (MMPI). Given that our approach to evaluation relies on observer analysis rather than self-report, participant disavowal of negative affect would be unlikely to contribute to the measure. Our rating approach does not require the participant's conscious endorsement of negative affect. It detects and gives weight to the leakage of negative affect even if it is not acknowledged by the participant.

COMPARISON OF COLLEGE AND ADULT ASSESSMENT PROCEDURES AND SCALES

The time orientation of the college interviews and the period of life they cover differ from those in the adult life histories in important ways. (Appendix 3 describes the interviews conducted in college and adulthood.) The college interviews focus on the current time and track experiences during the years of college as they unfold, as well as the whole life up to the start of college, whereas the adult interviews focus on the whole life, including the era covered by the college data, up to the interviews. The adult assessment restricts its focus to the time from after Harvard to the present, whereas the college assessment considers the four (more or less) years of undergraduate life and assesses the participant's brightness and darkness at the end of college. The bounded time periods prevented overlap, allowing cleaner comparison of two eras in the life history, but did not prevent earlier experiences from influencing the affective themes in the target periods.

Despite differences in present versus past orientation, in the span of time covered, and in the apparent immediacy of the events and experiences discussed in the two sets of interviews, the essential characteristics of the college and adult data lend themselves to the same assessment procedure, adapted to the college circumstances of the sample. The construct of intrapsychic brightness and darkness appeared in grounded analyses that were the basis of the college psychobiographical sketches of participants presented in this book.

In recognizing longitudinal trajectories in the sample, I have considered the possible effects of data differences. They may introduce some incomparability due to the effects of recency and memory, between the content and affective tendencies visible in the adult versus the college interviews. But I do not believe these are significant problems for the reliability of the two constructs or their comparisons.

The grounded analyses produced an analogous procedure to assess overall affect in college interviews, adapted to the college sample. It is shown in online appendix 6. Each of the steps of the adult assessment (explained earlier in the chapter) applied to the assessment of the college interviews. The two perspectives of life goals and domains were in principle identical, and so too was the concept of affect balance in determining summary tendencies of domains and college affect overall. Consequently, the spectrum of overall college affect for the sample followed the same dual numeric and thematic logic applied to the adult interviews. The positions on the scale capture the same gradations of overall affect and linked psychological characteristics.

The comparability of the two assessment procedures is the basis for the study's longitudinal determination that some participants seem relatively stable. Hovanec, for example, is observed to be a 5 in college with similar affective themes to those in his adult life history, at which time he was observed to be an averaged 5.67. The two assessments served as the basis for my psychobiographical sketch of Hovanec in chapter 2, showing these themes.

But the college assessment procedure differs from the adult procedure. The content of life goals and the common domains of affective experience in college reflect the reality of the Harvard College student, the earlier phase of the life course, and to some degree the historical era. (Its domains include family of origin, extended family, academic college life, extracurriculars, romantic relationships, social relationships, career development, intellectual development, mental health or health, and other important areas.) Hovanec's adult life goals appear in aspects of the family and the career that he has had, whereas his college life goals appear in his efforts in course work, athletics, dating, and career planning. Despite the different contexts in which they appear, his life goals show similar themes in college and adulthood. Hovanec was concerned with realizing his aspirations in career, family, and personal conduct.

Similarly, Hovanec's responses to unrealized life goals share themes in college and adulthood. The observer of Hovanec's college interviews describes Hovanec's focus on positive aspects of his college experiences and putting problems in perspective. These responses to unrealized life goals are habits of mind resonant with Hovanec's later response to difficulties in his marriage and his career as an adult.

The themes of college and adult assessments show change in the sample

TABLE 4.7. Exemplars of the College Scale

College Rating	Participant	Chapter Sketched
5	Payne	3
5	Hovanec	2
4	Costa	3
3	Russo	3
3	Fisher	3
2	Hoyt	3
2	Vaughn	7
2	Martin	2

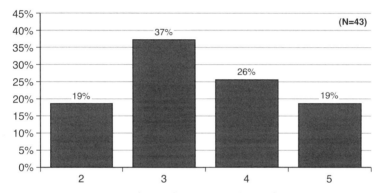

FIGURE 4.3. Intrapsychic Brightness and Darkness of College Participants

across time. Participants in college show a narrower range on the scale than in adulthood. They had not achieved their life goals, as they were just embarking on their adult lives, and there was enough uncertainty, anxiety, and lack of control, among even the brightest participants, that they did not appear to our research team to break out of the mixed category. The highest position on the scale was a 5. Similarly, participants who seemed overall dark had plenty of opportunities ahead of them and seemed to take that fact in; no one seemed to be a 1. That extreme of the "most dark" didn't appear until the adult sample. The uncertainty of youth and an unknown future restricted both ends of the scale in college. In chapter 3, I discussed the adult sample's affect elaboration relative to the college sample and linkage of this elaboration to Erikson's concept of reminiscence as well as other potentially contributing factors. Table 4.7 shows the college ratings for participants sketched in this book, while figure 4.3 shows the college sample's distribution of brightness and darkness.

As with the adult scale, the intervals of the *x* axis show the brightness and darkness along the positions, in this case 4, on our scale. The scale is ordinal, with thematic correlates that comprise a typology at each position analogous to the same positions in the adult scale.

Although the college scale range is narrower, there is a sufficient distribution to suggest that the distinct positions on the scale were viable conceptually and visible empirically to observers. More than the adult scale, the scale skews significantly toward the darker end. Nineteen percent of participants were evaluated to be in the mixed positive category and higher, as opposed to 57% who appear in the mixed negative category and lower. This skew reflects the restricted range of the college scale in light of the life course position of participants. College students had more difficulty with and were more uncertain about how their lives would proceed, and had a greater tendency toward the negative emotions, than were those in late midlife. Since no comparable data exist to compare this sample to others for this measure, it is not clear whether they are similar in this respect to other groups.

Reliability of College Observer Ratings

Given time and resource limitations, college evaluations were carried out by the two most experienced coders and me. For thirty-five of the forty-three college cases, one blind rater formulated and presented a completed case analysis in a conference with me. We made revisions to the analysis if there were omissions, incorrectly weighted considerations, or mischaracterizations recognizable to both of us. We used a standard of forced agreement in determining final ratings. This method produced ratings that we both agreed to and that were substantially blind and independent; the blind raters' premeeting ratings correlated at .857** with the final agreed ratings. This two-step process limited the potential contamination of the college ratings by my familiarity with adult participants, all of whom I had interviewed. My presence and contribution to the rating procedure is indicated by the fact that we revised nine of the thirty-five premeeting ratings.[12]

For eight cases, we lacked a blind rater. We rated five of these cases using the same method of conferring about a rater's premeeting analysis and reaching a shared conclusion. It is unlikely that our agreement about the remaining three cases was unreliable, given that they were central to our team's understanding of the college assessment procedure. Agreement about two cases had been reached during the grounded theoretical analysis and the development of the college coding procedure, and all three cases were part of the training that each coder undertook to gain proficiency in applying the procedure.

A moderate correlation with the adult ratings of all longitudinal cases ($N =$ 37) would be expected for the college measure, given that the psychobiographical sketches showed continuity for many participants and change for others. These ratings indeed correlate at .364*, further indicating that the college assessments were not heavily influenced by exposure to the adult cases.

Correlations with Other Measures

The college measure correlates with conceptually related survey questions completed by the interview sample near the end of college, as shown in table 4.8. Three Likert-scale questions on general mood and felt efficacy correlate significantly or nearly significantly in expected directions. Further, a twenty-five-item measure of self-esteem correlates positively. Finally, analogously to the adult measure, the MMPI K scale does not associate with this measure. The college assessment procedure considers negative affect, even that which is not consciously endorsed.

TABLE 4.8. Correlates of the College Scale of Intrapsychic Brightness and Darkness

	Pearson coefficient		N
Other General Measures of Mood and Felt Efficacy[a]			
While I have my ups and downs, my predominant feeling is a happy one.	0.40	*	41
I usually have the feeling that I am working successfully toward my life goals.	0.30	+	41
I have had (or would like to have) some form of psychotherapy or psychoanalysis.	−0.33	*	41
Self-Esteem			
Individual Rating Scale self-esteem ratings	0.34	*	43
Disavowal of Negative Affect			
Disavowal of distress, mistrust, social anxiety, and emotional dysregulation (MMPI K scale)	0.06		39

[a] Single-item Likert measures, standardized.

***$p < 0.001$; **$p < 0.01$; *$p < 0.05$; +$p < 0.1$

See appendix 5, Variables and Measures.

CREDIBILITY OF THE CONSTRUCT AND
THE PROCEDURE

This chapter's introduction of the procedure for assessing brightness and darkness across the two eras of the study has laid the groundwork for explaining patterns in the lives of the sample. My confidence in the procedure arises from numerous sources that I have suggested in this chapter.

- The procedure grew out of a grounded analysis.
- Independent observers agreed in assessing participants with varying presentations.
- Some participants showed longitudinal consistency in their psychological characteristics captured by the procedure; others did not. The procedure thus captured change and continuity over a period spanning forty-six years.
- Associations of the two measures of intrapsychic brightness and darkness with measures of other similar constructs lent support outside of the interview data.

The greatest source of support for the procedure and the construct it captures, however, is utility. In the rest of the book I will use data captured in both surveys and interviews to show how brightness and darkness captured at two separate times illumines the long-term trajectory of lives.

CHAPTER 5

The Stability Model

This chapter presents a model of human development that accounts for the dominant longitudinal pattern in the sample, that of relatively stable intrapsychic brightness and darkness. This model is needed because objectively measured career success is not the explanation for the sample's adult brightness and darkness. Martin and Hovanec and Fisher and Payne appeared relatively stable in their brightness and darkness from a time even before they began careers, suggesting that other forces are responsible. In this chapter I will argue that participants arrive at college with these forces already largely in place and that they overshadow competitive attainments in shaping well-being.

Two groups of participants make up the relatively stable group: those who are stable and those who change insignificantly. They account for 65% of the longitudinal interview sample ($N = 37$). Their proportions of the sample, stable (43%) and insignificant change (22%), are shown in figure 3.2 alongside participants who change significantly (35%), whom I refer to as *changers*. In this book I use the words *stable* and *relatively stable* to describe participants belonging to the 65% and the words *stability* and *relative stability* interchangeably to refer to their longitudinal patterns.

Figure 5.1 shows stable participants as squares on white space. Changers appear as deltas on the shaded background. They show a significant shift in their intrapsychic brightness and darkness against the current of the life course river, a trajectory that is accounted for in chapter 7.

The large proportion of stable participants in the sample raises the question of whether the best account of participants' development might simply be that

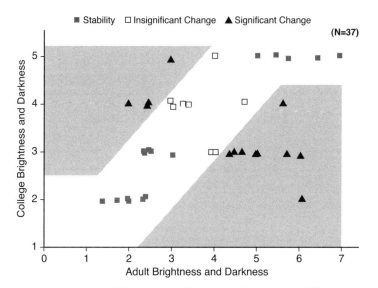

FIGURE 5.1. Longitudinal Trajectories of Intrapsychic Brightness and Darkness

Note: The scatterplot shows the numeric ratings of intrapsychic brightness and darkness across time assigned to college and adult participants. Points on the scale in each era of the study were designed to be comparable. (The scale is described in chapter 4.) The college scale range is from 2 to 5 and the adult scale range is from 1 to 7.

Squares represent participants whose adult rating is within 1 point of their college rating. Deltas represent participants whose adult rating is more than 1 point away from their college rating. The 1-point threshold was our operational definition of change determined by longitudinal qualitative analyses described in appendix 4, allowing for some error in ratings.

their lives in college predict how happy they are as adults. College and adult ratings of brightness and darkness are significantly correlated, at .364*.

Despite its appeal on the grounds of simplicity, this account does not explain the sample's adult brightness and darkness. The coefficient is not large; much variation is unexplained. Further, this story does not make sense. The reader will pause to reflect on his or her college experience. As the participants' stories illustrate, college is not a neutral context; it influences the thoughts, feelings, and experiences we have about our lives at that time, especially in relation to the college experience. College experiences do not provide a map of adult lives. They omit a large swath of the factors responsible for stable development, and they also do not account for participants who change in adulthood.

OVERVIEW OF THE STABILITY MODEL

This chapter leverages the full breadth of the study's qualitative data to account for the stable pattern; the model is depicted in figure 5.5 at the end of the chapter. A key concept is the *identity story*: the lens or worldview through which we all experience important situations and events, important others, ourselves, and the world at large. Crucially, the identity story at any given time is inextricably linked to intrapsychic brightness and darkness. This linkage makes the major influences on the identity story also major influences on how brightness and darkness develops across the adult years. The *Remembered Early Life*, or REL, a term I use to refer to an early version of the identity story, is the major influence on this development. It shapes our sample's identity stories from late adolescence to late midlife.

The first section of the chapter introduces the identity story and its key parts: (1) our strivings, made up of values and goals; (2) attributions we make in construing important situations and events, important others, ourselves, and the world at large; and (3) the affect inhering in our experiences. The concept helps explain why experiences of important situations or other people, for example, seem to repeat or to have similar qualities across time in the participant's life. Clinicians and intimates often notice these repeating patterns in how an individual looks at aspects of his or her life.

The second part of this chapter delineates three distinct versions of the identity story: one in college, one in adulthood, and a third one focused on a past era of the participant's life, his Remembered Early Life. This REL identity story is visible at separate times, in both the college era and the adult era of the study. It shapes both the college and adult identity stories.

One path of REL identity story influence on later identity stories is direct: its values and goals, attributions, and affect are habits that are enacted in the college and adult identity stories. Unless something intervenes, these habits remain. The second path of influence flows through normative life course behaviors in family formation and career. The REL identity story influences how participants approach these behaviors, which in turn lead to social reinforcement of the earlier worldview. Via these two paths the REL identity story, already visible early in college, exerts a long arm of influence in shaping the adult brightness and darkness of stable participants. These paths of influence reveal that the individual and social reinforcement work together to actively maintain the participant's position in the current of in the life course river.

THE IDENTITY STORY

Hovanec and Martin's psychobiographical sketches reveal a central organizing story for each man's life. This story captures his understanding of his experience in relation to the life course tasks he faces in each era of the study. I use the word *worldview* in this book, but there is much more to the identity story, as I explain later in this chapter. In short, Hovanec was trying to preserve and enact a vision he had for his life, and Martin was trying to feel adequate and earn respect in the eyes of his father.

Hovanec experienced college as a personal win in that he graduated with respectable grades, earned the high regard of his teammates and coaches, and maintained his code of personal responsibility. Harvard challenged the vision he as an outsider had for his life, but Hovanec left with the knowledge that his identity embodying this vision remained intact. In adulthood Hovanec repeated this experience. In spite of difficulties in corporate roles and in his own business, Hovanec recognized his accomplishments in each. In spite of some difficulties in his marriage, he and his wife raised a good family. Here, too, Hovanec felt he succeeded in getting through these challenges with his identity intact. A crowning satisfaction was his children, who shared his values of nuclear family and personal responsibility and his appreciation of the outdoors.

In college Martin was trying to maintain grades and performance that would redeem him in the eyes of his father. He never managed to succeed at this or in identifying a career that would earn him worthiness while drawing on his interests in the humanities. Pressure mounted on him over the college years. His relationship with his girlfriend offered a reprieve and a potential new direction in life, but the breakup led to a crisis. Martin left college with a pessimistic view of his future. As an adult Martin withdrew from his attempts in college to unburden himself of his sense of inadequacy and instead accommodated to it. He entered business as he believed his father wanted him to, although he did it in a field that had some resonance with his humanistic interests. He fought against the constant anxiety of failure in this business. His marriage was not clearly stable but long-lasting and estranged. Martin had internalized his father's critical judgment of him and had resigned to his inability to lift its weight from him. Martin seemed resigned to a general sense of failure about his life.

These brief summaries of how each man experienced his life in college and then again in adulthood portray something essentialized in each man's worldview, which is the identity story.[1] The identity story is the skeletal synthesis of a complex and expansive life experience represented in the person's life history. The identity story construes the larger reality in which the self is located, consisting of the most important categories of experience—important situations and events, important others, and the world, as well as the self—giving purpose and an interpretive framework to his strivings, experiences, and outcomes. It is a personal paradigm of meaning.

The identity story is the hidden factor implicated in brightness or darkness. Meaningful experiences were invested with significant affect. To recognize how bright or dark a participant was, our research team needed to recognize his most important life experiences, those comprising the identity story, and the affect in them. It is from this vantage that Hovanec shows his overall world-view infused with brightness and Martin, conversely, shows his infused with darkness.

The study's procedure for assessing brightness and darkness (described in chapter 4) provides a systematic guide to identifying and assessing these experiences and their affect. Events, people, situations, attributions, interpretations, goals, values, and other features are interconnected in narrative. The procedure isolates them and generates understanding of how they relate to each other and to intrapsychic brightness and darkness. The written product includes not only a numeric summary of affect in domains and in the identity story in summation, intrapsychic brightness and darkness. It also incorporates the coder's thick description (Geertz, 1973) distilling the web of meaning found in narrative into the individual's most important experiences on his terms.

Stability and the Identity Story

The identity story is essential to the explanation of stable intrapsychic brightness and darkness because it and its component parts, while dynamic, remain relatively stable across periods of the life course.

First, central strivings, made up of goals and values—called *life goals* in this book—serve as repeating standards by which experiences are interpreted. Across time, Hovanec was concerned with remaining true to his vision centered on nuclear family, the outdoors, and personal responsibility. Martin was concerned with measuring up to his father's example of career success in business and ameliorating the pain of unhappy relationships with his parents and then his wife.

Second, within the interpretive framework of life goals, each man made attributions to important situations and events, important others, himself, and the world at large. These construals characterized how he experienced these central features of his reality. For example, Martin saw himself as inadequate and ineffectual in both eras of the study. This is a repeating characteristic. So, too, was his dislike of women whom he felt were overly attentive to the needs of others. He felt that he needed to protect himself against a world at large that posed a threat to his well-being. During college this world at large took form as the Harvard world, and in adulthood it took the form of the business world, in which he struggled to stay afloat and manage the dangerous market conditions and anxiety of owning his own business. These themes and others contributed to the darkness of his affect as well as to the typical characters and situations within his story.

By contrast, repeating characteristics in Hovanec's construals included inhospitable corporate cultures incompatible with his values that he found over and over throughout his career. He in turn was someone who had not been compromised by accommodating to these cultures or by compromising his family life or personal responsibility in these roles. In harmony with his values, the outdoors served as a source of nourishment. He found great value in his steadfast adherence to his vision for his life. There is a quality of redemption to how his life turns out at the end of Harvard and at the end of midlife.

The interview assessment procedure, organized into analyses of life goals and domains, homes in on the key elements of the identity story—strivings, attributions, and affect—and shows them to be interlocking psychological characteristics that constitute a psychological system. Brightness and darkness is the central affective tendency that permeates this system, the identity story. The stability of its multiple elements help explain stability of both the system and intrapsychic brightness and darkness across time. Identity stories thus are a critical concept in explaining stable development, appearing as both a fundamental shaper of and a repository for the person's well-being.

SHAPING COLLEGE AND ADULT IDENTITY STORIES

What accounts for the stability observed in participants' identity stories? Identity stories come from somewhere before our participants enter the college years. Further, identity stories are not impervious to the conditions of adult life, sometimes changing (as will be explored in chapter 7). An as-yet unidentified influence launches and shapes the long-term trajectory of the identity story and its embedded affect.

The origin of the identity story for participants seems to precede their first encounter with the Harvard Student Study. There was a retrospective gaze—both explicit and implicit—in the adult and college interviews, a road leading backwards in time to the years growing up, the years before Harvard.

This period from birth to the arrival at Harvard is what the study refers to as the Remembered Early Life. It was here that the basic imprints were made, according to the empirical record. Hovanec found his inspired vision. Martin found his pain and burden. Both emerged from this period of their lives with psychological characteristics that were recognized in their psychobiographical sketches as relatively stable across their college and adult records, including their intrapsychic brightness and darkness. By the time they reached Harvard, Martin and Hovanec and other participants were already substantially engaged with and defined by identity stories set within the social contexts of their lives prevailing in the preceding years, at home and in family, in community and school, and in other contexts. It is these earlier social contexts—or the social context of life growing up, broadly construed—that places an indelible imprint on the identity stories of all participants over the course of their lives. (The imprint is especially pronounced for stable participants, but it is also central in the lives of participants who change.)[2]

If the research team were to replicate the coding procedure of the Harvard Student Study for a third period of participants' lives, namely their lives growing up, as participants remembered them, we would thus profile a third parallel identity story with affect embedded in it. Comparable to the college and adult years, the early years show goals and values, attributions, and affect that appear in age-appropriate contexts as they do in college and adult identity stories. Rather than in domains of college academics and career development, or adult marriage and parenting, experience transpires in family or community or school life and other domains to be described shortly.

An analysis of these early experiences using an adapted evaluation procedure, however, would be a different exercise from those we carried out with the college and adult evaluations. Rather than focusing on a life history leading to the present time, it would focus on a period of life prior to the interviews. I considered conducting this analysis of the Remembered Early Life and its brightness and darkness in each of the two eras of the study.[3] The REL identity story and its embedded affect were visible and central in shaping the experiences of participants in both eras.

In the adult era of the study, Hovanec's and Martin's early lives appeared far more formative than their college experiences, which comprised an encounter between this remembered early experience and the conditions and environment of Harvard College (in the domains I have identified, such as academics and social relationships). Similarly, in adult life, the long sweep of the years from after college to late midlife seemed to show a distinctive and prominent dynamic between the Remembered Early Life identity story and the conditions and circumstances of adult life (this time, in domains such as career and parenting). The participant brought his psychological past to the constraints, opportunities, and demands of the present domains of life. To a large extent, participants assimilated the conditions of their college and adult worlds into the terms of their lives known to them from their formative social context of another time, in the years growing up.[4]

In each era of the study, therefore—separately from each other—it was clear that the Remembered Early Life of participants was not simply another identity story among the three identity stories that we observed: early life, college, and adult. It was an identity story that functioned as an affective and psychological imprint on the later identity stories. The privileged position of the earliest identity story became visible in the interviews not only by their temporally preceding the college and adult experiences but by indications of their lasting psychological primacy.

Primacy of Remembered Early Life

Indications of the lasting affective primacy of the REL appeared in the interviews in three ways. In many instances, participants spontaneously volunteered formative experiences that they felt would shed light on an aspect of their more recent life history. For Hovanec, his children's appreciation of the values he had learned as a child were important, he made clear, because these values had always been important to him. He mentioned a childhood incident when he deviated from the expected standard of personal conduct and he was punished. In recounting an incident with one of his children who did not act with personal responsibility, Hovanec volunteered the observation that acting with personal responsibility served him well, and he wanted his children to live that way. This is an example of a participant sharing without prompting what he sees as the origins of his values and interpretation.

For Martin, who had been through psychoanalysis, the critical father of his youth was readily offered as a major formative influence on many of his adult life decisions and experiences, especially in his career. So, too, were disharmonious relations between his parents, the conflict he felt with them, and his mother's interpersonal style toward him. Martin and his wife declined to have children, he said, due to concerns about handling resurgent early parental dynamics and painful childhoods that would have emerged. Martin's experience in psychoanalysis likely led him to fashion explicit attributions to early life causes, but other darker and brighter participants independently made similar attributions.

More often than not, many of the early life influences on participant accounts were not visible to them but appeared to me, as an interviewer, and I sought to test them at an advanced stage of the interviewing. We had at this point covered participants' adult experiences and their accounts of growing up. If I noticed repeating themes in their adult experiences, I waited for an opening to ask about it. One participant was the primary caregiver to his children, and his wife was the primary breadwinner before they divorced. Later in the interviews, he mentioned "another role reversal" in a relationship that created an opening for me to ask about it. Growing up, girls were more available than boys as platonic friends, he said, much as his adult intimate relationships with women seemed to be platonic. Sometimes, if the participant did not present an opening, I would describe a theme and ask whether I had perceived this theme correctly. If affirmed or clarified with revision, I would then ask whether this theme was involved in other experiences. This was an associative probe, and we would spend as much time listing and reviewing the other experiences as occurred to the participant. In the course of this associative segment of interviewing, the dominant pattern was that the road would lead back to the early years, to a formative moment or situation. One participant who spent a lot of time alone as an adult attributed his solitariness to moving around a lot as a child and learning to be self-sufficient.

Early experiences revealed their lasting affective primacy in interviews in a third way, through unconscious display of patterns that did not need to be probed. A participant who wept during each of his interviews talking about painful experiences in work wound up talking about the trauma of a mentally ill family member and violence in his childhood home. The pain and terror were palpable as he related a particularly violent incident involving a weapon. Another participant, who had more energy and active engagements as an adult than almost anyone I've met (spanning marriage, parenting, work, artistic performance, religious community, hobbies), conveyed that engagement was a fundamental part of his coping strategy from early years. The study staff came to call him "the activity monger." He had learned to function this way to transcend (successfully) serious economic and emotional deprivation, and his energy is likely a major reason he got into Harvard. One participant, an introvert who had been left alone in his family of origin and who had delighted in creating clay models and doing experiments as a child, became a scientist as an undergraduate at Harvard.

This third way of observing the primacy of early experiences was applicable to the college interview record as well. The college interviewers sometimes asked explicitly about patterns—such as I did in the second approach—but most often basic psychological features and their connection to an early identity story were visible without probing. The major difference between the college record and the adult record in recognizing these early identity stories was one of elaboration. The older participants by and large presented more elaborate pictures of their lives growing up than the college students; this general difference in elaboration was visible broadly, not only in memories of the past. Most adult participants were more descriptive, concrete, and aware of characteristic patterns in themselves, their thoughts, feelings, behaviors, and actions, and in their life histories than they had been in college.[5]

In summary, the early life identity story stood out because it held primacy in the participant's own memory. It showed its impact on his subsequent identity story recounted in each era of the study's interviews. This early time in life was the destination of the participant's return to the original influences on him, both consciously and unconsciously. The early era of life is not merely a preceding era; it is an era that includes the earliest reaches of the person's memory and awareness. The memories vary across participants as to their fullness and vividness and recency and in myriad other cognitive and emotional ways. But for most participants, the emotional force of these earlier times was clear. Participants showed radiant affect in discussing these past formative times as though they were the deepest imprints, providing their own deepest sense of their goals and values, important situations and events, important others, themselves, and the world at large—as though they were defining of their lives. These precedents seemed to form the basis for how the participant understood the world and himself in it.

Social Sites of Remembered Early Life Experience: Concentric Circles

I now will be more specific about the content of these all-important remembered early self-in-world identity stories. Hovanec's and Martin's lives illustrate some of the common social sites where these early memories take place for the sample. They take place largely in family and school and community; these venues exist in region and country, and in history. Hovanec lived in an idyllic natural world with his parents and family. He recognized himself as a great athlete and a good student with little effort. His parents instilled in him high standards that he had to live up to. His father worked hard, and his mother was involved in the community. His town and his community, in which his family were nested, appreciated a rural way of life that enjoyed a natural balance. His family was respected by others in the community. He felt recognized by others and himself as going somewhere in life. His parents sacrificed to give him opportunities. He was not going to let them down. The entire story took place in and was imbued by a regional and historical context of the North American heartland of the 1950s.

By contrast, Martin lived in a suburb of a city. His father was a successful business executive who was engaged with his responsibilities, working and traveling a lot. Martin's mother was overly concerned with others and Martin preferred to keep his distance. Martin experienced his family in general as having conflict, and he sought distance from them. He went to boarding school, where he learned to be a good student and strived to earn his father's respect. After some behavioral difficulties, he learned to channel his energies into study. Martin's early life story took place in a US urban setting and eastern boarding school of the 1950s when corporate America was ascendant. Martin, like Hovanec, showed that the greatest concentration of his account took place in his family and school and, to some degree less than for Hovanec, in his home community.

These and other participants' stories of remembered early life suggest concentric circles of important early life experiences. As depicted in figure 5.2, the most important site at the center of the circles is the experiences participants have in relationships with parents. The next circle encompasses the family;

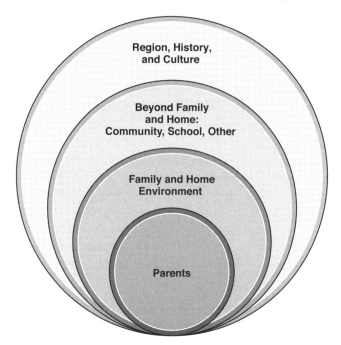

FIGURE 5.2. Overlapping Sites of Remembered Early Life Experience

it includes siblings and the functioning, structure, and culture of the family, although parents are central in shaping the meaning of these things. The third circle contains the sites of community and school. Community includes things like friendships and extended family and experiences in religious community and in the ethnic, class, and cultural milieu. There are regional and national contexts that matter as well, which might be placed in yet a fourth concentric circle, but my goal is not to develop a theory of the sites of remembered early life memories.[6] The diagram brings some structure to these sites of early experience and sets the stage for an expedient and powerful method of demonstrating the linkage between these early memories and participants' identity stories in college and in adulthood.

Themes that appear in the REL identity stories are presented in appendix 6. They were identified in grounded theoretical analysis of participants' life histories in adulthood and in college. Similar to the themes, by domain, appearing at the end of the adult and college coding procedure forms (online appendixes 5 and 6), also produced in the study's grounded analyses, this appendix offers a more complex picture of where affect shows up in Remembered Early Life identity stories. Themes in listed categories are not mutually exclusive and do not correspond precisely to the concentric circles, but they flesh out important areas in REL identity stories.

A LONGITUDINAL MODEL OF DEVELOPMENT

The identity story, its embedded affect, and the primacy of the Remembered Early Life identity story are cornerstones in understanding the relative stability of participants. This section of the chapter ties these pieces together.

In chapter 3 I used the metaphor of a river and its current to describe the longitudinal patterns of intrapsychic brightness and darkness in the sample. Close to one bank of the river was the darkest part of the current, and close to the other was the brightest part of the current. Participants could be paddling in these overall dark or overall bright places on the river, or they could be in the middle. In the middle they were subject to the mix of forces of brightness and darkness. Despite the vagaries of life and changing conditions over time, as participants advanced down the river they tended to stay in the same relative position of the current. The changers, a minority of the sample, relocated relative to the current. This analogy of the river depicts longitudinal trajectories of intrapsychic brightness and darkness, but it does not explain them.

The explanation is not simply inertia. The stability of the identity story appears to be motivated within the participant and actively maintained by social reinforcement. For participants who change, these forces are disrupted, resulting in change toward a brighter or darker central tendency.

The identity story, containing the balance of affect the participant experiences, exerts a powerful influence on behavior over time. In sociology, a pathway is a social platform rich with influences that multiply determine outcomes. For example, in explaining health over the life course, pathways are trajectories that show the unified cumulative effect of exposures, experiences, and interactions (Fine & Kotelchuk, 2010). I suggest that the identity story is a psychological as well as sociological platform on which a multitude of forces converge to exert a great but not deterministic influence on long-term adult behaviors in family formation and career observed by this study. If the Remembered Early Life identity story is the psychological imprint for later identity stories and affect embedded within them, it is also a strong agent in shaping life course behaviors in the sample.

Identification of Behaviors that Matter

The coding procedure for intrapsychic brightness and darkness in each era of the study specified domains where affect was displayed by participants. The three most important of these domains for most participants in adulthood are marriage/partnership, parenting, and career. It is no accident: these realms of life matter the most because they are where the adult participants are endeavoring to realize values, goals, and needs. The domains summarily describe areas where participants are invested. The grounded theoretical analysis provided the study team with a powerful snapshot of the range of the sample's concerns, and it landed our attention squarely on these as the essential concerns and aspirations for the sample.

In a sociological perspective on our sample, certain concerns in these realms would be identified as reflecting normative life course demands for this group.[7] Participants showed in their life histories that no one is immune from the expectation that they would partner or marry, have children, and carry out careers, and it was the rare participant who did not realize one or more of these expected outcomes. Participants themselves noted it as a kind of deviance and detriment, which they then explained. Martin explained his and his wife's decision not to have children, Fisher observed that his life was the poorer for not having a family, and another participant, single but successful in his career, said he "quit investing" in relationships about ten years earlier because he realized that his historical pattern of pulling away would ultimately sabotage any new relationship and lead to a breakup. He "totally ignored or to a large degree ignored the personal side of life. You know, family, children . . . having children . . . that's an inherent weakness that a fully rounded life should have had all those things."

Participants without careers also noted their deviance from norms and the detrimental effects. One, an accomplished amateur athlete, seemed to underscore his decision to forgo the continuation of his career as a satisfying choice but still a loss. Participants who felt thwarted from developing career trajectories normative for this group, such as Costa, took such outcomes to heart. There was no way around drawing the conclusion that they were trying and not succeeding. It was not that they had made other life choices and were not striving in this area of their lives.

Finally, even participants who had carried out normative career trajectories but who were forced into retirement or marginalized roles in later years (a group including doctors, lawyers, and educators) saw themselves as deviating from the expected course of life at some significant loss. Although external and organizational circumstances figured into their accounts, most of these participants implicated their own behavior and decisions in the distressing turn their careers had taken. An inappropriate sexual relationship, professional misconduct, or disregard for changing times or organizational culture had cut short a career.

Participants like Hovanec and Payne stood in stark contrast to these other participants. It was not only that they seemed to be intrapsychically brighter and largely on the brighter current of the life course river. It was also that their lives fit a more normative standard of forming families and carrying out careers. Over the years they had made and sustained investments in these roles and had seemed to surmount the obstacles—in both themselves and their environments—that might have thwarted or derailed them. These differences in behavior in participants like Hovanec and Martin are as unmistakable as the psychological differences between them. Using a measure presented in the next chapter, I will show that the fulfillment of these three normative life course behaviors is significantly associated with intrapsychic brightness and darkness in adulthood.[8]

Although being married and being a parent are not well-established criteria for well-being for all groups,[9] the finding that normative life course behaviors is associated with intrapsychic brightness and darkness is not necessarily surprising. Marriage, parenting, and career are more than sites of sociological demand—they offer important opportunities to fulfill basic needs during adulthood. They offer the potential for social support, community, and human connection; goal fulfillment and expression of values; generative investment in others and the next generation; a sense of meaning and purpose; structuring one's time and energy; fulfilling material and financial needs; and so on. There are innumerable paths of influence. At the same time, the sociological press (that is, environmental demands) to carry out these behaviors matters as well. Making and sustaining investment in these realms helps to avoid the self-doubts and feelings of stigma that often accompany deviance from the expected course of life.

The age and life course position of our sample contributes to the stark contrast in brightness and darkness between those who made and sustained these investments and those who did not. The adult sample is at the end of midlife and the end of the normative career period of life and on the cusp of old age. These investments are not, by and large, artifacts of the recent past but are instead long-term adult achievements. They reflect decades of how a life was spent. It would be difficult, although not impossible, to reverse the imprint of the accumulated record of these many years on a participant's current trajectory. It would be difficult for Fisher to change relational habits, partner, and father children, or for Costa to realize his aspirations for a creative occupation at this stage of his life. I do not mean to suggest a deterministic picture. Some participants divorced and remarried to their visible benefit. Some gave up on unrewarding aspects of their careers and invested in other, more rewarding directions. And some will likely successfully carry out major transitions in the years to come. But this stage of life presents fewer opportunities for shifting the weight of the historical record of the adult years from instability or abstention in one of these realms to sustained investment. The psychological past and biological age present significant constraints in refashioning the historical reality of the adult years for the late midlife sample.

The availability of interested partners and social resources for marrying and fathering children, for this privileged group of men, is not clearly a constraint needing attention, because the biological and psychological constraints are sufficient to demonstrate the restricted opportunity. The die has been cast and the record of the middle years is in.

But there is an obvious sociocultural constraint at work, amplifying the significance of the adult record in achieving or not achieving normative behaviors in family. Anticipating the transition to older age, retirement, and biological decline, participants seem to place a heightened sense of value on all relationships, but especially marital and parenting relationships, which are seen as especially important sources of support and connection that offer a continued sense of purpose and value to others. Career and the career world are receding as venues for meeting needs. This change in focus has particular impact for this group, given the rich opportunities they had educationally and occupationally until now. The legacy of decades of behavior, age, and restricted possibilities for altering trajectories are thus meeting in a landscape of opportunity located more focally in nonoccupational realms. In this context participants like Hovanec and Payne, who have invested in these realms all along, are well positioned to enter the next phase of life and to feel more positively about their current situation and their future and how they have spent their middle years. The present context of the transition to older age is thus amplifying the importance of the relational achievements of the middle years.

Two Orientations Embedded in the REL Identity Story

If these behaviors are so important to well-being among the sample in adulthood, and if the sample as a whole has come to place a higher premium on family relationships in recent years, why did all participants not make these investments in their adult years? The behaviors are not artifacts of the recent past; they reflect long-term engagements across the adult years. Did some participants abstain from these engagements simply because they made a conscious and deliberate choice to pursue other interests and goals? Was it a matter of values? Did it stem from religion or class background? Was it a matter of circumstances or available opportunities to marry or stay married, to form a family, or to engage with and stay engaged with a specific career trajectory? All these factors likely matter, but there is another prominent story in the longitudinal data, one that homes in on the dynamic interaction between the personal and the social across the adult years.

The answer is embedded in the affective and psychological imprint of early life. There are two distinct strategies for living[10] enacted by the brighter and darker participants. These strategies incorporate more than motivations: they are a cluster of the psychological habits carefully tracked throughout this book. They first appeared in the psychobiographical sketches of Hovanec and Martin and were developed further in the life history assessment procedure; in this chapter I have suggested that they cohere in the identity story. A select number of psychological habits are illustrated in figure 5.3. They combine repeating goals and values, attributions, and affect that structure a participant's worldview and help account for his brightness and darkness across time. These different strategies for living are enacted in the college and adult identity stories but seem to be outgrowths of the precedent of the Remembered Early Life.

In their launch into college and adult life, the happier participants are pursuing positive goals and values that they hope to realize in the important so-

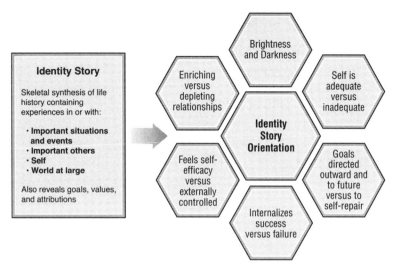

FIGURE 5.3. Identity Story

cially expected domains of life, whereas the less happy participants are pursuing what I have called self-repair goals, goals that look to correct the damage of the past and protect participants from further loss of value and further injury. The mixed participants show some combination of these tendencies.

Hovanec and Martin had markedly different dispositions, or orientations, encoded into their primary identity story from early life, and visible again in their college and adult identity stories. Hovanec inherited a treasured world and a treasured place in it that he was trying to preserve, replicate in his family life and career, and impart to his children. He was trying to live up to the best life that he could imagine. Martin inherited a sense of personal inadequacy and deficiency and an ever-present worry about falling into dysfunction. He lived in a narrower social radius and in a narrower psychological radius. He was trying to preserve the residual value that he felt he had and protect a vulnerable center against further erosion. The contrasting characteristics evident in their psychobiographical sketches now can be understood as part of a larger structure introduced in this chapter, as features of the identity story and a general orientation toward life encoded in it. These distinctive orientations of Hovanec and Martin generalize to other brighter and darker participants across time.

Social Reinforcement

The REL identity story's direct effect on a participant's orientation in the college and adult eras of his life is not its only path of influence. As noted above, participants are not traversing nearly fifty years of their lives on the force of inertia. The REL identity orientation—whether more outward and positive or more self-protective—meets another set of forces, also suggested by the metaphor of the river and its current. There are divergent patterns of social reinforcement—one a virtuous cycle and the other a vicious cycle—corresponding to the brighter or darker initial outlooks of the participant. Participants get feedback from the world over time, and this feedback reinforces the perspective on his life encoded in the REL identity story. This feedback is part of what gives the REL identity story its long arm of influence in shaping the college and adult identity stories. This social reinforcement is particularly evident in the main arenas of adult endeavor—work, marriage/partnership, and parenting. But it is visible already in the college era, a precursor to the adult era.

Observing the effect of social reinforcement across the course of the study requires recognizing the linkage between college and adult contexts of endeavor. I focus on two realms spanning both eras of the study, *achievement* and *relational life*. The achievement realm includes strivings and experiences in education and occupation across time. The college assessment procedure captures several domains in this realm: academics, extracurriculars, and figuring out and taking steps toward future education and career goals. It will become clear that these domains are a precursor to the participant's account of educational and career experiences forty years later. *Relational life* offers a second realm in which to track social reinforcement over time. It includes romantic relationships, social relationships, and extracurriculars (the social aspects of them) in college, and marriage/partnership and parenting domains in adulthood.

Patterns of social reinforcement described here may occur in many other contexts in which the individual makes and sustains normative long-term behavioral investments. These patterns also likely apply to short-term behaviors within a day or a week or a month, but that is not my focus here. (There is likely a lot more noise in these shorter-term contexts, making the effects harder to see.) I am distinctly concerned with reinforcement occurring across the life course and in the normative psychosocial roles and contexts that occur over periods of years and decades. This is why I focus on the central efforts of participants—what they are up to in life—in this regard, specifically in achieving and relating across the entire era of the study.

A key consideration shaping the cycle of social feedback is how the participant tries to invest in normative behaviors. The two different orientations of identity stories result in divergent social reinforcement. (In participants with mixed brightness and darkness, both patterns of social reinforcement are at work.) The outward orientation of brighter participants predisposes the individual with more promise for both gratification and stability in his efforts in achieving and relating. He is more likely to locate himself in roles and situations that meet his values, interests, and needs. He is more likely to feel enriched and fortified, which in turn leads to making and renewing long-term investments that work for him.

Conversely, a self-repair orientation predisposes a participant to feel invalidated in his efforts, especially compared with his more outwardly oriented counterparts. Feeling thwarted, unsupported, or misunderstood, he is more likely to find it difficult to maintain his energy and enthusiasm over the long term for achieving and relating experiences that deplete him. The invalidation confirms the identity story and the inadequacy of the self. It encourages him to conserve his limited resources, withdraw or abstain from further investment, and protect himself. These divergent processes of social reinforcement are suggested by the metaphor of the river of the adult life course and its brighter and darker currents. Figure 5.4 illustrates the two currents.

Reinforcing Pathways in Achievement

The beginnings of divergent patterns of social reinforcement are evident in the achieving contexts of the college years. A common problem for participants is how to deal with anxiety in the transition to adulthood and in the imperative to figure out their future educational and career plans. Strivings in course work, extracurriculars, career formation, and intellectual development are generally understood to be on the critical pathway toward one's future. This is simply part of the environment, which I briefly describe here.

Academically, achieving Gentleman's Cs would not lead to failing in this era at Harvard, but academic excellence was the underlying theme, even if a student chose not to pursue it. Average verbal SAT scores were 673 and average quantitative scores were 698. Many students came to Harvard as valedictorians of their high schools. Athletic, artistic, and organizational competence were also valued achievements in the Harvard environment. While no particular

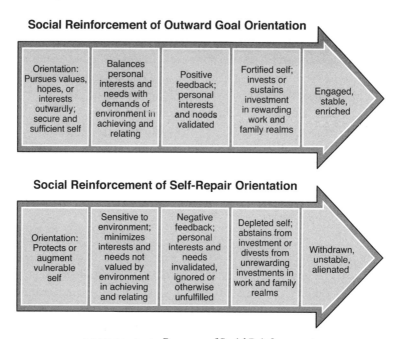

FIGURE 5.4. Processes of Social Reinforcement

form of excellence necessarily dominated the expectations of students, there was an expectation that students would excel and proceed to high-status careers. The socioeconomic background of students was generally middle or upper middle class (even though our sample and the classes from which they were drawn included a sizable number of nontraditional students). Family expectations dovetailed with Harvard expectations and contributed to pressures for students to enter the professional, managerial, or intellectual class for their careers. The fathers of many students had an advanced degree (48% at the master's level or higher) and were in such careers themselves. Harvard was seen as a gateway to these careers (King, 1973).

Darker participants, like Martin and Fisher, looked at these areas of endeavor through the prism of their doubts about their futures. They experienced more anxiety about their prospects than Payne and Hovanec. Payne and Hovanec spent their college years similarly, trying to figure out what they would do after college. Both were concerned with their course work and their extracurriculars. Payne even graduated without knowing what he would do. But he had a faith in the future that things would work out. The sense of inadequacy and invalidation that Martin and Fisher felt in their Remembered Early Lives predisposed them to be more highly attuned to perceiving problems in the life situations they encountered (inclined to internalize failure more than success) and to feel a sense of urgency to avert the threatening prospects they believed were signaled by these problems. Grade anxiety thus became personal anxiety. Anxiety about managing the multiplicity of demands during the college years thus became personal anxiety. Whereas Payne and Hovanec's faith derived from an REL identity story infused with reassurance (a personal sense of adequacy, a belief in his value to important others, the efficacy of his own actions), Martin and Fisher had doubts that the future would work out any differently than the past.

Thus, self-repairing participants felt anxiety carrying personal consequence in achieving endeavors that was dimmed for the outwardly oriented participants. Self-repairing participants generally had more difficulty with the anxiety of the college years. Hovanec and Payne diffused it, resolved it, or lived with it.

The response to this anxiety, an outgrowth of the identity story orientation, appears also in the darker participants' greater responsiveness to the demands and values of the environment. They seem to be in a race to get their prospects sorted out or, alternatively, they avoid engagement as a solution for their anxiety. Both strategies for expedient relief lead to instability and disaffection in the long term. Rather than tolerating uncertainty about their futures as they apply themselves in the present, self-repairing participants minimize or obscure from their view personal concerns and needs that diverge from demands and values pressed upon them by the environment.

To be specific, there are two basic variants of the self-repair strategy in the achievement realm: self-augmentation and self-protection. Self-repairing participants used these strategies as they contended with a demanding setting for the transition to young adulthood. Harvard College in the early 1960s emphasized competitive educational and occupational attainment, values manifest also in educational and career environments that most participants pursued after Harvard (King, 1973).

The first variant of self-repair strategy was favored by participants primarily focused on attaining status, power, and social recognition in their achievement strivings. In the Harvard environment common pursuits toward these ends included getting good grades and aspiring to academic distinction, majoring in a field that was reputable or at least respectable (that is, a field not regarded in the college community as requiring little work or intellectual ability) and that positions the individual for a desirable graduate school or employment trajectory, and participating and excelling in extracurricular activities that also create future opportunities. (Forming useful social connections that serve these goals was another part of the achievement realm.) These goals were not reserved only for participants pursuing self-repair strategies. (Nor are the manifest values necessarily unique to Harvard in this era or the only ones in currency at Harvard in this era.) But for those with a self-repair strategy, in contrast with the more outwardly goal-oriented participants, the centrality of these strivings was more out of balance with, and came at the expense of, other less publicly validated interests, values, and needs. In fact, it is not so much that Martin conveys a vivid picture of other neglected needs and aspirations; it is that these other parts of his life seemed obstructed or never to have developed, much less flourished, as they had for other participants.

Martin and other darker participants faced an urgent problem. The aim of their self-repair strategy was to augment the deficiency darker participants perceive in themselves, which they strived to do by gaining and conferring value upon themselves in socially validating ways. Fisher's academic achievement in high school, then in college, and finally in his academic career seemed to him, upon his adult reflection, to supplant freedom he wished he had had to do work that interested him. It was not a detraction to pursue academic achievement; it was a detraction to pursue it at the expense of other needs. He felt pressure in his early life—from parental expectations to pursue a professional career and from his sense of alienation from them—to work his way out of his problems through academic excellence. Fisher suggested that his urgent pursuit of academic attainment since a young age was a kind of Eriksonian foreclosure. He found a solution to the problem of his youth, but it did not serve his other needs in college or as an adult. He neither reached his aspirations in his career nor felt generally satisfied with the way he spent his time in his career. An imbalance embedded in the self-augmentation strategy in achieving is carried over from college into adulthood (and from the construal of early life).

The second, closely related, variant of the self-repair goal is self-protection. Less happy participants pursued comfort and security at the expense of stimulation and enrichment. Martin might be described in terms of the first variant, but I understand a large element of his motivation as the desire to protect himself from further loss of value and further injury. In college he was trying to avert a possible fall from the perch of academic success he felt he occupied at boarding school. This fall would derail the trajectory that he was on. To him, this trajectory looked to hold the key to long-term fulfillment. But it is clear that he was trying to respond to the inadequacy he felt from his life growing up. Succeeding academically insulated him from the pain of this invalidation. So, too, did Martin's minimization of his interests in the humanities to pursue a career that he thought his father would respect. The problem with Martin's solution, like Fisher's, is that it reinforces unresolved anxiety and feelings of inadequacy in the long term. It is a way of avoiding life rather than engaging it, and it left Martin feeling insecure and unfulfilled in his career. He did not internalize his success (even though objectively he was in some ways more successful than his father) because he was oriented toward averting negative outcomes. Such goals are never attained. This orientation omits too many of the individual's emotional and psychological needs and thus does not address them. It feels invalidating and unrewarding to him, which affirms the anxiety and personal insecurity of the identity story.

Neither of these motivations—the two variants of the less happy—is visible among the brighter participants. Hovanec was trying to be successful in his academics and athletics at Harvard, and he was trying to be successful in his corporate career, but these aims were tempered by other concerns. Hovanec said he would not be happy if he had sacrificed his marriage to be more successful in his career, nor would he have been happy to have shirked his personal responsibility in business roles to get ahead. The same is true of Payne. He seemed to want the long-term stability that Martin sought, but he pursued this aim while also selecting a career that was personally meaningful; he was deeply involved with those he served, his colleagues, and his community. Hovanec and Payne entered adult life with a different template for how to operate in their educational and career trajectories than Martin and Fisher. Their goals reflect a developed sense of personal values and concerns both within and beyond their careers.

Payne's uncertainty about career and postcollege plans did not tap a sense of personal inadequacy. He ended up exploring roles for some time after college. Later in his career, Payne made career choices that reflected his personal satisfactions and the needs of his family. He relocated for a period of years in support of a good opportunity for his wife. Hovanec moved from an urban to a more rural setting befitting his desire to share the natural world with his family, a move that dovetailed with his desire to run his own business but was not an urgent press to solve a personal deficit. In both cases personal concerns in and out of work combined with the pursuit of career success. Both men were sustained by feeling secure and knowing that they could solve their problems. They ended up feeling gratified and at peace with their decisions.

From a strictly behavioral point of view, Martin and Fisher had as much stability in their careers as Hovanec and Payne. (Some other darker participants have had less stable careers.) Where they show the principal difference as adults in the achievement realm is in disaffection versus enrichment in their careers. Hovanec is not as bright in his career as Payne, but neither of them experiences the sense of overall frustration and disappointment that Martin and Fisher do in their careers; to the contrary, they seem overall satisfied with their careers. The career experiences of the two intrapsychically darker men reinforce a sense of personal inadequacy. For the two brighter men, career experience figures into and extends a sense of personal adequacy present all along.

Reinforcing Pathways in Relational Life

Broadly construed, social interactions were a central part of college life and the transition to young adulthood. Relating to individuals, participating in activities and groups, and relating to Harvard as an institution and community are discernible presses during the college years. As with the domains involving achievement, opportunities for engagement varied, but students felt general pressure to relate. For example, dating was something that students did alone and in groups, and most participants understood it to be part of the college experience, whether they were partaking in it or not. The sites of social encounter with friends, acquaintances, and organizations were expansive. Getting along with roommates, selecting houses and room groups to live with, discussing courses and college life and career plans, punching (pledging) social clubs, eating with others and one's social group at dining halls, going to socials at nearby women's colleges, participating in extracurricular activities and intramural sports, having companions for outings and activities outside of studying, including vacations and bull sessions, are but a few of the common places that called for some social involvement and functioning.

Two aspects of the divergent social patterns during the college years carry over into the adult years. The first aspect is whether a participant met his relational and social needs sufficiently through engaging in mutually satisfying and stable involvements with others—referred to in this book as *social competence.*[11] Social competence is visible in some degree during the college years and shows up in adulthood particularly in satisfying and stable family experience. The second aspect is a participant's ability to pursue social involvements at the same time as the expected achievement strivings. This second aspect relates to balance discussed in the achievement realm, whether the participant pursues personal interests, values, and needs alongside publicly validated ones. Brighter participants seemed better able and more disposed to devote psychological resources to relationships and social involvement. This is especially true when considering the heavy concurrent demands of the achievement realm. In imprecise terms, this quality is what has been discussed as work-life balance (with "life" in this discussion denoting social involvements). It is a larger context for relational life during the college and adult years, referring to successful navigation of the multiple demands on a participant. It later appears in adulthood as the cumulative achievement of satisfying and stable investments in both achievement and relational realms.

A developmental lens provides context for observing relational life at the same time as achievement. Most participants had established themselves in achievement contexts to get into Harvard in this era but were not necessarily socially competent. Personal relationships and social involvements were indeed important to functioning in the college years, but they did not seem as uniformly differentiated among participants as their achievement abilities. For example, although it was not premature in the 1960s to begin to form a family during the college years, it was possible for members of this cohort to wait before marrying and having children. But by adulthood, and by late midlife, given the environmental demands they faced, participants would be expected to be operating in families. Social competence is not unimportant in educational and occupational contexts, but as Erikson pointed out, it is different from the competence required in intimacy (Erikson, 1950).

The relational lives of participants reveal divergent longitudinal patterns in both gratification and stability. These patterns can be seen when viewing relational life in isolation and when considering achievement and relational life together across time. A brighter or darker affective experience shows up in the college relational domains of dating, friendships, and other social involvements. Similarly, a brighter or darker affective experience shows up in adulthood in the domains of family life, marriage, and parenting. A linkage appears in a participant's relational life between the two eras, namely, that the college pattern of social competence seems to presage a participant's stable investment in family formation. This happens because the individual's REL identity story influences both eras of his relational life: its affect is extended into college and adult life and is replicated in each era's identity stories. There are two paths of influence: direct patterning of the intrapsychic and patterning through behavioral reinforcement.

Behaviorally, in college, participants like Martin and Fisher were less involved socially and more dissatisfied socially than Payne and Hovanec. Fisher was almost exclusively focused on academic excellence and felt the bite of his sacrifice when he graduated early and cut short the budding communal and social ties he was beginning to feel. He struggled with his inability to find the time or attention to be involved in social life at Harvard. Martin appeared to have phases during college. As a freshman he seemed drawn to his roommate and got involved in a social club. But over time his primary effort socially was devoted to dating and his main relationship and later ones turned out not to be stable. He described himself as overly dependent on his girlfriend. Their breakup triggered a crisis.

Intrapsychically, Martin and Fisher's relational lives in college exemplify a self-repair orientation that was evident in achievement contexts. Fisher was avoidant, seeming to husband his psychological resources for the pressing need he felt to excel academically and for protecting himself from experiencing his sense of failure and devaluation in social involvements. He was distinctly conscious of not having the skill and experience to date, and this worried him and made him think his parents also should be worried. This is one example of how he lacked social competence. His approach in his relational life is the self-protecting variant of self-repair.

Martin illustrates the self-augmentation variant of self-repair orientation in his relational life in college. Although he experienced some gratification from his involvement with his social club, he struggled to form friendships and date. He felt overly dependent on his girlfriend and seemed to seek out other relationships with an urgency to feel more stable and to escape a personal sense of inadequacy that he felt with his parents. His actions foreclosed on a more satisfying relational life just as Fisher's career actions ignored or subverted other needs and concerns to focus urgently on augmenting his perceived inadequacy.

The outcome was dissatisfaction and abstaining from stable investment. Fisher was frustrated and deprived of social gratification. Martin was overwhelmed by the painful consequences of relational setback and instability. This negative feedback bled into a general sense of personal failure and reaffirmed the personal deficiency embedded in each man's REL identity story.

Hovanec and Payne illustrated an outwardly oriented approach to relational life in college. Hovanec, active in numerous social venues of college life, had friends through his athletics and in his roommates; he dated, and he cultivated relationships with adults at Harvard. Harvard's culture posed great challenges, but he did not withdraw from trying to engage it. He did not rush to have sex or to fuse with girls he dated, and by the time he graduated, he seemed to have found someone for a life partner. He was both satisfied and invested. Payne dated and had friends during college. He used his time profitably outside of course work to explore possible future career directions and to participate in meaningful activities reflecting his values. Payne was trying to figure out his future and had not clarified it by the end of college. He was planful rather than avoidant. He determined it was unwise for him to marry before earning an advanced degree. Payne's experience of Harvard as a social community was not tainted as a site of struggle, as it was for Martin and Fisher. Importantly, neither Payne nor Hovanec personalized the setbacks they experienced in the social realm of college life. Martin's and Fisher's lack of social gratification fed the general sense of inadequacy in their REL identity stories.

These divergent patterns in college show up over the long sweep of relational life in adulthood. The presses were clearer by the time participants neared the end of midlife. Substantial psychological resources were required for participants to make and sustain investments in all three behavioral investments of interest here—marriage, parenting, and career—demarcating the participants on the brighter pathway. It was possible for almost every participant to invest in and sustain behaviors in one or two of these domains, but the third domain seemed out of reach as a long-term stable investment for most of the less happy participants. The unrealized domain most often was either a stable marriage/partnership or parenting children. Fisher excelled academically and in his career but did not partner or form a family. Martin sustained a career and a marriage but did not have children. This pattern is surprisingly robust across the sample. By contrast, brighter participants looked like Hovanec and Payne: they sustained investments in all three adult behaviors.

The self-repair orientation resulted in a more restricted social radius in college and in adulthood. It also deprived participants of the fortification that brighter participants experienced from enriching relationships and social involvements. The virtuous cycle of reinforcement in achieving and relating took the psychological resources endowed early and extended them, allowing and encouraging participants to invest in the manifest opportunities and presses for a normative life course. The vicious cycle of reinforcement in achieving and relating took its toll, depleting participants with disaffection and holding in place a disadvantaged self-repair orientation to engaging with life.

SUMMARY OF THE MODEL OF DEVELOPMENT

The REL identity story orientation patterns later brightness and darkness through two paths of influence. One is a direct patterning of the psychological/affective and the other is behavioral reinforcement, which in turn contributes to the psychological/affective. In both these ways, the identity story in adulthood comes to resemble, despite being half a lifetime apart, the Remembered Early Life identity story. Important situations and events, important others, oneself, and the world at large all take on a similar hue by virtue of the inter-

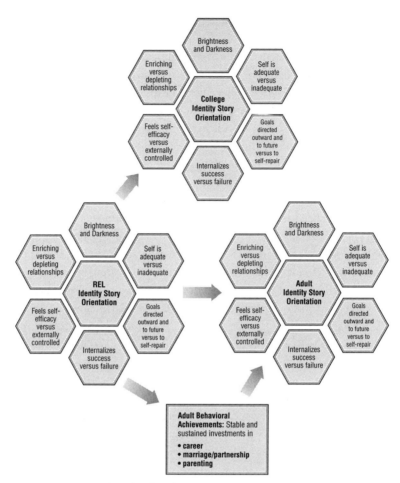

F I G U R E 5 . 5 . Remembered Early Life and Social Reinforcement Effects on Stable Trajectories

locking forces of the identity story and the replication of it in adult experiences. Happier participants are brighter because they experience fortification, connection, and enrichment; unhappy participants are darker because their struggles, sense of invalidation, and disconnection continue to deplete them.

Our study coined the expression *adding positives*. It is a shorthand way of describing both the emotional and behavioral dividends across time that are visible in the outward orientation of the brighter participants. Adding a positive is the consolidation of an emotional gain through a positive achievement or relational experience across years. Payne's career added a positive to his life, but Fisher's did not. So too did Payne's marriage and experience as a father, both of which are absent from Fisher's life. The concept captures the tendency of the brighter participants to have stable careers and stable marriages, to parent children, and to have positive experiences in these endeavors. Adding a positive, in turn, contributes to the well-being of the person. Participants who were not adding positives were getting drawn down the darker currents of the river. The ensuing frustration and alienation of these darker-pathway participants contributed to the ongoing reminder that their early identity stories were valid.

This model of development suggests that the college identity story orientation is patterned in the same ways, although I have not formally specified mediating behaviors in the college era as I have in the adult era. The model is depicted in figure 5.5.

The dominant pattern of relatively stable brightness and darkness provides a critical context for understanding lives in the sample. It shows the forces within and without that work together to uphold a central affective gestalt and central, long-term behaviors in career and family contexts across a large portion of a participant's life. Although I used an exhaustive qualitative analysis to make my case, in the next chapter I expand my argument to include another approach that shows quantitative support for this model.

CHAPTER 6

Stability Tested Quantitatively

The model of stable development presented in chapter 5 is a main finding of the study. It was produced after systematically considering many variables and potential explanations of the sample's adult brightness and darkness in a wide net of analysis that is a distinctive strength of qualitative research. This chapter focuses on key relationships in that model and retests them statistically in order to evaluate quantitative evidence for the model, to refine the model, and to place this research in conversation with quantitatively observed explanations of happiness and development. In moving from qualitative to quantitative analyses the chapter takes care to minimize introduction of unintended effects and noise. The focus of these statistical replication analyses is graphically represented by a simplified model in figure 6.1.

APPROACH TO TESTING THE MODEL

I test the effects of the Remembered Early Life (REL) identity story on later identity stories after operationalizing a measure of how bright or dark, how positive or negative, the affect is in this remembered early period of life prior to college. The study's measures of brightness and darkness of the college identity story and the adult identity story are available from the coded interview procedure.

The qualitative analyses found adult behaviors in career and family formation to be a mediating variable, part of the social reinforcement of Remembered Early Life Affect that comes to influence adult brightness and darkness. I test whether REL Affect shapes later behavioral achievements, whether these

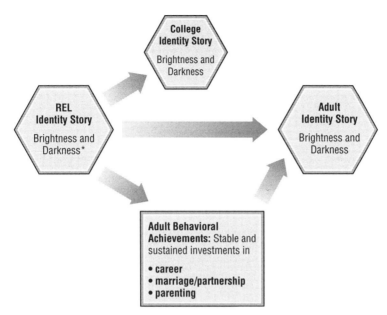

FIGURE 6.1. Statistically Tested Model of Development
*REL brightness and darkness is measured as REL Affect.

behaviors associate with adult brightness and darkness, and whether these behaviors mediate the effects of REL Affect on adult brightness and darkness.

Further, I consider the alternative explanation for the happiness of our participants posed at the outset of this project: their competitive success. In keeping with this chapter's quantitative examination of the long-term model of stable development, I restrict my focus to the adult component of competitive success, namely, objectively measured career success. I also consider alternative explanations for the happiness of adult participants advanced by other lines of research.

I test each of the following relationships as incremental steps in quantitatively testing aspects of the qualitative model. I test whether

1. REL Affect associates with college brightness and darkness.
2. REL Affect predicts adult behavioral achievements.
3. REL Affect predicts adult brightness and darkness with behavioral achievements as a mediator.
4. Objectively measured career success does not associate with adult brightness and darkness, both without controlling for and with controlling for

variables of the mediation model (REL Affect and adult behavioral achievements).

5. The association between college and adult measures of brightness and darkness is explained by common cause in REL Affect.

Because of the importance of REL Affect in the model as a distinct explanatory construct, I also test whether

6. REL Affect explains adult brightness and darkness better than five-factor model personality traits found to be associated with well-being. Specifically, this sixth step involves two questions:
    a. Are the five-factor model personality traits of neuroticism, extraversion, and conscientiousness (operationalized as deferred gratification) associated with REL Affect?
    b. Does REL Affect explain adult brightness and darkness better than neuroticism, extraversion, and conscientiousness (operationalized as deferred gratification)?

MEASURES

This section reviews each of the constructs in the model and their measurement. Variables and measures are summarized in a table in appendix 5.

Adult Behavioral Achievements

Participants expended a great deal of psychological energy in making and sustaining investments in marriages and partnerships, parenting, and career. Although each of these investments required resources, the cumulative demand of making and sustaining all three of them demarcated the participants on the brighter pathway.[1] These participants brought to bear the strengths of the brighter experience from remembered early life from which they were launched into college and adult life. These investments were rewarded with the experience of adding positives, contributing to the sustained investment and the social reinforcement of the brighter remembered early life experience. I therefore measured whether a participant fulfilled the sample's norms for all three investments.

I used responses to the adult survey instrument completed by the interview sample as well as survey participants. The three sets of norms in the interview sample also appear in the longitudinal survey sample ($N = 207$), each of which is fulfilled by roughly two-thirds to three-quarters of the two samples. They are

1. to be married or domestically partnered one or two times, currently married or partnered and living with one's spouse or partner;
2. to have two or more children rather than no children or one child;
3. to be working full time rather than being retired, working part time, being disabled, or being unemployed.

I controlled for other potential explanations of these behaviors, religious identity, and financial circumstances. Religious identity may influence family formation behaviors. Financial circumstances may influence the decision whether to continue working full time. But failure to realize any of these behaviors, as rough indices, can also be taken as a lack of stable investment in these realms and more generally a positioning at some distance from the brighter current of the river. Participants not invested in these behaviors more often than not were not realizing the dividends of the brighter current.

Figure 6.2 shows the distributions for the longitudinal survey sample.[2] At the center of the diagram, the overlap shows that only 43% are able to fulfill all three behaviors; in the longitudinal interview sample this figure is 38%. The measure of behavioral achievements captures the overlap of the three circles.

The numeric labels on the Venn diagram indicate the percentage of the longitudinal survey sample who realize *at least* the indicated behavior or behaviors. These figures do not exclude individuals who concurrently realize behaviors represented by other circles or regions of the Venn. For example, 77% of the sample realizes the marriage/partnership behavior, but this also includes some individuals who realize parenting and work behaviors as well. In another example, 55% of the sample realizes both the marriage/partnership and work behaviors, but this includes some individuals who also realize the parenting behavior. (The only exception is 4% of participants who realize none of the adult behavioral achievements.)

Remembered Early Life Affect Scale

The model proposes that remembered early life experience launches the pathway trajectories described in chapter 5. To test it, a measure from the earliest era of the study is needed, one that captures affect in the Remembered Early Life. Coding a measure from college interview data would have had the benefit of operationalizing the construct that had already been observed qual-

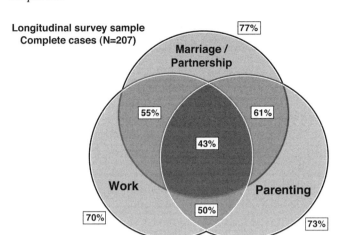

FIGURE 6.2. Adult Behavioral Achievements

Note: Venn diagram shows percentages of longitudinal survey participants who realized the sample's normative adult behavioral achievements. Each of the three achievements is denoted by its own circle and was realized by 70% or more of the sample; two were achieved by 50% to 61% of the sample. All three behaviors at the center of the Venn—which are characteristic of brighter adult participants—were achieved by only 43% of the sample. (Not depicted in the figure, 4% of participants achieved none of the behaviors.) The normative marriage/partnership behavior is defined as being married or domestically partnered one or two times, currently married, or partnered and living with one's spouse or partner. Parenting behavior is to have two or more children. Work behavior is to work full time rather than being retired, working part time, being disabled, or being unemployed.

itatively. However, creating the measure using archival survey data allowed for replication analyses using the full sample (carried out in chapter 9). It also did not entail coding multiple measures from the same source data, or a third labor-intensive, multiyear qualitative coding effort. I therefore selected archival survey measures on theoretical grounds and standardized them to create the REL Affect Scale described in appendix 7. My aim was efficient capture of individual differences in the affect of REL observed in the college interviews. The scale ranges from 1 to 3 and has a mean of 2.15 and a standard deviation of .67.

Standard Controls

My analyses control for basic demographic and person-level influences that might be or would be expected to impact the well-being or happiness of adult participants. There are two groups of possible influences, one applicable to the adult era and the other to the college era. In the adult era possible influences include religiosity and self-reported health. In the college era the possible influences are the socioeconomic background of family of origin (father's education),[3] religious background (whether from a Protestant family) and current religiosity, and the region of the country a student was from.[4] Several controls have special meaning for this Harvard cohort. Adjustment to the Harvard environment appeared more difficult for participants from "outsider" backgrounds: those not from the eastern United States, those not from Protestant families, and those from lower socioeconomic status. Although discernible qualitatively and therefore included in controls, these influences do not appear to be driving intrapsychic brightness and darkness or longitudinal patterns.

Objectively Measured Career Success

Objectively measured career success is captured using a measure of occupational prestige and a measure of household net worth. They were appropriate indices of accrued career success for the sample, whose career trajectories had already been established for several decades prior to this time.

I administered a measure of household net worth (assets minus debts) that reflects the levels of wealth expected in this population. Nine response categories reflect the range of wealth in this population observed in the study's interviews and include: negative; $0 to $100K; $100K to $400K; $400K to $1 million; $1 to 2 million; $2 to 4 million; $4 to 10 million; $10 to 25 million; over $25 million.

Household net worth might be affected by inheritance or spousal or partner wealth, but I do not see these as major confounds to a useful measure. Seventy-nine percent of respondents (87% of interview sample) report that one-quarter or less of their household net worth comes from inheritance. The vast majority of participants were the primary breadwinners in their families. Asking participants about and obtaining reliable accounting for the separate origins of household net worth is difficult. Household net worth likely largely reflects the participant's cumulative financial attainment. This attainment might come from multiple sources, including wages, bonuses, equity in a business or partnership, real estate, and investment returns. The small estimated portion of wealth from inheritance reported by the large majority of participants suggests that these other sources of wealth reflect in some reasonable measure for this sample the financial result of their career.

Other Theories and Considerations in Explaining Adult Happiness

I control for three other potential contributors theorized to shape adult happiness: personality traits and temperament, intelligence, and psychiatric intervention. I also control for college-era brightness and darkness to test whether, as observed qualitatively, it explains adult brightness and darkness better than Remembered Early Life Affect.

Personality and temperament. Extraversion and neuroticism are traits in the five-factor model of personality (McCrae & Costa, 1987, 1997) commonly found to be associated with subjective well-being (Diener et al., 2003; Libran, 2006). A third trait, conscientiousness, has also been found to be associated with subjective well-being (Lucas, 2008).

I include measures of each of these traits available in the archival data set. The first two use items from the Minnesota Multiphasic Personality Inventory (MMPI) (Hathaway & McKinley, 1951). The measure of extraversion is the sixty-nine-item Si scale (Drake, 1946), one of the clinical scales of the MMPI, and the measure of neuroticism is an eighty-seven-item measure developed by Johnson et al. (1984). A measure of deferred gratification seems to tap conscientiousness (John & Srivastava, 1999). Its sixteen-item scale sums responses to the Choice Behavior Questionnaire, an instrument asking the respondent to make choices in real-life scenarios between immediate satisfaction and greater future satisfaction (such as taking next weekend off work or having a longer period off sometime next month).

Research on subjective well-being firmly establishes genetic contribution to subjective well-being. Some scholars have placed this contribution as high as 80% of variability in the stable component of subjective well-being (Lykken & Tellegen, 1996), but other scholars offer more sober estimates, suggesting that 30%–50% of the variance in well-being at a single occasion can be explained by genetic effects (Lucas & Diener, 2015; Lucas, 2008; Lyubomirsky, 2007). The inclusion of personality measures should capture a large share of the hypothesized effect of genes on long-term happiness.

College-era brightness and darkness. I include this measure to test the qualitative finding that the Remembered Early Life and the affect contained within the identity story from that earlier period better explain adult brightness and darkness than does college brightness and darkness.

Intelligence and academic performance. Although prior scholarship suggests no relationship between standard measures of intelligence and well-being (Grossman et al., 2013), the US public suspects that adolescent intelligence and scholastic achievement have lasting effects on happiness in adult life. I therefore use Scholastic Aptitude Test scores as well as junior-year class rank at Harvard as controls for these factors.

Psychiatric intervention and mental illness. I control for psychiatric treatment in college and adulthood to make sure that brightness and darkness in each era, and the explanatory model, are not confounded by intervention. I use behavioral measures drawn from each era of the study. I also regard these behavioral measures as gross indices of psychiatric illness or psychiatric disturbance. Controlling for them provides further confidence that statistical results are not driven by outliers who are suffering mental illness.

I recoded two underlying questions in the college data set into a single measure of psychiatric usage. It captures whether either of the two questions was endorsed: one question asks the participant whether he ever used the Harvard psychiatric clinic, and another asks whether, while at Harvard, he consulted anyone for help with emotional problems (a psychiatrist, psychologist, counselors) other than members of the Harvard staff.

The adult measure is derived from a series of questions asking the respondent the length of time, since he was eighteen years old, that he received "outside help, assistance or treatment to address emotional, psychiatric, family or personal problems." The respondent specifies the length of time ("never," "less than one month," "two to six months," "seven months to one year," "over a year but less than two," "two to five years," "over five years") for each of the following: took prescribed medication; saw a psychiatrist, psychologist, social worker, marriage therapist, or another professional counselor; was an inpatient in a hospital, treatment facility, nursing home, or care facility for psychiatric or emotional problems; attended a self-help group; saw a minister, priest, rabbi, or other spiritual advisor for counseling. These responses were recoded to capture whether a participant received treatment by any modality for seven months or more. This cutoff excluded shorter-term engagements less likely to have an impact. I regard inpatient experiences as not comparable to the other interventions because of their intensity, but determined that there was no need for special treatment of them. Respondents utilizing inpatient services almost uniformly reported that they utilized other interventions for seven months or more.

RESULTS

Multivariate linear regressions lend support to the relationships observed qualitatively. I report regression results using standardized coefficients to allow for comparison of multiple explanatory variable relationships with the dependent measure. Results for each tested relationship are presented in stepwise fashion from left to right in tables and are discussed in sections that follow.

REL Affect Associates with College Brightness and Darkness

The qualitative model observes that REL Affect associates positively with brightness and darkness in the college era of the study. In analyzing this association quantitatively, I restrict the sample to thirty-seven longitudinal qualitative cases used in the development of the qualitative model.

The association of REL Affect with college brightness and darkness is supported by the regression results. This is true with the inclusion of standard controls: father's education, whether the student comes from the eastern part of the United States, whether the student identifies as Protestant, and whether he reports no religious identification. This finding is supported when including other possible explanations for college brightness and darkness as well: intelligence and academic performance, five-factor model personality traits, and psychiatric intervention during college. Other theorized explanations were entered individually in separate regression analyses, while the group of standard controls was always retained.

The relationship is an association rather than a prediction, since Remembered Early Life Affect operationalized as REL Affect Scale, and these other possible explanations were captured in the college era. (In the qualitative model in chapter 5, I conceptualize REL Affect as a relatively stable underlying trait that is causally prior to the college identity story. The Remembered Early Life identity story and its affect appear early in the college careers of participants and are relatively stable during college as well as between college and late midlife.)

Table 6.1 shows further that when controlling for REL Affect, none of the other covariates—intelligence and academic performance, five-factor model personality traits, and psychiatric intervention—associates significantly with brightness and darkness in college.

TABLE 6.1. Linear Regressions Testing Remembered Early Life Affect and Other Factors' Associations with College Brightness and Darkness

Dependent Variable: College Brightness and Darkness
Longitudinal interview subsample, complete cases
Standardized coefficients

Variable	Model 1		Model 2		Model 3		Model 4		Model 5	
Remembered Early Life Affect	0.59	***	0.60	**	0.62	**	0.57	**	0.50	*
Standard controls			x		x		x		x	
Intelligence and academic performance										
SAT score					−0.18					
Junior year academic class rank					0.06					
Personality traits										
Neuroticism							0.00			
Extraversion							0.01			
Conscientiousness (deferred gratification)							0.10			
Psychiatric intervention										
Received psychiatric help during college									−0.15	
N	35		34		33		33		32	
Adjusted R^2	0.32		0.28		0.26		0.15		0.26	

Note: Columns are multivariate linear regressions testing whether any of intelligence and academic performance, personality traits, or psychiatric intervention associates with college brightness and darkness, entered with Remembered Early Life Affect as a control and, as denoted by x, standard controls.

***$p < 0.001$; **$p < 0.01$; *$p < 0.05$; +$p < 0.1$

See appendix 5, Variables and Measures.

REL Affect Predicts Adult Behavioral Achievements

The qualitative model observes that REL Affect predicts the adult behavioral achievements, and these achievements associate with being among the brighter participants. Regression results support this qualitative finding, when including standard controls and potential alternative explanations for the realization of these behaviors.

TABLE 6.2. Linear Regressions Predicting Adult Behavioral Achievements with Remembered Early Life Affect

Dependent Variable: Adult Behavioral Achievements
Longitudinal interview subsample, complete cases
Standardized coefficients

Variable	Model 1		Model 2		Model 3		Model 4	
Remembered Early Life Affect	0.34	*	0.39	+	0.39	+	0.42	*
Standard controls			x		x		x	
Personality traits								
Neuroticism					0.20			
Extraversion					0.09			
Conscientiousness (deferred gratification)					−0.21			
Psychiatric usage since 18 years old for 7+ months							0.16	
N	35		35		33		32	
Adjusted R^2	0.09		0.01		−0.09		0.06	

Note: Columns are multivariate linear regressions testing whether Remembered Early Life Affect predicts adult behavioral achievements, entered alone, and with standard controls and personality traits and psychiatric intervention as controls where denoted by x. Low and negative adjusted R-squared values indicate merely that these measures are not strong predictors.

***$p < 0.001$; **$p < 0.01$; *$p < 0.05$; +$p < 0.1$

See appendix 5, Variables and Measures.

Standard controls (listed above) were restricted to college era only, since behaviors reflect investments spanning the course of adulthood. These controls were theorized as potentially being able to explain the relationship between REL Affect and behavioral investments. No adult-era controls were used, because the timing of measures such as self-reported health or religiosity was unclear and could potentially explain or be explained by the dependent measure.

Alternative explanations included in the regressions are five-factor model personality traits and adult psychiatric intervention. The measure of adult psychiatric intervention spans the same period when adult behavioral achievements would have been realized. It is difficult to know theoretically how to interpret this measure; it may follow or precede the realization of behaviors. But since it may potentially explain the realization of behaviors, I include the regression in table 6.2 to show that psychiatric intervention is not altering REL Affect's prediction of adult behavioral achievements.

REL Affect Predicts Adult Brightness and Darkness with Behavioral Achievements as a Mediator

The qualitative model observes that REL Affect predicts adult brightness and darkness and that adult behavioral achievements act as a mediating variable (see table 6.3). The regression results support this qualitative finding, when including standard controls and when controlling for various other possible explanations. The estimated effects of behavioral achievements and REL Affect remain large and fairly stable across regression specifications, providing evidence for the direct effect of REL Affect and the mediating effect of behavioral achievements.

Controls applicable to the college era are the standard controls: father's education, whether the student comes from the eastern part of the United States, whether the student identifies as Protestant, and whether he reports no religious identification. Adult-era controls include self-reported health, adult psychiatric intervention, and adult religiosity.

Alternative explanations included in the regressions are objectively measured career success, college brightness and darkness, intelligence and academic performance, five-factor model personality traits, and psychiatric intervention in college and adulthood.

Objectively Measured Career Success Does Not Associate with Adult Brightness and Darkness

The animating research question for this book is whether competitive success explains adult happiness. The adult component of competitive success, objectively measured career success, was observed qualitatively not to associate with adult happiness. An alternative explanation, the mediation model, better explained adult brightness and darkness in multivariate regression analyses as well as qualitatively. I now give full quantitative consideration to the question of whether objectively measured career success explains adult brightness and darkness.

For this analysis, I entered measures of objectively measured career success (household net worth and occupational prestige) first alone, then including standard controls, and thirdly including the variables of the mediation model (REL Affect and adult behavioral achievements). The regression results displayed in table 6.4 concur with the qualitative finding showing no support for objectively measured career success as an explanation of adult brightness and darkness.

TABLE 6.3. Linear Regressions Predicting Adult Brightness and Darkness with Remembered Early Life Affect and Adult Behavioral Achievements as a Mediator

Dependent Variable: Adult Brightness and Darkness
Longitudinal interview subsample, complete cases
Standardized coefficients

Variable	Model 1	Model 2	Model 3	Model 4	Model 5	Model 6	Model 7	Model 8	Model 9
REL Affect	0.64 ***		0.47 ***	0.39 *	0.36 *	0.43 *	0.47 **	0.35 +	0.38 +
Behavioral achievements		0.67 ***	0.51 ***	0.57 ***	0.63 ***	0.57 ***	0.63 ***	0.56 **	0.59 **
Standard controls				x	x	x	x	x	x
Objective career success									
Occupational prestige					−0.13				
Household net worth					0.18				
College brightness and darkness						−0.06			
Intelligence and academic performance									
SAT score							0.25		
Junior year academic class rank							0.15		
Personality traits									
Neuroticism								0.15	
Extraversion								0.22	
Conscientiousness (deferred gratification)								−0.25	
Psychiatric intervention									
Received psychiatric help during college									0.00
Psychiatric usage since 18 years old for 7+ months									−0.30 +
N	35	35	35	32	32	32	31	31	30
Adjusted R^2	0.39	0.43	0.62	0.55	0.56	0.53	0.61	0.55	0.56

Note: Columns are multivariate linear regressions testing whether Remembered Early Life Affect predicts adult brightness and darkness, entered alone and with behavioral achievements (together comprising the book's mediation model) and where denoted by x, both entered with standard controls and controls of (models 5–9): objective career success, college brightness and darkness, intelligence and academic performance, personality traits, and psychiatric intervention.

***$p < 0.001$; **$p < 0.01$; *$p < 0.05$; +$p < 0.1$

See appendix 5, Variables and Measures.

The Association between College and Adult Measures of Brightness and Darkness Is Explained by a Common Cause in REL Affect

Although analyses have shown the role of REL Affect in influencing brightness and darkness in each of the college and adult identity stories, I now consider explicitly another finding of the qualitative model: that the observed correlation of adult brightness and darkness with college brightness and darkness is explained by REL Affect, which is causally prior to the adult measure of

TABLE 6.4. Linear Regressions Predicting Adult Brightness and Darkness with Objectively Measured Career Success

Dependent Variable: Adult Brightness and Darkness
Longitudinal interview subsample, complete cases
Standardized coefficients

Variable	Model 1	Model 2	Model 3	
Remembered Early Life Affect			0.36	*
Behavioral achievements			0.63	***
Standard controls		x	x	
Objective career success				
Occupational prestige	0.04	0.01	−0.13	
Household net worth	0.09	0.11	0.18	
N	38	36	32	
Adjusted R^2	−0.05	−0.08	0.56	

Note: Columns are multivariate linear regressions testing whether objectively measured career success predicts adult brightness and darkness entered alone, with standard controls as denoted by x, and with this book's mediation model as a control (REL Affect and adult behavioral achievements). Negative adjusted R-squared values (models 1 and 2) indicate merely that measures are not strong predictors.

***$p < 0.001$; **$p < 0.01$; *$p < 0.05$; +$p < 0.1$

See appendix 5, Variables and Measures.

brightness and darkness and which I understand to be causally prior to the college measure of brightness and darkness.

For this analysis, I entered college brightness and darkness first alone, then including standard controls, thirdly including REL Affect with standard controls, and fourthly including both variables of the mediation model (REL Affect and behavioral achievements) with the controls. Regression results in table 6.5 show that college brightness and darkness and adult brightness and darkness have a common cause in REL Affect, which appears to explain the observed correlation between the two measures of brightness and darkness.

TABLE 6.5. Linear Regressions Testing College Brightness and Darkness as a Mediator of the Effect of Remembered Early Life Affect on Adult Brightness and Darkness

Dependent Variable: Adult Brightness and Darkness
Longitudinal interview subsample, complete cases
Standardized coefficients

Variable	Model 1		Model 2		Model 3		Model 4	
Remembered Early Life Affect					0.58	*	0.43	*
Behavioral achievements							0.57	***
Standard controls			x		x		x	
College brightness and darkness	0.36	*	0.36	*	0.04		−0.06	
N	36		33		32		32	
Adjusted R^2	0.11		0.05		0.23		0.53	

Note: Columns are multivariate linear regressions testing whether college brightness and darkness predicts adult brightness and darkness, entered alone, with standard controls as denoted by x, with REL Affect, and with this book's mediation model (REL Affect and behavioral achievements) as a control. Low adjusted R-squared values (models 1 and 2) indicate merely that measures are not strong predictors.

***$p < 0.001$; **$p < 0.01$; *$p < 0.05$; +$p < 0.1$

See appendix 5, Variables and Measures.

REL AFFECT EXPLAINS ADULT BRIGHTNESS AND DARKNESS BETTER THAN FIVE-FACTOR MODEL PERSONALITY TRAITS OF NEUROTICISM, EXTRAVERSION, AND CONSCIENTIOUSNESS

Neuroticism and extraversion are associated with REL Affect operationalized as REL Affect Scale; conscientiousness (measured as deferred gratification) is not. The qualitative analyses found that the Remembered Early Life identity story exerts an affective and psychological imprint on the college and adult identity stories. This conception of the explanatory construct raises the question of whether established five-factor model conceptions of personality might be more efficient or better explanations of the adult happiness of participants. There is something distinctively "personality-sounding" about the Remembered Early Life identity story's central affective tendency. Indeed, it is a personality conception, and the operationalized construct of its central affective tendency sounds akin to the broad and diffuse trait constructs characterized by the five-factor model of personality. It would be reasonable to wonder: Is the REL Affect Scale simply picking up traits found to be associated with long-term subjective well-being, namely neuroticism, extraversion, and conscientiousness? These traits would be expected to capture something of brightness and darkness.

To answer this question, I carried out two analyses. First, I determined whether the three selected personality traits are associated with the REL Affect Scale. I analyzed each available measure of personality separately, first alone and then with controls, in a multivariate linear regression with the REL Affect Scale as the dependent measure. Controls for these analyses were the standard college controls (father's education and so on). Given the small size of the longitudinal interview sample and the availability of a larger sample, I carried out these analyses a second time with the longitudinal survey sample.

The results suggest that two of the three five-factor model measures are probably associated with the REL Affect Scale. Extraversion is significantly associated in both samples and when including controls. Neuroticism is associated in the larger sample with and without controls and seems marginally associated in the smaller sample, with a p value of slightly higher than .05 and not when adding controls. Conscientiousness (measured as deferred gratification) shows no association when including controls in either sample. The modest correlation coefficients of the two associated personality trait measures suggest that there is only some shared variation with the REL Affect Scale (table 6.6). This makes sense, given the very different empirical context—qualitative examination of a specialized sample—in which this scale's underlying construct was observed. It also makes sense given this study's specific and delineated social context for observing the construct—the Remembered Early Life—rather than the context-free conception of personality presumed in the five-factor model. Finally, it makes sense in light of this study's use of available archival measures rather than a contemporary instrument to measure five-factor model traits such as the NEO-PI-R personality inventory (Costa & McCrae, 1992). These measures are not the gold standard for capturing five-factor model traits, although the two that associate have been found to be valid measures of their respective constructs.

REL Affect explains adult brightness and darkness better than five-factor model personality traits of neuroticism, extraversion, and conscientiousness (measured as deferred gratification). A second set of analyses is suggested by the finding that REL Affect explains adult brightness and darkness better than specific five-factor model personality traits. This finding raises the question: Is the

T A B L E 6 . 6 . Linear Regressions Testing Association of Five-Factor Model Personality Traits with Remembered Early Life Affect

Dependent Variable: Remembered Early Life Affect Scale
Standardized coefficients

Longitudinal interview subsample, complete cases

Variable	Model 1		Model 2		Model 3		Model 4		Model 5		Model 6
Personality traits											
Neuroticism	−0.31	+	−0.25								
Extraversion					0.45	**	0.39	*			
Conscientiousness (deferred gratification)									0.31	+	0.14
Standard controls			x				x				x
N	33		33		34		34		35		34
Adjusted R^2	0.07		0.10		0.18		0.18		0.07		0.06

Longitudinal survey sample, complete cases

Variable	Model 1		Model 2		Model 3		Model 4		Model 5		Model 6
Personality traits											
Neuroticism	−0.34	***	−0.32	***							
Extraversion					0.33	***	0.32	***			
Conscientiousness (deferred gratification)									0.15	*	0.10
Standard controls			x				x				x
N	192		192		203		202		192		190
Adjusted R^2	0.11		0.12		0.10		0.11		0.02		0.02

Note: Columns are multivariate linear regressions testing whether for the longitudinal interview sample (top half) and for the longitudinal survey sample (bottom half) five-factor model personality traits associate with Remembered Early Life Affect alone and when entering standard controls as denoted by x. Low adjusted R-squared values indicate merely that measures are not strong predictors.

***p < 0.001; **p < 0.01; *p < 0.05; +p < 0.1

See appendix 5, Variables and Measures.

TABLE 6.7. Linear Regressions Predicting Adult Brightness and Darkness with Five-Factor Model Personality Traits and REL Affect

Dependent Variable: Adult Brightness and Darkness
Longitudinal interview subsample, complete cases
Standardized coefficients

Variable	Model 1	Model 2	Model 3	Model 4	Model 5	Model 6	Model 7
Personality traits							
Neuroticism	−0.15				0.18		
Extraversion		0.34				0.09	
Conscientiousness			−0.14				−0.24
(deferred gratification)							
REL Affect				0.61 **	0.60 **	0.58 **	0.64 **
Standard controls	x	x	x	x	x	x	x
N	31	32	32	32	31	32	32
Adjusted R^2	−0.06	−0.02	−0.09	0.26	0.20	0.23	0.28

Note: Columns are multivariate linear regressions testing whether five-factor model personality traits and Remembered Early Life Affect predict adult brightness and darkness entered with standard controls as denoted by x, and with each other as a control. Low and negative adjusted R-squared values indicate merely that measures are not strong predictors.

***p < 0.001; **p < 0.01; *p < 0.05; +p < 0.1

See appendix 5, Variables and Measures.

REL Affect Scale picking up the effects of five-factor model traits on adult brightness and darkness? I therefore evaluated each trait measure in explaining adult brightness and darkness with standard controls and with REL Affect as a control. This analysis was possible using only the longitudinal interview sample for which brightness and darkness was coded. Standard controls for these analyses included the standard college controls and adult self-reported health and adult religiosity. None of the traits appears to predict adult brightness and darkness when entering standard controls and REL Affect as a control, as shown in table 6.7. However, REL Affect predicts adult brightness and darkness with standard controls and with these five-factor model personality traits as controls. (Incidentally, none of the five-factor model measures associates with college brightness and darkness as a dependent measure when entered with controls and REL Affect.)

These findings suggest that the construct of REL Affect captures something unique of college-era person-level effects that explains later happiness, although likely containing some element of the trait measures. The early life context as the target for narrative recollection likely functions as a repository for affective experience but is more specifically situated than traits conceptualized by the five-factor model. It is more specific in context both for its focus on a bounded period of life with a discrete social context and for its focus on narrative autobiographical memory. It explains the affective dimension of the narrative identities—the college and adult identity stories—of participants in college and adulthood, whereas the trait measures do not.

This chapter statistically retested and found support for key relationships in the qualitative model explaining longitudinal stability in brightness and darkness (presented in chapter 5). More than half of the variation in adult brightness and darkness is explained by this theoretical model (table 6.3). REL Affect predicts adult brightness and darkness with normative life course behaviors as a mediator; REL Affect is the common factor that explains the association between college and adult measures of brightness and darkness; the model better explains adult brightness and darkness than other explanations, including objectively measured career success, which does not associate with adult brightness and darkness. Finally, REL Affect explains adult brightness and darkness better than five-factor model personality trait measures (neuroticism, extraversion, and conscientiousness).

CHAPTER 7

The Change Model

Although relative stability is the dominant pattern in the longitudinal interview sample, roughly one-third of participants change significantly. In this chapter I account for this change. Changers move across the life course river to a significantly brighter or darker location in the current. Disruptions to socially reinforcing pathways in adulthood leave them with relatively permanent gains or losses in the overall intrapsychic brightness and darkness they experienced in college.

In formulating a model of change, I rely on data about thirteen participants who changed. Depth and redundancy in their saturated life histories clearly demarcate their trajectories from the trajectories of other longitudinal interview participants. The rich case data and the larger sample's contrasting trajectories help to offset the limitation of the small number of changers.[1] In explaining change, I also implicitly further my description of the stable portion of the sample and underscore the explanatory power of the stable model of development.

Change, I argue, reflects an interaction between the environment and the individual, rather than arising solely within him or solely in the conditions outside of him. The change process is most easily demonstrable in a handful of the most dramatic changers. They exhibit a nearly wholesale departure from their prior affect balance. Other, less dramatic, significant changers show the same factors at work, but to a lesser degree. The small group of changers and smaller group of dramatic changers underscore how infrequent significant change is. Even for these participants, much in their lives, and much about the themes figuring into their affect balance, remains the same. (Affect balance, explained in chapter 4, is another way of describing *overall bright-ness and darkness.*)

CHANGE IN THREE LIVES

Lawrence Hoyt's psychobiographical sketch (see chapter 3) revealed him to be a person who traversed much of the breadth of the life course river from college to late midlife. His life gained greater brightness after his relative's death. The shifts in his life occurred in three discernible dimensions: intrapsychically, behaviorally, and in his environment. Hoyt changed careers, married, had children, divorced, and formed a satisfying long-term relationship. Over this time he changed from feeling disoriented in his life direction, alienated from others, and ineffectual and thwarted, to becoming a central figure, a force for good, in his work and family. The disruption in Hoyt's life was not to his intrapsychic brightness and darkness, narrowly speaking, but rather to the system of inter-acting forces that maintained the status quo ante. By the time Hoyt reached late middle age, he was among the brightest participants in the sample.

Although Hoyt came from means, Jerome Vaughn, raised in very different economic circumstances, made a similar, and arguably more dramatic, tra-verse from overall darkness in college to overall brightness in late midlife. He had no friends and seemed lost and aimless during college and for at least fifteen years afterwards. He was alienated from his parents and siblings, who were marginalized because they lost status and cultural proficiency when they immigrated to the United States when he was a child. For fifteen years after college he traveled internationally, got odd jobs to pay his way, and seemed to be living the exotic life of a free-spirited traveler untethered to external roles or relationships. But he seemed also to be running from pain and alienation. In his thirties he came back to the United States more frequently and found work as a craftsman. A series of mentors taught him a disciplined work ethic. He began to feel productive. As his fortieth birthday approached, he heeded the warning of a relative that if he did not marry soon, he would never marry. By late midlife, he had several children with his wife and was thriving as a father and a craftsman working in a small business. He had become among the hap-piest men in the sample. The change in Vaughn's life, as in Hoyt's, occurred in three dimensions: intrapsychically, behaviorally, and in his environment.

Vincent Costa's life illustrates change moving in the other direction, toward greater darkness. Costa left college torn about whether to enter the social world offered by his Harvard education and to establish distance from his ethnic working-class beginnings. His ambivalence during Harvard had him enjoying something of both worlds while refraining from embracing either world for his future. He lost the perch of his college opportunity slowly over the next several decades. Thwarted romantic and career pursuits highlighted moments of disillusion in this process. By the time of late midlife, a decidedly mixed affective presentation in college had devolved into a decidedly dark sense of alienation, frustration, and sense of failure. Costa's change, like the others', occurred intrapsychically, behaviorally, and in his environment.

Intrapsychic, Behavioral, and Environmental Aspects of Change and Their Linkages in the Change Process

After his relative's death Hoyt came to feel that he wanted children. He no longer wanted to operate within what he began to feel were the restrictive goals valued by his father. He underwent a change in a central organizing motivation or life goal, an intrapsychic change. Hoyt changed his career first and then formed a family. His behavior changed, reflecting his new motivation.

The feedback Hoyt received also changed, reflecting how others valued him and his new disposition to internalize their response to him. Hoyt had felt unsuccessful and not valued in his former career, but in his new role he was appreciated by the people helped by his work. Hoyt had another new role, father, and his children needed him and appreciated him. The validation and appreciation registered with Hoyt because it aligned with his new motivation. If he had had children without wanting to have children and be an involved father, for example, Hoyt would have been less inclined to appreciate, and even to recognize, his value to his children. The change in Hoyt's environment in concert with his new motivation comprise a tandem internal-external shift resulting in changed feedback. It conferred a newfound sense of value to his life.

The new feedback contributed to Hoyt's identity story. It showed up in his domains (of career and parenting) and in his life goals. Hoyt felt more efficacious, more appreciated by others, enriched and validated by his contributions, and more adequate. This accrual of effects contributed to a cycle of positive reinforcement in which Hoyt fell under the sway of the new equilibrium of forces drawing him down the brighter current of the river.

FACTORS IN CHANGE

This brief account highlights factors in Hoyt's change that beg more precision. How do Hoyt's and other participants' motivations change? What is the nature of the change in the environment? The study's data, while not conclusive, are able to show more granular factors in both change and relative stability than those presented in previous chapters.

I introduce a subtle shift in my language from my previous discussion of the identity story. I refer to the identity story as an *intrapsychic organization* of the person, hoping, despite the predominance of stability in the sample across the forty-six years of the study, to highlight the person's psychological malleability and contingency on a constellation of person-environment factors that can change.

I also introduce the concept of *identifications* to refer to smaller forms of intrapsychic organization visible within the identity story—linked to people and social contexts—that contain the participant's experience of important situations and events, important others, the world, and himself. The word *identification* has many definitions and usages in psychological theories. My usage is intended to denote that the individual feels an emotional connection to an interpersonal or social experience that retains a lasting formative presence in his identity story.[2]

Identifications in the identity story of Martin were his experience of his relationship with his father and his experience of his parents as a unit and their invalidating way of relating to him. An identification in Hovanec's identity story was his experience of his parents, of whom he was proud and to whom he was grateful for the values they gave him. An identification in Costa's identity story was his family's proud ethnic working-class background, which both enriched and oriented him while also limiting him.

Multiple identifications are visible in most participants' identity stories in each era of the study. These major components of a participant's identity story organize a large swath of outlook, affect, and behavior.

Five factors are visible in the life histories of all changing participants:

1. An early life identification with a parent, parents, family of origin, another human actor, or social context which has the potential, if engaged or activated, to gain more influence in organizing the person intrapsychically and behaviorally.
2. A distancing from an identification or constellation of identifications shaping the person's active intrapsychic organization.
3. A slow change or a shock in the adult environment that occurs outside of the person, especially a gain or loss interpersonally, or a change in the person's value in the environment.
4. Different feedback refracting the changed external environment through

the changed internal organization, especially in motivations / life goals and how a person responds to setbacks.

5. The approach toward or eventual arrival at a new equilibrium, one that includes a new orientation and a new balance of brightness and darkness.

Hoyt's narrative illustrates how these factors shift an identity story. (See chapter 5 for a contrasting model of development in which social reinforcement helps foster stability in an identity story.)[3] Hoyt was pursuing self-repair in college and during his early adult years as he fought against the gravity of his father's expectations for how his life would proceed, especially in his future career. In contrast with brighter mixed participants, Hoyt was not as much working toward a positive vision for his future as he was fighting against the predetermination of his future.

Hoyt's father was a successful professional and wanted Hoyt to follow suit. His father's social posture toward other people and his children seemed to exude a worldview centered on career ambition. Hoyt felt pressure to pursue a competitive life and to adopt the same kind of competitive identity as his father had done. Hoyt experienced his father as critical and distant.

Hoyt fought against this vision for his life but during the college years found himself unable to withstand the gravity-like pull toward the field and identity his father had chosen for him. Strikingly, by the end of his Harvard career, Hoyt spoke the words that he had declared himself opposed to for years. He now said he would enter his father's professional field (but hoped it would not be permanent).

Self-repair goals—as shown among the sample, Hoyt's life included—often end up being counterproductive. The fight can tire the individual into submission to a psychic orientation that is defensive and self-protective. The person struggles against a problem rather than pursuing positive goals. This orientation turns into a vicious cycle of reinforcement of the problem. The effort to overcome primes the person to expect and to notice the problem and his own inefficacy in combatting it, leading to more of the same. The reinforcement and repetition[4] include self-doubt, a sense of inadequacy and failure, and a sense of alienation, offset only by the survival of some measure of hope; this is a mixed experience at risk of sliding into overall darkness.

Before Hoyt was jarred by the death of his relative, Hoyt was trying to resist the agenda his father had for him but felt that he was fighting a losing battle. He felt unfulfilled, unsuccessful, and stuck, and he felt a general distance from people. He felt overshadowed by his father's success. His adult narrative conveyed that his feelings in this period were much like his feelings during college.

Up to this point Hoyt appeared to fit the pattern of relative stability in brightness and darkness. But the death of Hoyt's relative destabilized his holding pattern, and the cascading consequences accrued into a process of change that spanned decades. Hoyt recognized the ramifications and could not imagine how his life would have turned out without this trigger. It released him from his self-repair aspiration and reoriented him toward the pursuit of another set of goals.

The first externally visible step was Hoyt's departure from his professional career. In college he had several times considered but not fully entertained careers in education and service roles. One perceives in the younger Hoyt's dismissal of these possibilities the strength of his father's thinly veiled critical voice. As an adult, Hoyt gave language to the psychological thwarting. He felt he lacked permission to pursue such possibilities before he began to reorient toward a new agenda.

Hoyt showed a very positive response to the positive feedback he received in his new career role. It was not merely that he was effective in this role. Hoyt was disposed to recognize his contribution because it reflected a motivation he sat easily with, one that infused him with hope and the sense that his efforts were valuable. His prior motivation was a self-repair effort that depleted and demoralized him. This psychological-social alteration of feedback following the death of Hoyt's relative diminished Hoyt's father's psychological influence by loosening the grip of Hoyt's identification with his father, thereby creating an opening for a new identification.

But a shift in Hoyt's career was only the first step in his transformation. Hoyt married and fathered children. His marriage was at first rewarding but then developed into another invalidating experience that ended in divorce.

If the account ended here, this experience would have reinforced Hoyt's prior experience in relationships. But the entire experience was not invalidating. Hoyt was grateful for his children. The desire to have children and a family had been an emergent goal while Hoyt was struggling with his father's agenda for him. Having children represented the realization of a positive life goal. His marriage was a means to children.

But what led to Hoyt's new striving to have a family? I have already suggested that Hoyt's desire to be in a service role was visible long before he acted upon it, but the same cannot be said of his desire to have a family. As a freshman Hoyt said he had given no thought to a future family, and as he was leaving college Hoyt planned to push back having a family until he was thirty-five. The organization of Hoyt's strivings in college was dominated by the values and expectations of his father. But another intrapsychic potentiality, an identification early in Hoyt's life, was waiting and available to be activated—although not inevitably. There was no way to foretell that Hoyt's relative's death would create the clearing that it did. Nor was there a way to predict that this clearing would be filled by this potential force. With the benefit of the study's perspective on all those who changed significantly, however, it is clear that change depends on this force and its potential to alter the course of a life.

Hoyt's vision to have a family is linked to his memory of his beloved mother. Her warm and maternal presence created a family life until her death, which Hoyt cherished. Hoyt's emotional memory of her was rich both in college and adulthood. This memory was not previously central in organizing Hoyt's strivings. Hoyt's identification with his father precluded an identification with his mother from actively governing his life because his father devalued and even invalidated it. The life Hoyt knew with his mother showed him the value of family life and its potential to contribute to feelings of self-esteem, personal fulfillment, and a positive general outlook. Hoyt felt these things in his family when she was alive and he wanted to reexperience them as an adult. This time, a remembered experience stood as a kind of intrapsychic organization. It was not active or reinforced when Hoyt was younger and striving to realize his father's agenda for him. To the contrary, it was dormant and impermissible. But it was sufficiently developed and present that the disruptive event, Hoyt's relative's death, could allow oxygen to reach the embers.

The developments following this event—Hoyt's receding identification with his father, his emerging identification with his mother, a career change, marriage, and fathering children—began to shift Hoyt's central tendency as he added positives to his life. The process of accrual continued. It launched a trajectory to the present era of Hoyt's life.

By the end of midlife it was clear that Hoyt's children were the prize of his life. His new long-term relationship offered a fulfillment that he had never experienced in an adult relationship. Hoyt experienced family life as having resonance with the one he knew when his mother was alive. Hoyt also felt enriched and validated in his career. Hoyt learned to have a closeness with others that was antithetical to his father's example and expectations. The vicious cycle of negative reinforcement in Hoyt's earlier life had given way to a virtuous cycle of positive reinforcement. Hoyt was now enjoying his life and wanted to live as long as he could to continue to enjoy it.

Hoyt's example illustrates the five factors in the model of change.

An early life identification with the potential to be activated. This intrapsychic potentiality is linked to a past interpersonal or social experience, which in Hoyt's case was with his beloved mother. It has the potential, if engaged or activated, to gain more influence in organizing the person intrapsychically and behaviorally.

This past experience is not a marginal episode but rather central and formative in the participant's life growing up. But it is not currently active because it was superseded by a later formative experience. It thus stands at a distance from the prevailing emotional tendency and intrapsychic organization. This is true for participants who change toward greater brightness and for those who change toward greater darkness, as illustrated in the example of Costa in the next section.

This factor is necessary but not sufficient for change; some nonchangers show it in their pasts as well. Martin, for example, experienced a more positive period in his life prior to his family's move to the city in which they eventually settled, but this positive experience was overshadowed by the problems in his relationship with his parents as an older child.

Distancing from an active identification. Second, change requires distance from an active intrapsychic organization of the participant's strivings and experiences. For Hoyt this distance appeared after his relative's death, as his identification with his father receded. Distancing from such an active organization is not possible if there is no alternative available for activation. A vision for Hoyt's life connected with Hoyt's mother created the possibility of an opening.

Other participants, who do not change, cling tenaciously to their organization, no matter how unfavorable or favorable, in the absence of other potential patterns to live through and organize themselves around. This is how self-repair orientations gain force. The participant perceives no better option for living. Hoyt's relative's death might not have had the effect it did if another intrapsychic potentiality was not allowed into the clearing. Hoyt's ability to let go and move on was premised on an alternative intrapsychic organization capable of filling the void.

It might be said, then, that an element of change requires malleability, or perhaps fragility, in the present intrapsychic organization, so that exogenous events and shocks can trigger disruptions. (The exogenous influence does not have to be abrupt or come as a shock. For many participants, it was a long-term process. This is discussed below.)

A change in the environment. Third, importantly, Hoyt's change did not occur as a foregone conclusion. Chance was involved. Hoyt was the first to recognize that the event that triggered his change had a salutary effect on him. He could not have imagined how his life would have turned out if his relative had not died.

If the logic were extended, however, the analysis might get muddled in an infinite web of contingencies that are good and bad luck. It is difficult, when considering all the contingencies, to know whether luck was helpful or hurtful. This analysis would apply to Hoyt's identification with his father, the triggering event, and even the circumstances of later developments, such as Hoyt's marriage, children, and new long-term relationship; chance operated for both better and worse.

Still, the particular shock that disrupted Hoyt's intrapsychic patterns happened to be well targeted to create an opening. It led to the collapse of Hoyt's intrapsychic patterns organized around his prevailing strivings as a younger man.

The events in the lives of participants who move toward darkness also reflect a measure of luck. Costa's life could be told in terms of bad luck, such as unrequited love. Costa's difficulty getting traction both in a career and in a relationship could be attributed to chance in the situations he encountered, and to his working-class background that deprived him of advantages. But chance is at work constantly in lives. It is at once an undeniable factor and not the only factor. Hoyt's interpersonal loss or the thwarting of Costa's relational and career initiatives must be a factor substantial enough to provoke internal reorganization.

External triggers appear sometimes as an exogenous shock and sometimes as a slow and long-term environmental change. Costa's triggers seemed to be more of an accrual than a decisive moment, but this is a matter of perspective, since there were decisive moments of rejection. Frequently, events consolidate an environmental shift under way, such as when a divorce consolidates the long-term dysfunction in a marriage. Among the thirteen changers, abrupt disruptions such as Hoyt's relative's death appear less commonly than slower shifts in the environment contributing to change.

I do not have sufficient data or cases to bring a sociological perspective to the structure and predictability of such environmental changes. Within a life history they appear to be unpredicted and external to the person's purview; common cases include a new relationship, loss of a loved one or a relationship, or a shift of one's currency in the environment.

Different feedback refracted through the changed environment-intrapsychic organization, and a new equilibrium. Fourth and fifth, there is a new pattern of social reinforcement. New motivations and values lead to the person's registering his value in the environment differently. Sometimes, as with Hoyt, the person visibly initiates new behaviors and role choices. Even without the person's active role, the environment can shift and regard the person differently. Both developments result in the person's perception of his increased or decreased value in the environment.

This pattern is the opposite of what was described in chapter 5, in explaining stability. The interaction between the internal and external are not mutually reinforcing in cases of participants who change significantly; instead, the internal or the external—or both—starts out being disruptive. Once begun, the disruption launches a mutual volley of subsequent disruptions that eventually settle the person in a new equilibrium—particularly in family and work roles. This messy process eventually takes form as a distinguishable accretion.

This new equilibrium emerges over a long period (or it may still be emerging, as with many modestly changing participants); the new equilibrium explains why the person comes to look like other participants in the same position in the current of the life course. These other participants came to this new equilibrium by way of a relatively stable trajectory, whereas changers came to it by way of change. Someone like Hoyt ends up looking brighter: he is now enjoying the virtuous cycle of positive reinforcement in his new work and family life. Someone like Costa ends up looking darker: he is now suffering from the vicious cycle of negative reinforcement, the contraction in his life resulting from the forces within and without that thwarted his ability to add positives to his life.

FURTHER ILLUSTRATIONS OF THE CHANGE MODEL

Vaughn's wandering life at Harvard and after became disrupted when he began to value and feel valued by a mentor and employer teaching him a craft. He showed a potential for such a positive relationship in his recollection of the early years of his life before his family immigrated to the United States. His family, and in particular his father, had held a socioeconomically and culturally favorable position in their home society, but his father lost a large measure of his competence and influence in the immigration to the United States. Vaughn saw his father as inefficacious and a source of shame and sadness and saw the period prior to immigration as more satisfying and functional for everyone in the family. This more favorable emotional past, and his loss of it after immigration, are visible in Vaughn's accounts both in college and adulthood.

Vaughn showed an emergent motivation, a wish for greater discipline, productivity, and self-efficacy, in tandem with increased skill and competence and being appreciated as a craftsman. The cycle of feedback was beginning to change. Vaughn could not have been disposed to this tandem internal-external shift were it not for his capacity to value his new work experiences.

Vaughn showed another shift in his personal life. Strikingly similar to the intrapsychic organization that guided Hoyt to marriage and parenting, Vaughn showed the potential for such a reorganized life. His favorable experience of family life prior to immigration was an unrealized potentiality. Vaughn's age and his relative's admonishment not to delay marriage were decisive "external" catalysts. These were not surprises or shocks, like the death of Hoyt's relative was to Hoyt. Vaughn's behavior changed. He married and fathered children. He found connection, validation, and joy in the family that he formed, which he had not found in his adult relationships previously.

Vaughn's openness to and interest in changes in career and family life, and his responsiveness to environmental encouragement, had intrapsychic roots in his past. Vaughn felt that things in his life had been right before immigrating to the United States. He had a more positive feeling about himself and the world. Vaughn's long and expansive travels might be seen in this context in part as seeking out a return to this prior life. Without this potential alternative life in waiting, and capacity to experience his life in these different terms, Vaughn might not have settled down. He might have come to look more like Costa as an adult. Further, without gaining distance from the alienation of postimmigration life in the United States, Vaughn might have continued on his alienated and aimless course.

Costa illustrates the same factors of change but, sadly, in the opposite direction. He grew up in a socioeconomically and to some degree emotionally impoverished experience. He recognized himself as an outlier with intellectual and artistic interests not shared by his family or friends. He hoped to transcend the restrictive conditions of his youth and the terrifying rut he saw in his class-bound future, especially in work. The environment had affirmed in him that he had the potential to do so; he had made it to Harvard.

But this affirmation did not coalesce into a new, long-term cycle of positive reinforcement. Costa faced a severe deficit of skills, knowledge, and social support in carrying out a potential transition into a new social and cultural world. In college the threat of inertia mounted as he faced difficulties excelling in academics and sports and in forming social connections as he had done in high school. These difficulties continued after college as Costa tried but met great disappointment in his forays romantically and with his career. A new cycle of positive reinforcement was solidified for some participants from disadvantaged backgrounds who went to Harvard. But the intrapsychic potential of a debilitating force that existed in Costa's past discouraged him and held him back when he met real resistance and difficulty in finding his footing. His steps in college were more tentative than those of other participants from similar backgrounds, and in adulthood they became more halting with each rejection, devolving, over time, into a retreat and hopelessness. This retreat was a return to an earlier experience that he had fought against in his youth. In making it to Harvard and while at Harvard, Costa showed potential for a later intrapsychic organization to supplant this earlier experience. But Harvard turned out to be an exceptional period in his life. The earlier reality was well developed and primed. It might be said that Costa did not so much change as not change, since his life reverted to an earlier and darker intrapsychic organization.

SHARED ELEMENTS OF THE TWO MODELS OF DEVELOPMENT

Two factors in the model of change appear also in relative stability: early life identifications and adult environmental forces. I briefly compare and expand them in the two models.

The Stability of Remembered Early Life Identity Story

The central emotional experiences of the Remembered Early Life (REL) in college do not appear to be lost to participants with the passing of time and the changing of circumstance in adult life. This is true for changers and non-changers alike. Both show stability in these broad emotional outlines of their REL identity story. Hoyt, for example, in spite of his dramatic change as an adult, does not seem substantially to alter his REL identity story from college to adulthood. The death of his beloved mother remains central. The ensuing competition with his father and emotional deprivation remain central.

Instead, what changes is the present salience of themes of the REL identity story. Some seem to recede in importance and new ones emerge as important in their place. Change reflects a shift in active identifications. For Hoyt and other changers inactive identifications do not disappear wholesale from memory as a result of adult change, just as emergent identifications were not absent in earlier REL identity stories. They appear in the participant's memory and experience even while their salience changes.

Organizing Identifications

The emergent identifications of changers have much in common with those that organize stable participants. Hoyt's intrapsychic organization linked to his mother, Vaughn's life prior to his family's fall from grace, and Costa's class-limiting inertia each fit into the social sites of REL, depicted by concentric circles, introduced in chapter 5 when explaining relatively stable participants. Hovanec's aspiration to form a family and impart a treasured set of values comes primarily from his experience in a nuclear family. Martin's alienation, withdrawal, and self-protection come primarily from his experience with his parents, especially his father's depreciation of him. Fisher's scholastic ambition and interpersonal alienation link to his experience of an invalidating mother and absent father.

Changers have required us to parse the Remembered Early Life into these more specific elements. These elements, or identifications, are visible among nonchangers as well. Changers help to highlight that the impact of the early experience on the present runs through a relational or social context.

The psychobiographical sketches preserve the complexity in these lives. Here I depart from that complexity for the sake of analytic clarity and, at the risk of being overly reductive, hazard in table 7.1 a list of some of the REL identifications that the exemplars of change and of relative stability exhibit in their adult life histories. These are the easiest to identify and present, although there are others for each listed participant and in the sample as a whole. This list underscores the centrality of home and family life as the site of the most affectively formative experiences for nonchangers and changers alike. But it also shows other important sites as well.

Predicting Adult Identity Stories from Early Identifications

This sampling of common early life identifications does not reveal how these influences will affect a participant in adulthood. The thematic analyses the study carried out show far too large a variety of patterns in these respects to be formulaic. Even when looking at the small sampling for the participants listed in table 7.1, it is not possible to predict how the threads of influence will weave together within the REL identity story itself, much less how they will be active in organizing the adult identity story.

TABLE 7.1. Common Remembered Early Life Experiences that Organize Adults

A Sampling of Common REL Experiences (Identifications) That Organize Adults	Hovanec	Martin	Fisher	Payne	Hoyt	Vaughn	Costa
Validating or invalidating experiences in relating to the same-sex or opposite-sex parent or parent figure	x	x	x	x	x		
Validating or invalidating experiences with both parents as a unit or with the family as a nuclear unit	x	x	x	x	x	x	x
Ethnic, national, religious, or regional identification, which often includes pride as well as a mixed proposition, for it often entails hardship in both preserving and transcending it as it is embodied in the family's history	x		x			x	x
Parental expectation that one will marry and have children and reproduce a nuclear family, sometimes infused by religious or ethnic values held by parents	x	x	x	x	x	x	x
Class identification that places a heavy burden to realize a class aspiration, whether it is overcoming disadvantage, realizing a middle-class aspiration, or perpetuating a legacy	x	x	x	x	x		x
A central value of educational and career achievement held by one or both parents (often a more concrete expression of class identification and aspiration)	x	x	x		x		
The expectation that one will follow a specific educational or career path (e.g., go to Harvard, enter business or law) valued by a parent (also a concrete expression of class aspiration in many cases)		x	x		x		
The expectation that one will serve others or otherwise carry out altruistic pursuits such as "giving back to society" or generative aims such as "helping others"	x			x	x		

For example, for a given participant it would not be clear how an ethnic identification would combine with an invalidating experience with parents or class disadvantage to shape life goals and values as a whole. Costa, for example, seemed poised to break out of his class background as a Harvard student; but it is not impossible to imagine that he would have latched onto his ethnic identity as a cherished value and not have been as centrally concerned with upward mobility. What goals and values the participant pursues come together in idiosyncratic and personal ways. Activities, domains of striving, responses to setbacks, and the central affective tendency are not predetermined by these identifications.

The participant's life history showed how his life came together into a holistic picture, the identity story. Knowing the specific elements, the identifications, was not enough to know how they shaped the identity story or were integrated into it.

Given the predominance of relative stability in the sample, a participant has more of a chance of remaining affectively stable from college to late midlife than of changing against the current of the life course river. However, likelihood is not certainty. The analysis of change shows that the past does not predetermine the present. The REL identity story does not predetermine a trajectory in adulthood. The lines of influence between the REL and adult identity stories are manifold, and the environmental interaction with active and inactive identifications may reinforce or disrupt the lines of influence.

Environmental Influences in the Change Model

I have been asked what my research reveals about what factors in adult life or in the adult environment "cause change." I hope my disagreement with the premise of the question is now clear. My research demonstrates that change is the product of intrapsychic-environmental interaction.

Environmental factors take on meaning only in the context of the intrapsychic organization of the person. Two participants lost a parent to suicide in the first fifteen years out of Harvard. Both were deeply stricken, but one rebounded to a prior overall brightness, whereas the other seemed to retreat to a darker current in the life course river. Was the suicide of a parent the same event for each man outside of its meaning to him and his life? No. This is why it does not make sense to decouple the intrapsychic from the environmental in asking what causes change.

Similarly, the intrapsychic organization of the person takes on meaning in the context of environmental factors. Costa and Vaughn both seem to pursue a lower-status career trajectory than most participants, but its meaning in each man's circumstances is dramatically different. Vaughn found validation for his career among appreciative mentors and employers and his career further conferred stability upon his life as a husband and provider in a family. For Costa his career path was the mark of thwarted ambitions and realized fears of getting stuck in an unsatisfying job (if not a working-class rut), which reverberated with Costa's general experience of frustrated initiatives and social isolation as an adult.

It is possible to note the *sites of environmental factors that contribute to change* of changers. The three all-important domains of social reinforcement in nonchangers' lives—career, marriage/partnership, and parenting—are implicated in change as well. Hoyt and Vaughn illustrate the salutary effect of these areas in change to more brightness, and Costa illustrates their deleterious effects in contributing to change to more darkness.

Our small thirteen-person sample size and the variability of sites of change do not permit generalizations except to note that these three areas are the important ones where environmental effects contribute, as shown in table 7.2.

THE MOST DRAMATIC CHANGERS

Hoyt, Vaughn, and Costa illustrate change in all three areas of their lives. Behaviorally in these areas, as well as intrapsychically, they come to realize—or not to realize—the behaviors that reinforce the orientation of their emergent identity stories. In both respects they come to look like nonchangers whose current of the river they come to share in adulthood. I presented these changers' lives in this chapter because they offer more vivid illustrations than many other changers' lives. Their shift in overall affect balance is relatively extreme. For example, in tables 7.1 and 7.2, note that only five of thirteen changers show environmental influences in their change in all three areas of their lives.

But this is not how I identified the participants whom I call the most "dramatic changers." Three participants, including Hoyt and Vaughn, show the largest magnitude of shift in their overall affect balance, exceeding 2.5 points from their college to adult rating. Costa shifts by two points. Hoyt and Vaughn show less in common with their college affective themes than Costa does. Costa illustrated key concepts, and his change is unquestionably significant, however, which is why I include him as an example. Table 7.3 shows the variation in changers by their degree of change.

I am reluctant to make too much of this quantification, since the group is so small and the underlying measures are ordinal, meaning that the size of change across time is hard to interpret. But it is one way of suggesting variation among changers. The difference between dramatic and less dramatic changers is a matter of degree, not a matter of the mechanisms at work.

Hoyt and Vaughn, as dramatic changers, show almost a wholesale substitution or replacement of an active with an inactive intrapsychic organization. In their cases, it is almost as if there is a government in waiting that comes into power. By contrast, for more modest changers, a dormant identification emerges more subtly and in integration with other active identifications. There is a fragility or malleability to the intrapsychic organization of more dramatic changers. The life histories of less dramatic changers show less of a divide between their active and inactive identifications. I offer this characterization cautiously, recognizing that the environment might have affected dramatic

TABLE 7.2. Sites of Environmental Influences in Change

Change to More Brightness (N = 9)	Affected Changers	Change to More Darkness (N = 4)	Affected Changers
Experience of marriage, especially a good second one (4 participants), contributed to change to more brightness. [For 2 unmarried participants, one divorced and the other never married, this fact dampened their change to more brightness.]	6	Experience of marriage (2 participants), divorce (1 participant), or not marrying (1 participant) contributed to change to more darkness.	4
Experience as parent contributed to change to more brightness. [Problems in a child's development, in relating to a child, or in feeling adequate as a father overall had mixed effects on 3 participants' change to more brightness. Not having children dampened change to more brightness for 1 participant.]	5	Experience as parent (1 participant) or not being a parent (1 participant) contributed to change to more darkness. [For 2 participants, being a parent had mixed effect on change to more darkness.]	2
Career experience contributed to change to more brightness. [Career detracted from 3 participants' change to more brightness.]	6	Career experience contributed to change to more darkness. [For 2 participants career dampened the change to more darkness.]	2
All three sites—marriage, parenting, and career—contributed to change to more brightness.	4	All three sites—marriage, parenting, and career—contributed to change to more darkness.	1

Note:
• This table lists participants multiple times, as multiple environmental sites affect a changing partici-pant's brightness and darkness.
• The top three rows of the table list all changers whose identity stories and brightness and darkness are affected by that site of environmental influence (marriage, parenting, and career). The site of influence is not necessarily affecting the participant's brightness and darkness in the same direction as the par-ticipant's overall change. (For example, his career may be a site of negative affect even while he changes to more brightness.) Further, these three rows indicate only that the specified site of influence has an effect; other influences may also be having an effect.
• In contrast with the top three rows, the bottom row lists participants for whom all three sites inde-pendently contribute to the participant's movement toward greater brightness or greater darkness. I include this third row to underscore its infrequency. The examples of changers presented in this chap-ter, Hoyt, Vaughn, and Costa, fall into this category. The effects of the three sites of influence act in con-cert, making the participant's change more dramatic. More of the identity story shifts. (A participant's having all three sites of environmental influence work in concert is not the formal criterion by which I delineate between dramatic changers and others, as explained below.)

TABLE 7.3. Variation in Changers by Their Degree of Change

Degree of Significant Change	Significant Movement against Current from College to Adulthood	N	Examples
Most dramatic	Greater than 2.5 points (on the spectrum of brightness and darkness)	3	Hoyt Vaughn
Middle group	2 points	4	Costa
Least dramatic	Between 1 and 2 points	6	Russo

changers differently in adulthood. Still, were it not for this quality of intrapsychic potential, such environmental effects would have generated a smaller degree of change.

The Adult Identity Story's Reflexive Stance

The participants I described in this chapter illustrate change more evocatively for another reason: they give more voice and visibility to their change than many other changers in describing their adult life experiences. This quality is shared by the dramatic changers and select others, such as Costa. There is a ready availability of the participant's conclusion that his life has changed. It is a central part of his story. The adult life accounts of these participants demarcate their present lives from a time in the past when they felt differently. The study reached the same conclusion about their lives by comparing their college and adult presentations.

This reflexivity is not visible in the life histories of some less dramatic changers and is absent from the saturated interviews of the nonchangers. This small number of changers reveals an important heuristic that marks their adult life histories, which is simply this: they are not necessarily clear why they changed, but they know that they have changed to a brighter or darker orientation to their lives. Costa feels that his best days are behind him, Hoyt and Vaughn that their worst days are behind them.

Adult life has been formative for these participants and they recognize it. Dramatic change reverberates throughout their adult interviews in two unmistakable ways, even without looking at the college record.

First, such changers do not engage in open-ended discussion aloud about whether they have changed, nor do they explore it in discussion curiously, as a possibility. They are certain that they have changed and leave no room for question. This presentation is in contrast with relatively stable participants and some lesser changers who debate aloud whether they have changed. (This debate is a reflection, I believe, of a strong cultural incentive to convey that a person has authored his life and changed favorably as a result of his efforts, even if he has not.) Stable participants often invoke complicated psychological reasoning that is removed from a visceral sense of having changed. It sounds like a debate of what might be true rather than a report of felt experience.

Second, the break with their former life has a special quality for unequivocal changers. They have reached a point of no return to a prior life. Participants who changed to greater brightness do not feel or convey that they might some-how slip back into the earlier pattern that was darker and more uncomfortable. There is no fear of regression from the current life, because they do not feel their gains are situational or temporary. This contrasts with others for whom there is a lingering anxiety that their gains may be sitting atop situational or reversible factors, such as a recent remarriage. This sense of irreversibility is also true for unequivocal changers, like Costa, who have changed to greater darkness. Their former lives feel to them out of reach.

This reflexive feature especially separates dramatic changers to more brightness from false positives of such change. True dramatic changers provide a decisive answer when asked whether they have changed. They provide this answer without being asked, and have done so long before they would have been asked, at the end of the interviews. This answer is a key frame of their life history. They weave this answer through their interviews and their perspective on the domains of their lives and their lives overall. There is no question in their mind that they have changed. There is no question that their former lives stand on the other side of a clear break in the history of their lives. And there is no question that the change is here to stay—they have crossed over into a new life. Other participants do not offer such resounding conviction of transformation.

THE MODEL OF CHANGE CONTRASTED WITH RELATIVE STABILITY

The model of change outlined in this chapter helps to explain the lives and the intrapsychic brightness or darkness of the thirteen participants who changed significantly against the current of the river from college to late midlife. It is a process model that shows a disruptive set of forces at work, in contrast with the model of reinforcement explaining the outcomes of the nonchangers. The effect of the REL identity story on later affect and later behavior is disrupted in the lives of changers. Another REL intrapsychic potentiality is activated and links to a new adult social reality in the all-important domains of career and family formation. In this sense adult life is formative for them, whereas for the nonchangers the earlier formation of intrapsychic organization visible in college remains largely intact.

Changers end up looking like other adult participants who share their level of intrapsychic brightness and darkness. Affectively and behaviorally, changers come to exhibit the patterns of nonchangers on the same current of the life course river. They just got there by a different route. For changers, the disruptive processes disconfirmed and altered the old identity story.

This model of change is descriptive rather than predictive because it is based on a small number of cases and it is the exception to the dominant pattern in the sample. The model of relative stability is both descriptive and predictive because it suggests the intrapsychic and behavioral outcomes that are more likely for the sample, based on their college evidence, as they traverse adult life. The two models together provide a fuller understanding of the sample and the trajectory of their lives.

PLACING CHANGE IN CONTEXT

I presented a model of change for completeness in describing the sample, but I have run a risk of misrepresentation. I isolated a small group who deviate from the dominant pattern, and I presented the most dramatic examples of them to illustrate the model. Change, even among most changers, is not without stability. It is difficult to weigh change and stability side by side. By observing the whole sample, and each participant's life in great depth in saturated interviews, this study recognizes only a few participants as dramatically crossing the life course river to a new overall affect balance. For most changers there is a strong legacy of affective themes, and the overall affect balance does not seem to break with the past more than it seems to retain its connection. For most participants, change occurs on the margin, and the central affective tendency does not appear to shift a great deal.

Still, it ultimately is a philosophic question and a matter of perspective whether the change in any given life or in the sample is significant. For the person living the life, it is. Most people would readily accept the incremental brightness and resist the incremental darkness that changers show. But at the same time, this study has a privileged vantage point on the sample and their long-term patterns of experience.

Robert White (1975) follows the life and personality development of Hartley Hale, physician and scientist, from college to late midlife in *Lives in Progress*. He concludes his close case analysis this way: "Studying natural growth means being on the lookout for change, but change in personality occurs against the background of much that stays constant" (White, 1975, p. 86). Hale was part of a cohort of Harvard students White was studying several generations earlier. White's statement summarizes what is true for participants in this study. Even among lives that change in this study's central construct, there is much that stays constant.[5] White's admonition holds forth not only in lives that change but in the sample as a whole.

CHAPTER 8

Beyond Success:
The Relationship between Career
and Happiness

I now return to the question that animated the study: How does competitive success affect the happiness of participants? Chapters 5, 6, and 7, with their analytic focus on the adult experiences of participants, suggested an answer by explaining adult brightness and darkness through two models of development, beginning with patterns starting in college. These models show the importance of affect, behavior, and remembered early life experience in adult outcomes; they also show that career success does not have an important influence on these outcomes. Although well supported, this perspective seems counterintuitive. In a study sample so heavily invested in their careers, how is it possible that career success does not show impact on late midlife happiness? To consider the finding from different angles that might either invalidate or clarify it, I have undertaken post hoc analyses, using both qualitative and quantitative data. This chapter raises five questions whose answers provide further insight into the forces responsible for adult brightness and darkness. In so doing, the chapter not only ties up loose ends but broadens the study's argument beyond the models of development presented in the previous three chapters.

As I have argued, the sample's happiness and socioeconomic attainment in career are not associated. This chapter shows how social comparison—a gaze directed toward others who serve as a standard for evaluating one's own achievements and merit—impedes competitive success from conferring significant well-being benefits, even for participants from socioeconomically disadvantaged family backgrounds. Further contextualizing the book's developmental argument, this chapter makes a broader claim: career experience more generally is circumscribed in its impact on the brightness and darkness of adult participants. Adult brightness and darkness is shaped primarily by experiences in adult family rather than in career.

EXCEPTIONAL CASES

The first of the five critical questions is this: Are there participants who are exceptions to the finding that socioeconomic attainment in career does not associate with late midlife happiness and, if so, what makes their pattern different from the pattern of the overall group?

Three participants are notable exceptions to the study's finding that socioeconomic attainment in career does not associate with late midlife happiness. What these three men have in common is that their careers far exceeded their wildest expectations for how successful they would be. They looked to their Harvard peers, others in their fields, and their fathers as reference points to establish their expectations; they had done much better than the reference points they had internalized.

Two were just about at the pinnacle of their fields. One was a nationally prominent scholar who shaped social policy and was responsible for a nonprofit employing several hundred researchers. Another was not only CEO of a publicly traded corporation but also among the wealthiest in the sample. A third participant, Russo, held a senior appointment at a well-respected academic institution; although not at the pinnacle of his field, he had risen well beyond his working-class beginnings.

These three men's level of socioeconomic attainment in career was decisive in altering their identity story and, along with it, overall brightness and darkness. In this regard they are exceptions to the study's main finding, underscoring the idea that pursuing socioeconomic attainment in career was a risky strategy for contributing to well-being in this sample.

THE ENVIRONMENT:
A PULL FOR BIFURCATED SELF-ESTEEM

The second question is: What environmental and selection effects—of going to Harvard and the competitive career world after Harvard—help explain the lack of association between socioeconomic attainment in career and happiness for this group?

I speculate that the competitive playing field in which the participants operated is one factor contributing to why socioeconomic attainment in career rarely impacted their happiness. Entering a career through this highly competitive world of Harvard did not guarantee that a participant would obtain a high level of objectively measured career success; nor was attaining a high level of objectively measured career success guaranteed to favorably affect his happiness. Selection into this world placed participants into a rarified level of competition with other top contenders in their fields. They found it hard to distinguish themselves and feel successful.

The intensity of the competition appeared almost immediately upon arrival at Harvard. Many participants experienced shock as their new status dawned on them. They had mostly been top students or athletes and had held leadership positions in their secondary schools and communities, but now they were not the biggest fish in their ponds—or even necessarily big fish. They looked around in their freshmen seminars or on the athletic fields and saw that the pond had turned into an ocean full of big fish. They couldn't get the grades they were used to or join the teams they wanted. Hovanec had difficulty getting athletic play his freshman year, for example, and Fisher struggled with grades his freshman year. Many never achieved big-fish status during their college years.

Participants experienced another jarring reality when they went home during summer vacations after their freshman and sophomore years, or through contact with high school friends or girlfriends. Most participants were changing; they found themselves increasingly distant from the common life trajectories of people from home communities. Moreover, they were treated by others as being different from what they had been. They belonged to a future elite occupational class, a future status almost guaranteed now that they were undergraduates at Harvard. These young men often felt uncomfortable with their changing status but could not help seeing their former communities and peers in a new light—often as parochial or unintellectual. They did not share the same future as adults and peers from home. Further, many parents who did not go to Harvard or another high-status undergraduate institution wondered what effect Harvard would have on their sons, and importantly, what effect it would have on their relationships with their sons. There was fear, not unfounded, of distance. Indications of these changes in status came out frequently in the interviews study participants gave after their freshman and sophomore summers.

What began to emerge during the Harvard years is a concept I call *a pull for bifurcated self-esteem*. Participants commonly remained big fish in the ponds from which they came, but they were small fish in relation to the Harvard social world they were entering. When they were at home, or when they considered their lives and their abilities and their prospects in relation to their home communities, they could more easily feel favorably; when they considered their lives and abilities and prospects at Harvard in relation to their new peers, they could more easily feel unfavorably.

This pull toward bifurcated self-esteem affected participants differently. Those coming from more emotionally unsettling backgrounds were more susceptible to its influence. Participants whose intrapsychic tendencies mapped onto the darker current of the river tended to show more insecurity in and vulnerability to their new environment at Harvard: grade anxiety, frustration and anxiety in relationships, and lack of confidence about their future career direction and future success. This pull was part of the Harvard environment. Harvard was thus not a neutral force. A participant's competence and prospects and even self-worth were brought into focus and, for many, into question. The brighter participants were less responsive to the darker part of this pull.

There was an analogue in adulthood: social comparison tended to deflate participants' sense of career success in relation to other Harvard graduates and other high-performing competitors. Participants entering competitive fields looked at others in their fields as well as others from Harvard; participants entering less competitive fields looked at others from Harvard. They directed their gaze to the highly successful men they had come to know as college students and adults—not only their fathers and brothers, if they were successful, but also other successful men in their communities. Even many participants who were successful by objective standards in relation to others in their fields or from Harvard seemed to feel their accomplishments lessened by the standard they were using. It was telling that Leo Mullin, former CEO of Delta Airlines, and Michael Crichton, a well-known novelist, had become public figures within one Harvard class. They were icons of successful Harvard graduates. Among participants in this class, unprompted, many mentioned their names; many more mentioned their names, among others, when I asked them to compare themselves to other Harvard graduates. Participants commonly conveyed themselves as feeling below average in the harsh light of social comparison—a mathematical impossibility.

Thus, Harvard and the adult career worlds that participants entered socialized them into standards of achievement that were rarefied and difficult to attain. This socialization had less effect on some participants from disadvantaged backgrounds than it did on participants from privileged backgrounds, since the former had a second standard to fall back on, that of their fathers and peers from their working-class communities. This phenomenon helps explain Russo's reaction to his career success, which did not place him at the top of the competitive hierarchy for either Harvard graduates or his field, but which far exceeded the attainment of others in the world he grew up in. Men from privileged backgrounds experienced reinforcement of the standards with which they had been socialized prior to arriving at Harvard. Sometimes it was prep school; other times it was their fathers or the cultural milieu of places like Greenwich, Connecticut, or Manhattan that showed them what was possible.

Pursuit of Socioeconomic Attainment: Low Probability of Contributing to Happiness

But the strongest dividing force was not socioeconomic background prior to Harvard. It was how participants reacted to the pressure and opportunity presented by Harvard. What was possible for a Harvard graduate presented a strong case for action; what was possible suggested itself as the standard to which participants *should* strive. Participants who did not adopt this standard, or who were able to maintain balance in their perspective, were generally less responsive to the environment, less concerned with self-repair, more focused on living with an outward orientation in achievements and relationships rather than protecting and augmenting themselves. They were participants who entered the Harvard world and their adult lives on brighter currents in the river. These participants resisted something that was widely felt: what was possible for socioeconomic attainment became what was expected.

It is therefore not surprising that *only three participants* among the longitudinal sample of thirty-seven experienced socioeconomic attainment in their careers as having a major effect on their brightness and darkness. Most participants did not feel that they had been as successful as they could have been or had wanted to be in their careers. Fisher's sentiment—that his career success was suboptimal—was common. Participants' standards were not purely the product of Harvard's influence; they preceded and succeeded Harvard in the competitive environments of education and occupation in which these men traveled. But alone and in conjunction with these other socializing influences, their experiences at Harvard suggested aspirations that most felt unable to meet.

Given the steep competition, the elevated standards, and the upward social comparison, the strategy of striving for career success for these Harvard graduates seemed to offer bad odds for feeling successful. It seemed a hard way to come to experience positive feelings about their careers or their lives.

Participants from Disadvantaged Backgrounds: Socioeconomic Attainment Still Shows Low Probability of Contributing to Happiness

Participants from disadvantaged backgrounds deserve special consideration for how socioeconomic attainment affected their happiness. Slightly more than a quarter of the longitudinal interview sample had fathers who did not complete high school. Even though the educational and occupational achievements of fathers, brothers, and other men in home communities offered a more forgiving standard for social comparison relative to more privileged participants, it was often an inactive standard, having been largely overtaken by standards in the competitive world these participants entered through Harvard.

It is nevertheless noteworthy that two of the three participants discussed earlier as exceptions to the finding that socioeconomic attainment in career does not associate with late midlife happiness came to Harvard from disadvantaged family backgrounds. The salutatory effect of socioeconomic attainment in career on their happiness came from far exceeding their expectations for how successful they would be. Even though they, too, looked at Harvard peers and others in their fields as reference points in establishing their expectations, their working-class fathers were particularly important influences on their standards. While exceeding expectations initially forged in disadvantaged backgrounds showed a significant benefit to happiness for surprisingly few participants from disadvantaged backgrounds, it is a mechanism for how socioeconomic attainment might possibly affect happiness. (General samples, however, show a similar pattern of long-term well-being not being significantly altered by gains in circumstances.)

Participants from disadvantaged backgrounds fit the overall patterns of well-being and development observed in this study even while showing some different qualities of experience from other participants. The salutary effects on happiness of their socioeconomic gains—less stress from having greater material resources and perceived life opportunities, enrichment, pride in achievements, and a feeling of greater respect from others—were counterbalanced by complicated feelings often including guilt and shame and a nostalgic sense of loss at widening social and emotional distance from families and communities of origin. As with other participants, as adults they followed the current of the life course river on which they entered Harvard. Their worldviews, organized by their remembered early lives, continued to shape how they felt long after they transcended its conditions. In chapter 10 I return to these observations about participants from socioeconomically disadvantaged backgrounds. There, I note that these participants' patterns show linkage with patterns observed in general samples and that their patterns may help explain the limited effect of circumstances, including competitive educational attainments, on happiness.

THE EFFECT OF CAREER EXPERIENCE, MORE GENERALLY, ON BRIGHTNESS AND DARKNESS

The third question examining the finding that socioeconomic attainment in career and happiness are not associated in the sample asks: Does career experience more generally, besides socioeconomic attainment, influence happiness?

It would be surprising if this cohort of Harvard men experienced no contribution from their careers to their overall brightness and darkness, even if socioeconomic attainment in careers had no effect. Indeed, when the focus turns to the career as a whole—and is not restricted to the effect of socioeconomic attainment in the career—career appears as an affectively important domain for almost all participants. It contributed to their overall brightness or darkness.[1]

However, the effect of this domain is circumscribed when one looks at the career in the context of the rest of participants' lives. For the sample as a whole—with a small number of exceptions—the deciding factor between a brighter or darker current of the adult life course river was affect experienced in family life, not in career. Martin's and Hovanec's lives diverged on the life course river in adulthood primarily because of Hovanec's positive family experience. Hovanec's career was brighter than Martin's as well, but without his positive family experience, Hovanec likely would have come to resemble nearly all participants who did not have a positive family experience. These participants travel the darker currents of the life course river.

A positive experience of family life overall came from a participant's experience as a husband (or partner), as a parent, or in both roles. It was not necessary for each role experience to be overall positive, only for family experience as a whole to be overall positive, for a participant to be located in the brighter current of the life course river. The affect that participants experienced in their careers made a difference only by enhancing or inhibiting the overall affective tendency determined by a participant's family experience. Fisher was on the darker current of the river, but the measure of satisfaction he got from his career kept him from sliding into overall darkness, as Martin did. Hovanec was on the brighter current of the river but his career did not carry him to the brightest reaches of the river, as Payne's career did for him. The affect that participants experienced in their families was the decisive pivot between the two broad paths down the river of adult life, whereas career accentuated or dampened the overall affective tendency.

THE EXPERIENCE OF CHANGERS: HOW CAREER EXPERIENCE AFFECTS BRIGHTNESS AND DARKNESS

The fourth question asks whether, if changers are different from nonchangers in the longitudinal model of their development, are they different also in how career experience affects their happiness?

Career experience functioned differently and played a larger role in the overall affect of changers than it did for nonchangers.

For a small group of changers, career experience was a catalyst for and/ or worked synergistically with experiences in family in a process of change. Vaughn and Hoyt both experienced important shifts in their careers early in their transitions toward greater brightness. For Vaughn it was the powerful effect of a mentor, and for Hoyt it was permission to pursue a career that he wanted, experiences enriched for both men by positive feedback. Conversely, Costa's frustrated attempts to gain a foothold in a career trajectory occurred concurrently and seemed in a negative synergy with his thwarted romantic efforts. These men's careers did not exceed the influence of their family lives. The primary influence on each of these men's overall brightness or darkness by late midlife was his family or relational life, but career helped to advance the change.

For five of thirteen changers, career experience appeared to equal or exceed the impact on brightness and darkness of family life. Table 8.1 shows the relative importance of family life and career domains in influencing brightness and darkness for changers. It differs from table 7.2, which indicates for how many changers each domain (marriage, parenting, and career) is a site of influence affecting adult brightness or darkness. Table 8.1 consolidates the two family life domains (marriage and parenting) and sets them up against career.

Of the five, three have already been described—the exceptional cases for whom socioeconomic attainment in their careers substantially contributed to their increased brightness. They are exceptional cases in a second sense as well: contrary to the large majority of the sample, their career experience overall (not merely socioeconomic attainment in career) equaled or exceeded family life in contributing affectively to overall brightness and darkness.[2] Two changers to greater darkness also show this exceptional pattern.

The exceptional pattern of career experience equaling or exceeding family life in its influence on brightness and darkness reveals some variation but un-

TABLE 8.1. Changers: Domains Influencing Brightness and Darkness

Longitudinal subsample changers

	More Brightness	More Darkness	Total
Family life is clearly dominant influence	6	2	8
Career experience equals or exceeds influence of family life	3	2	5
All changers	9	4	13

derscores the dominant pattern in the overall sample: family life exerted the decisive impact on adult brightness and darkness. This finding broadens the claims of the study by suggesting that career experience as a whole—a concept distinct from socioeconomic attainment in career—although important, had a secondary and circumscribed impact on the sample's happiness.

CAREER FAILURE AND MENTAL ILLNESS

There is a fifth and final puzzling question: How is it possible that socioeconomic attainment in career does not associate with happiness, given what we know about the profoundly deleterious effect of socioeconomic hardship, such as protracted unemployment?

This finding seems at odds with common sense and scholarship. There are plenty of bad things that can happen to people socioeconomically in a career: losing a job, prolonged unemployment or underemployment, demotion to a lower-status position, or thwarting of career ambitions. Is it not the case that such career circumstances make participants dark?

In answering this question, I distinguish *career failure* as a significant decrement in occupational prestige and financial attainment compared to the large majority of the sample. Career failure in this sample, given the advantages of a Harvard education and the opportunities it creates, is nonnormative. It requires special circumstances and a special explanation.

Most participants attain a relatively high level of occupational prestige in business, academia, medicine, law, and other fields. By contrast, some participants have lost their jobs and remain unemployed or have difficulty maintaining stable employment or hold positions well below average levels of prestige for their peer group nationally and especially for their peers from Harvard. Some are in low-wage and low-skill positions, such as a taxi driver or research assistant, not by choice.[3] The participants in these circumstances comprise a small portion, 6.3%, of the longitudinal survey sample (as measured by a method I describe below).

My impression of these participants is that they are doing as well as they can; it is clear that their relatively low occupational prestige and financial attainment compared with the rest of the group is the result of psychiatric illness. They have struggled for long periods with unipolar or bipolar depression or obsessive-compulsive tendencies or psychotic or delusional disorders or borderline or other personality disorders or challenges.

Some of these men never find their footing in work. Some find their footing in stable, lower-stress positions or in positions that are more manageable for them. Some seem successful, only to be demoted or forced into unplanned retirement toward the ends of their careers because of their own conduct—fallout of an affair or allegations of fraud or another kind of misconduct. They lose their jobs and cannot—in their late fifties and sixties—find new employment.

Mental Illness Explains Career Failure as Part of Darker Current in River

The outcomes of participants experiencing what I am calling career failure do not appear in the middle years suddenly, without antecedents. The longitudinal trajectories of these participants are shaped by mental illness much more than other participants in the sample. This is a special variation of the darker current of the river. Some participants with chronic mental illness do better than others, but the small number of men I am referring to here are the most challenged and reveal that career failure is a symptom of long-term mental illness.

Career failure is an extreme version of an inability to sustain stable investment in a career. (Stable investment in a career is one of three behavioral achievements discussed in chapter 6 that demarcate the brighter current of the life course river.) Most participants who do not sustain stable investment in a career nonetheless continue to maintain a relatively high occupational status compared to the US population. Career failure, by contrast, is an inability to function occupationally in a full-time role or in a role of normative status for this Harvard group or even for the general population.

In college, participants with psychiatric difficulty already show their tendency toward the future outcome of career failure. Their psychiatric distress tends to place these participants in the darkest currents of the river. As adults, it is harder for them to add positives and to feel good about their lives. Psychiatric difficulty in college, in fact, predicts career failure. The odds of ending up

TABLE 8.2. Cross-Tabulation of College Psychiatric Usage and Career Failure in Late Midlife

Longitudinal survey sample, complete cases

| | | Experiencing career failure by late midlife | | | | | |
| | | Yes | | No | | Total | |
		percent	N	percent	N	percent	N
Received psychiatric help in	Yes	16%	6	84%	31	100%	37
college	No	4%	5	96%	134	100%	139
	Total		11		165		176

Note: The table shows the proportion of participants experiencing career failure by late midlife based on whether they received psychiatric help in college. This table uses the longitudinal survey sample, having first observed an association between psychiatric difficulties and career failure in the longitudinal interview subsample. Career failure is operationalized as the respondent reporting any of the following conditions in late midlife: unemployed or disabled, household net worth is negative or less than $100K, occupational prestige is in bottom 15% of same-age male national population as measured in the 2004 General Social Survey (Smith et al., 1972–2016). Received psychiatric help in college is operationalized as respondent reporting senior year that during college he was a patient at the University Health Services psychiatric clinic or he consulted a psychiatrist, psychologist, or counselor for help with emotional problems. See appendix 5, Variables and Measures.

with career failure by late midlife—unemployed or disabled, or with relatively modest financial resources, or in a low-status position—is 5.2 times ($p < .05$) greater if a participant received psychiatric help during college (see table 8.2). Odds are 7.5 times ($p < .05$) greater when entering standard controls. I suspect this ratio predicting career failure in the sample to be conservative, given likely underreporting of career failure and psychiatric usage.

Because affect in family life in adulthood is decisive in dividing darker and brighter currents of the river, it is not surprising that participants with career failure are also less likely than others to add positives in marriage and parenting domains of their lives. They also show symptoms of depression. Table 8.3 illustrates the differences between participants with career failure and all other participants.

Participants with chronic mental illness are a subset of participants traveling the darker currents of the river. I separate them for two reasons. First, the potential for biology or social deviance to be prominent factors in their darker lives is made more obvious by their psychiatric illness. These same factors

TABLE 8.3. Emotional and Behavioral Correlates of Career Failure

Longitudinal survey sample, complete cases

			Experiencing Career Failure						
			Yes		No		Total	*Test Comparing Difference*	*Significance*
			percent/ mean	*N*	*percent/ mean*	*N*	*N*		
Depressed and unhappy	1	Proportion of depressed (2+ symptoms on CES-D)a	55%	11	7%	187	198	Pearson Chi-squared test	$p < .001$
	2	Mean happiness (reported on SWLS, range 5–35)	18.7	11	25.3	188	199	Mean difference t-test (2-tailed)	$p < .001$
Adult behavioral achievements outside career	3	Proportion with 2+ children	33%	12	75%	190	202	Pearson Chi-squared test	$p < .01$
	4	Proportion married, living together, in first or second marriage	25%	12	80%	189	201	Pearson Chi-squared test	$p < .001$

Note: Rows compare adult participants experiencing career failure with other adult participants for emotional and behavioral variables. Analysis is restricted to complete cases in the longitudinal survey sample. All variables show significant differences.

aThe CES-D scale: A self-report depression scale for research in the general population (Radloff, 1977).

See appendix 5, Variables and Measures.

may be at work in other participants' lives, but I have not explicitly used these concepts to explain the longitudinal patterns. Persons who have psychiatric illness are studied extensively in other literatures and are not the central focus of this study as a separate subgroup. Some unique factors may explain their development, but they nonetheless figure into the overall dark pattern of development described in this book.

Second, I separate participants with chronic mental illness and career failure to delineate the difference between career failure, explained by mental illness, and an individual's perceived shortage of socioeconomic attainment in career. The vast majority of participants felt that they could have achieved more in their careers. Very few experienced career failure.

A number of participants shared surprisingly candid concerns about the possibility of failing in their careers—ending up homeless or bankrupt, without resources, and without an ability to get back on their feet should such circumstances develop. Martin spoke of the possibility that his business would go bankrupt, and Hovanec's account of his business difficulties raised concern about his economic viability. The fear of such a dire outcome was far more prevalent than the outcome itself. This mismatch seemed analogous to the often-cited dream of forgetting about or otherwise not showing up for a test in college. Few people fail to show up for a test; many more worry about it. (Some participants with worries about career failure mentioned having a version of this dream as well.)

These fears are important to address because they make it difficult to communicate the empirical reality. Despite a high level of career attainment relative to the population, many participants fell short of the highest levels of career attainment that they imagined themselves capable of achieving and that they observed others achieving, in upward social comparison. Better understood as unrealized career ambition than as the special circumstance of career failure, this outcome is the most common in the longitudinal interview sample. Career failure contributes to the deleterious effect of preexisting mental illness, reinforcing intrapsychic darkness, but unlike unrealized career ambition, it is not common. Both career failure and unrealized career ambition reinforce the identity story long in place (except where it is part of significant change).

Psychiatric illness does not inevitably put a participant on the darker current of the river or result in career failure. Many brighter participants, such as Russo and Payne, experienced depression or anxiety or another psychiatric problem and utilized psychiatric services. Some participants who had psychiatric illnesses managed to function over the course of their careers but then lost traction toward the end. Still, psychiatric illness, especially chronic psychiatric illness, is associated more with the darker current of the river than the brighter. In darker participants' lives, the distress is more frequent than for brighter participants who experience episodes of illness. For the darker participants the periods are less time limited and seem to accentuate—rather than break with—their central affective tendencies in their life histories.

STATISTICAL REPLICATION OF QUALITATIVE OBSERVATION: AFFECT IN CAREER IS NOT PRIMARY EXPLANATION FOR INTRAPSYCHIC BRIGHTNESS AND DARKNESS

Moving beyond the mostly qualitative post hoc analyses presented so far of why socioeconomic attainment in career does not associate with happiness, I now deepen the account with quantitative analysis. Specifically, I retest the three main qualitative findings that career is of secondary importance in affecting brightness and darkness. I test whether

1. Participant perception of career success associates with brightness and darkness. (Qualitatively, it does not.)
2. Positive and negative affect experienced in career associates with brightness and darkness. (Qualitatively, it does not.)
3. Positive and negative affect experienced in family life significantly associates with brightness and darkness. (Qualitatively, it does.)

I use multivariate linear regressions to test these relationships, and I do so in light of the mediation model of relatively stable development presented in earlier chapters as a baseline account of adult brightness and darkness. Appendix 5 lists all measures described below and used in these regressions. I report regression results using standardized coefficients to allow for comparison of multiple explanatory variable relationships with the dependent measure.

Measures and Controls

I described the mediation model explaining adult brightness and darkness in chapters 5 and 6 and present the regression analyses testing this model in chapter 6. I begin with the same model as the basis for testing the additional effects of career and family life. The measures of the baseline model include REL Affect, adult behavioral achievements, and standard controls. In table 8.4, column 1 displays this mediation model.

I use the same measures of objective career success (occupational prestige and household net worth) presented in chapter 6.

Subjective career success. To measure subjectively perceived career success, I administered this survey question: "On a scale of 1 to 10, how would you rate your career success compared to that of others by the standards in your field?"

TABLE 8.4. Linear Regression Models Predicting Adult Brightness and Darkness with Subjective (and Objective) Career Dimensions and Satisfaction with Family Life

Dependent Variable: Brightness and Darkness
Longitudinal interview subsample, complete cases
Standardized coefficients

Variable	Model 1		Model 2		Model 3		Model 4		Model 5		Model 6		Model 7		Model 8	
Remembered Early Life Affect	0.39	*	0.36	*	0.35	*	0.36	*	0.49	**	0.44	**	0.52	**	0.51	**
Behavioral achievements	0.57	***	0.63	***	0.55	**	0.54	**	0.38	*	0.46	**	0.39	*	0.38	*
Standard controls	x		x		x		x		x		x		x		x	
Satisfaction with family life									0.36	*	0.34	*	0.36	*	0.37	*
Siegel prestige scores			−0.13								−0.14					
Household current net worth			0.18								0.12					
Subjective career success					0.12								−0.08			
Satisfaction with career							0.11								−0.05	
N	32		32		31		32		29		29		28		29	
Adjusted R^2	0.55		0.56		0.52		0.54		0.65		0.64		0.61		0.63	

Note: Columns are stepwise multivariate linear regressions testing whether career dimensions (in addition to objectively measured career success) or satisfaction with family life associate with adult brightness and darkness. The baseline mediation model explaining adult brightness and darkness (see chapters 5 and 6) with standard controls is entered first (model 1), then career and family life effects individually (models 2–5), and then each career effect along with the family life effect as controls for each other (models 6–8).

***$p < 0.001$; **$p < 0.01$; *$p < 0.05$; +$p < 0.1$

See appendix 5, Variables and Measures.

(Following the response, the participant is asked to specify in an open-ended format the standards in his field, which helps to ground his response.)

Career satisfaction and family life satisfaction. I use survey questions about domain satisfactions to stand in for the qualitative concept of affect in domains, specifically career satisfaction and family life satisfaction. The questions follow the format of the Health and Retirement Study's (Juster & Suzman, 1995) survey questions about domain satisfactions. The question about family life satisfaction is repeated from the 1992 wave of the Health and Retirement Study, whereas the question about career satisfaction was created for this study's adult survey. The questions ask, "How satisfied or dissatisfied are you with each of the following aspects of your life (where applicable)?" and give five response choices ranging from "very dissatisfied" to "very satisfied." For family life, an additional choice of "not applicable" is given. The domains—"Your family life" and "The career you have had"—are embedded in a series of queried domains.[4]

Results

The regression analyses lend support to the qualitative findings.

Neither subjective career success nor career satisfaction associate with adult brightness and darkness. Results for models 3 and 4 in table 8.4 show quantitative support for this qualitative observation about the sample, extending the study's main finding that objective career success does not associate with adult brightness and darkness.

Family life satisfaction associates with brightness and darkness. The columns for models 5, 6, 7, and 8 in table 8.4 show quantitative support for this qualitative finding, even when controlling for career effects: objective career success, subjective career success, and career satisfaction. This association also appeared qualitatively when considering these possible career effects.

These results observed in both qualitative and quantitative analyses contextualize and show a limit to the effect of career experience on adult brightness and darkness: affect in career extends or inhibits the primary affective tendency associated with family life.

This chapter clarified why socioeconomic attainment in career does not explain brightness and darkness of the adult sample. The chapter went beyond the models of development presented in the previous three chapters and addressed special considerations: exceptional cases, the competitive dynamics of Harvard and career environments, the effect on happiness of career experience as a whole (a concept distinct from socioeconomic attainment in career), special considerations of significant changers, and career failure—as distinct from unrealized career ambition—and psychiatric illness. These special considerations filled out the study's developmental account of brightness and darkness.

Specifically, post hoc qualitative analyses and quantitative replications revealed family life to be the primary site differentiating brighter and darker adult participants. Career experience extends or inhibits the brightness or darkness determined by family life experience. This finding further contextualized the lack of effect that socioeconomic attainment in career has on brightness and darkness by showing the circumscribed effect of career experience as a whole.

Finally, qualitative and quantitative analyses in this chapter accounted for career failure, an infrequent outcome contributing deleteriously to well-being. Career failure is significantly explained by the psychiatric difficulties that preceded the career and that placed the participant on the darker currents of the life course river.

The chapter focused principally on adult experiences in career and family that do and do not foster late midlife well-being. In doing so, it observed factors already at work in college that limit the benefit of both competitive educational success and later competitive career success to the sample's well-being across time: social comparison and the social forces featured in the book's developmental account. I return to considering factors shaping well-being in chapter 10, leveraging research about general samples to show evidence for this book's developmental account beyond the Harvard sample. In the next chapter I consider how this study of human development and its main findings would have turned out if we had used a conventional approach to studying happiness.

* 3 *

Comparison and Summary

CHAPTER 9

A Conventional Measure of Happiness: A Reexamination

This book describes a newly developed qualitative approach to the investigation of happiness, which was carried out longitudinally and which led to a new conception of happiness. This approach integrates the person rather than dividing him or her into parts, shows a developmental history leading up to happiness, and links this history to behavior. These efforts, applied to participants in the underlying study, fulfill the study's aim to understand what their lives have been like and are like and to examine the effect of competitive success on their happiness. But two questions remain: What would have been found had the study relied on a conventional approach to assessing happiness, and how do this study's findings about a specialized sample relate to other lives? This chapter addresses the first question, and chapter 10 addresses the second.

This chapter replicates the main statistical analyses of the study using a conventional and widely used measure of happiness, the Satisfaction with Life Scale (SWLS) (Diener, Emmons, Larsen, and Griffin, 1985; Diener, 2009b), as a dependent measure. While the replication analyses reveal areas of convergence between the SWLS and the Scale of Intrapsychic Brightness and Darkness, the study would have resulted in different findings if the SWLS had been used as the measure of happiness in the study. Using additional analyses, I trace the source of these different findings. My analyses suggest caution in drawing conclusions from the use of the SWLS without additional knowledge of the sample.

This chapter retests findings generated qualitatively and already replicated statistically using the Scale of Intrapsychic Brightness and Darkness as a dependent measure. These final replications using the SWLS analyze the following:

1. The book's mediation model, in which Remembered Early Life Affect explains brightness and darkness directly and through the mediating variable of adult behavioral achievements. (See chapter 6.)
2. No support for an association between objective career success and brightness and darkness. (See chapter 6.)
3. The association between satisfaction with family life and brightness and darkness, even when controlling for career effects on brightness and darkness, namely, objective career success, subjective career success, and career satisfaction. (See chapter 8.)
4. No support for the association of the additional career effects of subjective career success and career satisfaction with brightness and darkness. (See chapter 8.)

The replication results, presented in table 9.1, support parts of the longitudinal model and the effect of family life satisfaction on happiness but diverge in finding no mediation of behaviors in the longitudinal model as well as in finding significant effects of career variables. Personality and cultural influences, not accounted for by the SWLS, are accounted for by the brightness and darkness measure. These differences reflect more generally the conceptual and empirical differences between the two approaches to capturing happiness.

To carry out the most complete replication analyses, I use both the longitudinal interview sample ($N = 37$) and the larger longitudinal survey sample ($N = 207$). The larger sample provides more statistical power to detect significant associations, whereas the smaller sample holds constant the group that is being analyzed with the two measures of happiness.

REPLICATION ANALYSES USING SWLS

Replication analyses using the SWLS lend support for two of the three relationships in the longitudinal model of development, illustrated in figure 9.1.

More positive REL Affect predicts higher SWLS scores for both the longitudinal survey sample and the longitudinal interview sample, as shown in the regression results in table 9.2.[1] This is true when entering controls and alternative explanations (models 4 through 8 for both samples and model 9 for the interview sample). More positive REL Affect predicts greater realization

TABLE 9.1. Summary: Results of Replication Analyses Using the Satisfaction with Life Scale as Dependent Measure

Main Findings of Qualitative Study and Linear Regressions Using Scale of Intrapsychic Brightness and Darkness	Component Findings	Results of Replications with SWLS
1) A mediation model in which Remembered Early Life Affect explains brightness and darkness directly and through the mediating variable of adult behavioral achievements. (Chapter 6)	1a. REL Affect predicts brightness and darkness.	Same finding.
	1b. REL Affect predicts adult behavioral achievements.	Same finding.
	1c. Adult behavioral achievements mediate the effect of REL Affect on adult brightness and darkness.	Divergent finding: adult behavioral achievements do not associate with SWLS.
2) No support for an association between objective career success and brightness and darkness. (Chapter 6)		Divergent finding: objective career success associates with SWLS.
3) An association between satisfaction with family life and brightness and darkness, even when controlling for career effects on brightness and darkness, namely, objective career success, subjective career success, and career satisfaction. (Chapter 8)	Family life satisfaction associates with brightness and darkness.	Same finding.
4) No support for the association of the additional career effects of subjective career success and career satisfaction with brightness and darkness. (Chapter 8)	4a. Subjective career success does not associate with brightness and darkness.	Divergent finding: subjective career success associates with SWLS.
	4b. Career satisfaction does not associate with brightness and darkness.	Divergent finding: career satisfaction associates with SWLS.

of adult behavioral achievements for the full sample (as it did for the interview sample, as described in chapter 6), presented in table 9.3. However, adult behavioral achievements do not associate with the SWLS. Unlike the regression results using adult brightness and darkness as a dependent measure, adult behavioral achievements do not mediate the effect of REL Affect on SWLS (when including controls).

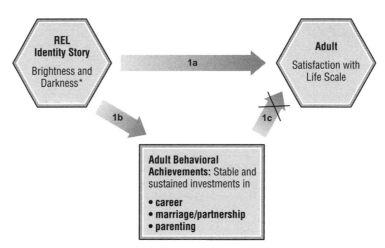

FIGURE 9.1. Support for Longitudinal Model Using the SWLS

EFFECT OF CAREER AND FAMILY LIFE ON
SATISFACTION WITH LIFE

The survey sample analyses (models 5 through 8 in table 9.4) show that family satisfaction associates positively with SWLS, but the interview subsample (models 5 through 8 in table 9.5) shows a weaker effect, in a smaller (but still meaningful) coefficient and significance levels mostly just above the $p < .05$ threshold. Together, these results suggest that SWLS is picking up the effect of family life satisfaction on happiness, an effect observed also using brightness and darkness as a dependent variable.

However, the SWLS shows a different relationship with career effects than the brightness and darkness measure does. The survey sample shows that three of four career variables associate positively with SWLS (net worth, subjective career success, and career satisfaction), but the subsample results show that subjective career success does not and that net worth does not (when controlling for family life satisfaction). In general, career effects seem to associate with SWLS, given the results in the full sample, but the smaller sample doesn't pick them up as robustly and may have some sample differences with the full sample. This diverges from the Scale of Intrapsychic Brightness and Darkness regressions, wherein these career variables (net worth, subjective career success, and career satisfaction) do not associate with the dependent measure.

TABLE 9.2. Linear Regressions Predicting Adult Satisfaction with Life Scale Responses with Remembered Early Life Affect and Behavioral Achievements

Dependent Variable: Satisfaction with Life Scale
Standardized coefficients

Longitudinal survey sample, complete cases

Variable	Model 1	Model 2	Model 3	Model 4	Model 5	Model 6	Model 7	Model 8	Model 9
REL Affect	0.32 ***		0.31 ***	0.24 **	0.22 **	0.25 **	0.10	0.23 **	
Behavioral achievements		0.12 +	0.03	0.02	0.01	0.00	0.00	0.02	
Standard controls				x	x	x	x	x	x
Objective career success					x				
Intelligence or academic performance						x			
Personality traits							x		
Psychiatric intervention								x	
College brightness and darkness									x
N	203	203	203	200	193	196	175	173	
Adjusted R^2	0.10	0.01	0.09	0.16	0.22	0.16	0.13	0.16	

Longitudinal interview subsample, complete cases

Variable	Model 1	Model 2	Model 3	Model 4	Model 5	Model 6	Model 7	Model 8	Model 9
REL Affect	0.50 **		0.44 *	0.59 ***	0.54 ***	0.61 **	0.75 **	0.57 *	0.66 **
Behavioral achievements		0.33 +	0.20	0.15	0.22	0.18	0.06	0.14	0.17
Standard controls				x	x	x	x	x	x
Objective career success					x				
Intelligence or academic performance						x			
Personality traits							x		
Psychiatric intervention								x	
College brightness and darkness									x
N	34	34	34	32	32	31	31	30	32
Adjusted R^2	0.22	0.08	0.23	0.55	0.63	0.52	0.51	0.50	0.54

Note: Analyses retest findings 1a and 1c in table 9.1, as shown in the mediation model in figure 9.1. Columns are stepwise multivariate linear regressions using the longitudinal survey and interview samples and the SWLS as a dependent measure to retest the book's mediation model explaining the adult Scale of Intrapsychic Brightness and Darkness as a dependent measure. In that model Remembered Early Life Affect explains the dependent measure directly and with adult behavioral achievements as a mediator. These variables are first entered alone, then together, and where denoted by x, together with standard controls and controls of objective career success, intelligence and academic performance, personality traits, psychiatric intervention, and for the interview sample, college brightness and darkness.

*** $p < 0.001$; ** $p < 0.01$; * $p < 0.05$; + $p < 0.1$

See appendix 5, Variables and Measures.

TABLE 9.3. Survey Sample Linear Regressions Predicting Adult Behavioral Achievements with Remembered Early Life Affect

Dependent Variable: Adult Behavioral Achievements
Longitudinal survey sample, complete cases
Standardized coefficients

Variable	Model 1		Model 2		Model 3		Model 4	
Remembered Early Life Affect	0.30	***	0.28	***	0.27	**	0.29	***
Standard controls			x		x		x	
Personality traits					x			
Psychiatric intervention							x	
N	206		206		179		177	
Adjusted R^2	0.09		0.08		0.06		0.06	

Note: Analyses retest finding 1b in table 9.1, as shown in the mediation model in figure 9.1. Columns are multivariate linear regressions using the longitudinal survey sample to test whether Remembered Early Life Affect predicts adult behavioral achievements, entered alone, and where denoted by x, with standard controls and personality traits and psychiatric intervention as controls.

***$p < 0.001$; **$p < 0.01$; *$p < 0.05$; +$p < 0.1$

See appendix 5, Variables and Measures.

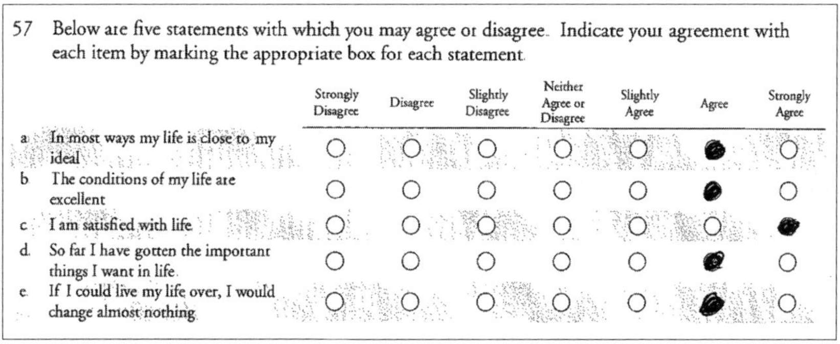
57 Below are five statements with which you may agree or disagree. Indicate your agreement with each item by marking the appropriate box for each statement.

	Strongly Disagree	Disagree	Slightly Disagree	Neither Agree or Disagree	Slightly Agree	Agree	Strongly Agree
a. In most ways my life is close to my ideal							
b. The conditions of my life are excellent							
c. I am satisfied with life							
d. So far I have gotten the important things I want in life							
e. If I could live my life over, I would change almost nothing							

FIGURE 9.2. Satisfaction with Life Scale, Excerpted from Harvard Student Study Adult Survey

TABLE 9.4. Survey Sample Linear Regressions Predicting Adult Satisfaction with Life Scale Responses with Career and Family Life Variables

Dependent Variable: Satisfaction with Life Scale
Longitudinal survey sample, complete cases
Standardized coefficients

Variable	Model 1		Model 2		Model 3		Model 4		Model 5		Model 6		Model 7		Model 8	
Remembered Early Life Affect	0.24	**	0.22	**	0.11	+	0.14	*	0.23	***	0.21	**	0.13	*	0.16	**
Behavioral achievements	0.02		0.01		0.01		0.00		0.01		0.00		0.00		−0.01	
Standard controls	x		x		x		x		x		x		x		x	
Satisfaction with family life									0.45	***	0.39	***	0.38	***	0.31	***
Siegel prestige scores			0.06								0.02					
Household current net worth			0.23	**							0.19	**				
Subjective career success					0.46	***							0.42	***		
Satisfaction with career							0.56	***							0.47	***
N	200		193		197		198		193		187		191		191	
Adjusted R^2	0.16		0.22		0.36		0.45		0.35		0.36		0.50		0.54	

Note: Analyses retest findings 2, 3, 4a, and 4b in table 9.1. Columns are stepwise multivariate linear regressions using the longitudinal survey sample to test the association of career and family variables with adult Satisfaction with Life Scale responses. The baseline mediation model explaining the adult Scale of Intrapsychic Brightness and Darkness and standard controls are entered first (model 1), then career and family life effects individually (models 2–5), and then each career effect along with the family life effect as controls for each other (models 6–8).

***$p < 0.001$; **$p < 0.01$; *$p < 0.05$; +$p < 0.1$

See appendix 5, Variables and Measures.

ACCOUNTING FOR DIFFERENCES IN THE TWO DEPENDENT MEASURES

The replication findings provide further support for the long arm of REL Affect in influencing both adult happiness and behaviors and for the association of family life satisfaction with happiness. The combination of findings across modalities and measures suggests robust support.

But the two dependent measures diverge in showing effects from life course behaviors and career variables. The explanation lies in what the two measures of happiness are capturing and what their differences are.

TABLE 9.5. Interview Sample Linear Regressions Predicting Adult Satisfaction with Life Scale Responses with Career and Family Life Variables

Dependent Variable: Satisfaction with Life Scale
Longitudinal interview subsample, complete cases
Standardized coefficients

Variable	Model 1		Model 2		Model 3		Model 4		Model 5		Model 6		Model 7		Model 8	
Remembered Early Life Affect	0.59	***	0.54	***	0.50	**	0.46	**	0.60	**	0.54	**	0.58	***	0.46	**
Behavioral achievements	0.15		0.22		0.11		0.07		0.07		0.16		0.07		0.05	
Standard controls	x		x		x		x		x		x		x		x	
Satisfaction with family life									0.31	+	0.25		0.22	+	0.23	+
Siegel prestige scores			−0.05								−0.03					
Household current net worth			0.31	*							0.22					
Subjective career success					0.20								0.01			
Satisfaction with career							0.39	**							0.35	*
N	32		32		31		32		29		29		28		29	
Adjusted R^2	0.55		0.63		0.74		0.68		0.63		0.65		0.80		0.72	

Note: Analyses retest findings 2, 3, 4a, and 4b in table 9.1. Columns are stepwise multivariate linear regressions using the longitudinal interview sample to test the association of career and family variables with adult Satisfaction with Life Scale responses. The baseline mediation model explaining the adult Scale of Intrapsychic Brightness and Darkness and standard controls are entered first (model 1), then career and family life effects individually (models 2–5), and then each career effect along with the family life effect as controls for each other (models 6–8).

***$p < 0.001$; **$p < 0.01$; *$p < 0.05$; +$p < 0.1$

See appendix 5, Variables and Measures.

The Conceptual Aims of the Two Measures and Their Overlap

The SWLS is a measure of subjective well-being, asking respondents five questions that presumably tap how they think about their lives. The responses are scaled from 1 to 7 and are summed up into an overall scale from 5 to 35. The items ask the respondent how much he agrees with such broad statements as "In most ways my life is close to my ideal" and "The conditions of my life are excellent." The five items are shown in figure 9.2, as they were asked in the study's survey.

The Scale of Intrapsychic Brightness and Darkness observes a similar construct differently. Data are collected in clinical life history interviews (see online appendix 2) that reach a point of saturation. The coders assess the affective content of the life history, conveyed in statements and (implicitly)

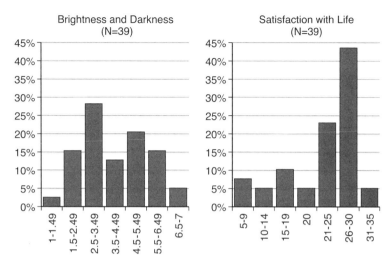

FIGURE 9.3. Distributions of SWLS and the Scale of Intrapsychic Brightness and Darkness

in narrative. The life history and assessment procedures systematically cover the different areas of a participant's life shown affectively and cognitively to be important to him; at the same time, they guide both the participant and the observer to review certain areas that might potentially be important, even if not recognized or directed there by the participant. The qualitative assessment weighs the different areas and combines them into an overall synthesis using a systematic procedure; the procedure uses the standards that the participant shows to be important to him in looking at his life.

Although the SWLS and the brightness and darkness measure are quite different approaches, they both defer to the participant's determination of what aspects of his life are important to him. It is a surprise and somewhat validating that they seem to succeed in capturing a similar underlying construct, as indicated by their common variance. The two measures correlate at roughly .49 (p < .01) for the adult interview sample (N = 39). Depending on whether one looks at the glass as half full or half empty, this association may appear to show that the two measures are capturing the same construct or not. Looking at the glass as half full and stopping the comparison there, it might seem that the qualitative approach is an unnecessary investment of time and resources. The SWLS is assumed to require about "one minute" of a respondent's time to complete, the study's interviews take seven to nine hours, and the coding procedure takes another fifteen hours for each participant.

But it is already clear that this argument overlooks divergent regression results, which need to be explained, and that half of each measure's variance

TABLE 9.6. Interpretation of Each Measure's Responses: SWLS and the Scale of Intrapsychic Brightness and Darkness

Satisfaction with Life Scale		Scale of Intrapsychic Brightness and Darkness	
Very satisfied	31–35	5.5–7.0	Overall bright
Satisfied	26–30		
Slightly satisfied	21–25	4.5–5.49	Mixed positive
Neutral	20	3.5–4.49	Evenly mixed
Slightly dissatisfied	15–19	2.5–3.49	Mixed negative
Dissatisfied	10–14	1.0–2.49	Overall dark
Very dissatisfied	5–9		

Source: Pavot, W., & Diener, E. (1993). Review of the Satisfaction with Life Scale. *Psychological Assessment*, 5, 164–172.

See appendix 5, Variables and Measures.

is not shared with the other measure. The devil is in the details, specifically in these "details" and what they tell us about the happiness of participants. Comparing the two measures for the adult interview sample ($N = 39$) exposes some central reasons for these divergences.

Different Distributions

The distributions for the two measures show the divergence. The SWLS distribution skews somewhat to the right and is not as evenly distributed as the Scale of Intrapsychic Brightness and Darkness (see figure 9.3).

The left skew of the SWLS scores suggest systematically more positive life assessments than those assigned by the brightness and darkness measure. The semantic interpretations given to participant scores by each measure show this at work. The mean SWLS score for the adult interview sample is 23.3, or "slightly satisfied" (Pavot & Diener, 1993), whereas the mean score of brightness and darkness is 3.9, or "evenly mixed." More than three-quarters (77%) of respondents are in the neutral and positive half (20 and above) of the SWLS range, whereas only one-half (51%) are in the neutral and positive half (4 and above) of the brightness and darkness measure's range.

Table 9.6 shows corresponding ranges of score for the two measures, based on their meanings or semantic interpretation.

It might appear that the different distributions of the two measures are inconsequential, simply locating the sample's distributions at different parts of their ranges. This would make sense, given that the SWLS was developed for general use with many populations, whereas the Scale of Intrapsychic Brightness and Darkness was developed in this study and applied to its sample. The lower half of the SWLS's range would be expected to capture populations less satisfied than this Harvard sample.

The validation literature for the SWLS lends some support to this argument. I draw primarily on Pavot and Diener's 1993 article reviewing the Satisfaction with Life Scale. Groups that score lower on the scale include psychiatric inpatients (mean = 11.8, N = 52), clinical outpatients (mean = 14.4, N = 27), and male prison inmates (mean = 12.3, N = 75). The means of most nonclinical groups fall in the "slightly satisfied" to "satisfied" range (Pavot & Diener, 1993). This finding is widely replicated (Diener & Suh, 1999) and indicates that the Harvard sample is typical of most nonclinical groups and, as might be expected, is concentrated in the more satisfied half of the SWLS's range.

If this argument explained the differences between the two measures, it would suggest that the foregoing semantic comparison of the two scales is not founded, because the brightness and darkness measure is calibrated to a generally overall satisfied group. This would mean that the differences between the two measures might simply be an artifact of their different semantic classifications of well-being levels. Further, a criticism of the brightness and darkness measure might be warranted; the qualitative assessment of participants' well-being might simply be tilted toward a more negative semantic interpretation.

But this account does not hold up to scrutiny. Few groups are reported to be in the lower half of the SWLS range, and most of the reported means fall into the middle to higher range of the SWLS. Further, if the SWLS locates nonclinical populations at the higher end of its range, the question might be asked why groups that fall into the lower half of its range, such as psychiatric inpatients, are not found to be more unhappy. One inpatient sample's mean of 12.3 classifies the sample as "dissatisfied" rather than "very dissatisfied" (Pavot & Diener, 1993). An inpatient psychiatric group would be expected to be among the most unhappy or dissatisfied groups in the general population. They are suffering from psychiatric distress and require hospitalization to help them manage. Participants in the Harvard sample actively suffering from mental illness (who were not inpatients) were qualitatively found to be overall dark.

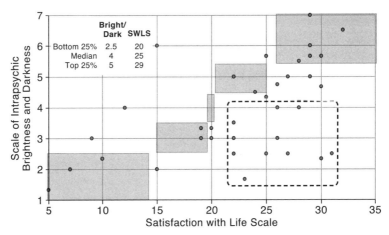

FIGURE 9.4. Individual Participant Scores on the SWLS versus the Scale of Intrapsychic Brightness and Darkness (*N* = 39)

Note: Figure compares participant scores on the SWLS to the Scale of Intrapsychic Brightness and Darkness using each measure's semantic meaning shown in table 9.6. Shaded boxes contain participants for whom the two measures seem to match (33%). The participants to the right of these boxes are those for whom the SWLS value is higher than their measured brightness and darkness (56%), and the participants to the left of these boxes are those with SWLS scores lower than their measured brightness and darkness (10%). The encircled points represent thirteen participants showing the most elevation in Satisfaction with Life Scale responses compared with Intrapsychic Brightness and Darkness ratings. (Two of eleven cases are not visible in the encircled area because of overlapping scores.)

Another source of concern with the SWLS is that it finds little variation in the Harvard sample's level of satisfaction. There seem to be few individual differences in the level of happiness participants report on the SWLS. Only 13% of the interview sample is found to have some degree of dissatisfaction. This is obviously not the case when one looks at the interviews of the sample, as the team of raters determined. The raters' assessments utilized the darker end of the qualitative measure's range about as frequently as the brighter end of its range.

The SWLS paints a rosier picture of the well-being of the sample, and it is not merely an artifact of scale calibration or semantics. Other factors are responsible for the divergent levels of happiness found using the two measures.

INDIVIDUAL SCORES PINPOINT DIFFERENCES

Examination of differences between the two measures at the level of individual participants reveal other factors at work. Figure 9.4 shows the participants who are responsible for the different distributions. The shaded boxes in the scatterplot are participants for whom the two measures seem to match. The participants to the right of these boxes are those for whom the SWLS value is higher than their measured brightness and darkness, and the participants to the left of these boxes are those with SWLS scores lower than their measured brightness and darkness. The mismatch in responses is significant. Using this chapter's semantic method of comparison, most of the sample (56%) has a higher SWLS score, very little of the sample (10%) reports lower SWLS scores, and only 33% of the sample seems to match.

Unequal Distribution of Score Differences

While there appears to be some general elevation of the sample's scores on the SWLS compared with brightness and darkness, the mismatch is not distributed equally across the sample. I draw a dotted line around the scores of participants ($N = 13$) in the scatterplot (figure 9.4) who show the greatest mismatch in the positive direction. These participants' SWLS scores locate them two or more semantic categories happier than their brightness and darkness score. Participants in the bottom half of the range of brightness and darkness show the highest such mismatch. Among these participants, those at 3 and below are of greatest interest. Dark or mixed dark, they are also satisfied in some degree (slightly satisfied, satisfied, and very satisfied). This difference is not the result of semantic differences between the two scales, as evidenced by 43% of the sample who do not conform to this pattern. What accounts for such contradictory conclusions about their well-being?

Why Some Participants Show Highly Elevated SWLS Scores

An analysis of the interviews with these thirteen participants offers an answer. One research participant's responses to the SWLS are shown in figure 9.2. This participant seemed to be in an estranged marriage (his wife had had an affair), his children had struggled with drug and alcohol problems, and he was emotionally wrought, tearing up with sadness during two of our three interviews. He seemed very sad and still traumatized by a mentally ill family member and violence in his home growing up. Qualitatively, he was one of the most unhappy participants in the study. Our research team assessed him at a 2.5 on a scale of 1 to 7.

Yet in responding to the SWLS measure, he strongly endorsed positive statements about his life (four responses of "agree" and one response of "strongly agree"), and overall he came out as the second happiest participant in the sample. According to the semantic meaning of his responses, his SWLS score (31) meant that he is "very satisfied."

The interviews show where this participant does not attend to his negative feelings as he speaks about and assesses key areas of his life. This is the phenomenon of "leakage" described in the interview assessment procedure. For example, he appraised his marriage overall as positive even though it seemed like an estranged marriage—as one coder said, "It isn't a terribly happy relationship." This observer noticed that the participant tended to avoid focusing on negative aspects of his life (in his interviews and in his life) and that his efforts to do so were not successful. She said they "are not strong enough to counter his tendency for self-blame and a generally depressed outlook."

Each of the thirteen participants with elevated SWLS scores showed leakage. The leakage in David Martin's interviews was described in chapter 2. Although Martin came across to the study team as decidedly overall dark, his SWLS responses indicated that he was "slightly satisfied" (23). Another participant, the first participant in the section titled "Capture the Filters in Interviews" in chapter 4, showed leakage in both career and marital experiences and was seen by raters as overall dark (2.33). But his SWLS responses placed him at the high end of the "satisfied" range (30). Leakage was a central factor confounding judgments that less happy participants made about their lives. These participants restricted their view to the more favorable aspects of their lives.

Without data that allow detection of leakage, it would be impossible to know whether any of these participants were as happy as they reported themselves to be on the SWLS. Without leakage, their self-reports appeared as happy as other participants'. The SWLS does not account for such distortions in assessing the happiness of the respondent.

CONSTRUCT DIFFERENCES

The qualitative assessment approach used by the study differs from the SWLS in the target of its captured construct. Derived from a grounded theoretical analysis, the construct of brightness and darkness does not make a formal distinction between life satisfaction judgments and the affective content of life histories. This distinction is not indicated in the qualitative data because of the many linkages between affect and judgments, the central one of which is the saturation of affect in the identity story. The identity story is the participant's skeletal psychological structure through which he construes himself and his life, and it is shot through with affect.[2] Darkness in the identity story also influences how the participant pays attention to his affect: it motivates the participant to turn away from negative affect, as was seen with leakage in the interviews and as is now seen in the selective elevation of SWLS scores of darker participants.

The distinction between cognitive judgments of life satisfaction on one hand and positive and negative affect on the other is a central distinction in the scholarship on subjective well-being. Although the issue is finessed, the two sets of constructs have been found to be distinct but related (Diener, Emmons, Larsen, and Griffin, 1985; Pavot & Diener, 1993; Diener, 1984, 2000, 2009a). The creation of the SWLS measure was in part an attempt to refocus research toward the neglected construct of life satisfaction, since most subjective well-being research up to that time had captured well-being as an affective construct (Diener, Emmons, Larsen, and Griffin, 1985).

It might seem feasible to attribute the elevated SWLS scores and differential regression results to this distinction and bring closure to this account. Measures of life satisfaction have been found to associate differently with other variables than have measures of positive and negative affect (Diener, Emmons, Larsen, and Griffin, 1985; Pavot & Diener, 1993). It would thus make sense that brightness and darkness—incorporating both affect and cognitive judgments—would yield different findings than the SWLS.

But this account would leave unanswered a critical question: Can and should SWLS's cognitive assessments of life satisfaction be treated as being independent of respondent affect? The study's clinical life history interviews show that affective distortions of judgments are responsible for the unequally elevated SWLS responses.

SOCIAL DESIRABILITY BIAS

Social desirability bias has been discussed in different terms in a long literature in social science research. Fastame and Penna (2012), following Johnson and Fendrich (2002) and Paulhus (1984), define social desirability bias as the "tendency of individuals to regulate their answers to establish a positive impression, avoid criticism or satisfy a need for social approval" (p. 239). This definition speaks to the incongruence observed in interviews, denoted by the study's concept of leakage.

Research into social desirability bias has ebbed and flowed in half a century of debate over its true effects on the validity of survey measures and, in particular, on well-being measures. The resolution of this debate among psychologists has been to find insufficient evidence to warrant concern.

Carstensen and Cone (1983) found that two widely used measures of life satisfaction, The Philadelphia Geriatric Center Morale Scale (Lawton, 1975) and the Life Satisfaction Index B (Neugarten et al., 1961), correlated with a measure of social desirability at .70 and .58 respectively.[3] However, their critique was rebutted, principally by McCrae (1986) and McCrae and Costa (1983), who argued that social desirability is part of the construct being measured (Paulhus, 1991; Kozma & Stones, 1987). This resolution mirrored the resolution produced by Block in a similar debate two decades earlier (Block, 1965).

Following these resolutions, Diener (2009a) has argued similarly that social desirability is an aspect of personality that is a part of the construct of interest, namely subjective well-being, targeted by the Satisfaction with Life Scale. "Thus, controlling for social desirability scores," Diener argues, "may simultaneously reduce the effects of impression management and also substantive personality influences on well-being, with no net increase in validity" (p. 33).

This conclusion is at odds with the study's evidence. The darker participants are not happier because of their efforts to avoid or exclude negative affect from their presentation, awareness, or appraisals. This affect would not have been visible to the study had these participants not displayed it in their life histories. These participants were implicitly reporting experience that they were not reporting explicitly. This phenomenon applied to some participants and not others, thereby detracting from the SWLS's capture of the intended construct of life satisfaction.

One problem in accounting for social desirability bias is the dearth of quantitative evidence using survey measures of the construct. Carstensen and Cone (1983) relied on a measure of social desirability (the Marlowe-Crowne Social Desirability Scale) (Crowne & Marlowe, 1960) that was criticized for confounding the construct of interest, well-being, with biased self-reporting. The vast majority of attempts to discern social desirability bias in survey responses have relied on other survey measures. I believe this poses an unreasonably high demand on the demonstration of the phenomenon, given the difficulty of detecting it in this modality of data collection.

The qualitative approach used by this study, though original because of its grounded theoretical derivation, is resonant with other qualitative scholarship. The distorting effects of the individual's psychological process on his awareness and presentation have been documented in psychoanalytic psychology

TABLE 9.7. Correlations of Disavowal (K Scale) with the Scale of Intrapsychic Brightness and Darkness and SWLS

	Pearson coefficients		N
Longitudinal survey sample			
Satisfaction with Life	0.49	***	196
Interview subsample			
Satisfaction with Life	0.31	+	37
Brightness and darkness	0.05		37

***p < 0.001; **p < 0.01; *p < 0.05; +p < 0.1

See appendix 5, Variables and Measures.

from its earliest to its most recent theorists of defensive processes and coping mechanisms (A. Freud, 1937; Haan, 1977; Vaillant, 1994; Vaillant et al., 1986). The experiencing subject shows incongruence between conscious awareness and unconscious experience (Westen, 1998). Clinicians, who rely on narrative data to understand patients, are constantly dealing with the incongruence between what a patient says and what he shows himself to feel about certain aspects of his life (Schafer, 1994).

If this study were to have used strictly a survey measure of social desirability bias to mount support for the phenomenon, this effort would have provided insufficient evidence. I administered the K scale on the Minnesota Multiphasic Personality Inventory (Hathaway & McKinley, 1951), a well-established psychological instrument used for personality and clinical assessment. The K scale is used to correct clinical scores of respondents who seem to downplay symptoms or distress. I found that it correlates with the SWLS but not with the qualitative measure, as shown in table 9.7 (although this differential association does not hold in regression analyses when entering the variables of the longitudinal model of the study: REL Affect, adult behavioral achievements, and standard controls).

The K scale was not designed for use in the nonclinical context in which I applied it, but my analyses indicate, not surprisingly, that it shares common variance with the SWLS. I believe this measure, like others, would be vulnerable to Diener's critique that it is capturing part of the intended construct. It captures the respondent's disavowal of various types of distress, such as the distress of emotional dysregulation. But the experience of such distress, it could be argued, is part of ill-being, and its disavowal part of well-being. This critique seems almost impossible to avoid using any survey measure of social desirability bias. Further, the psychological processes at work in social desirability bias may simply be too difficult to capture using a self-report method. It is difficult for a measure of distortion to get around distortion in responses to questions about it. Put differently, the responses are confounded by the very phenomenon that they are seeking to capture.

Having inadequate measures of social desirability bias does not mean that social desirability bias does not exist and that it does not affect responses to the Satisfaction with Life Scale.

The less happy participants displayed leakage or social desirability bias in their interview presentation. Not confined to a single moment or an instance of reporting, leakage was part of far-reaching and saturated interviews. The same distorting habits of presentation appeared across multiple interviews and in multiple reported aspects of a participant's adult life. The broad sampling of interview behavior used by the assessment procedure provided multiple instances of redundant evidence for the phenomenon.

Equally critically, participants displayed behavioral patterns across the adult life course that associate with their qualitatively observed well-being but not with their SWLS-reported well-being. This finding anchors the Scale of Intrapsychic Brightness and Darkness in an external reality. These decades-long behavioral achievements are unlikely to be subject to social desirability distortions in self-reporting. It is unlikely that most participants would misreport such visible features of their lives as being divorced or not having children. The SWLS was not anchored in this external reality.

The measure of brightness and darkness, therefore, was not merely an artifact of narrative production detached from the participant's experienced well-being at other times. His behaviors outside the interviews were intertwined with how he felt in and out of the interviews. This means, in turn, that social desirability bias (or leakage) is not merely an aspect of personality, which, as Diener suggests, is an appropriate part of the construct intended to be captured by the SWLS. Without accounting for these distorting effects, the measure of brightness and darkness would have done a much poorer job of distinguishing brighter from darker participants.

Failing to account for the distorting effects of leakage or social desirability, the SWLS did not pick up as fully the variation in well-being among participants. This is a weakness of the SWLS when used with this sample and may apply more broadly. Other survey self-report measures of happiness may have the same weakness. For example, a qualitative examination of another survey self-report measure of subjective well-being in an international context (N = 500) observed a similar elevation of scores for some respondents compared with narrated experience, warning researchers of "positivity bias" and over-estimates of well-being (Ponocny et al., 2016). However, that research does not explain the phenomenon's greater manifestation among some participants compared with others, as this book does. The study's less happy participants are not aware of the disconnect between their conscious appraisals of affective experience and their felt affect. The SWLS does not attend to this disparity.

WHY BEHAVIORAL ACHIEVEMENTS DO NOT ASSOCIATE WITH SWLS

The SWLS's lack of control for social desirability effects may explain why it does not show a significant association with adult behavioral achievements. With only a few exceptions, only the brighter participants in the study realized all three behavioral achievements. The elevated SWLS self-reports of darker participants diminished the measure's variation in the sample, likely obscuring an association with behavioral achievements revealed using the qualitative measure.

As described in the longitudinal model of development in chapter 5, less happy participants ignored or turned their attention away from stable investments in family and career over the course of their adult lives. Some or all of these areas of their lives were problematic for them and contributed negative affect, reinforcing their disengagement with these areas. In the data collection situation of interviews, participants regulated their attention away from these areas just as they did in life. It is likely that these participants ignored or turned their attention away from the more negative aspects of their lives in responding to the SWLS.

SWLS PULLS FOR RESPONDENTS' BELIEFS ABOUT HAPPINESS

Social desirability bias is not strictly a factor of personality. It interacts with cultural influences affecting participant responses to the SWLS—namely, ideas about what is socially desirable. Being happy, or reporting oneself as being reasonably happy, is only one of these ideas. Culturally saturated folk theories of happiness are another. These theories gain influence in the data collection situation of the SWLS.

The Data Collection Situation

Imagine trying to answer the five questions that go into the Satisfaction with Life Scale. You have one minute before you must move on to other questions in the survey you are taking or to other tasks. You have to figure out what each question is asking and what your life experience has been. In answering the first question, for example, you face the challenge of determining what the question means. How much do you agree or disagree with the statement "In most ways my life is close to my ideal"? Many parts of this question are vaguely worded. It is not clear what is meant by "in most ways," "my ideal" and "close to my ideal," not to mention "I agree." This vagueness is part of the open-ended design of the question. The respondent is invited to determine his or her own criteria and the experiences in his or her life that he or she will use in answering the question (Diener, Horwitz, & Emmons, 1985; Pavot & Diener, 1993).

However, this vagueness introduces significant problems for both the researcher and the respondent. The researcher does not know what people are thinking when they are answering these questions. Further, the cognitive burden on the respondent exceeds what is reasonable to assume a person is capable of handling in the allotted minute. I would go further and suggest that it exceeds what is reasonable to assume most people are capable of handling in any amount of time, without receiving help in reviewing their lives. The situation created by the SWLS is one of cognitive overload, induced not only by time pressure but also by oversimplification. One participant conveyed this sense when he wrote in the margin next to the third item of the measure: "How do I score a good life in a broken world?"[4]

This situation of cognitive overload resembles one many people experience daily. When someone asks, "How are you?," most people do not provide a full accounting. Doing so would be too difficult, because so much context would have to be established to know what is meant by the question, to determine the answer, and to report the answer. (The study's long interviews underscored the Herculean effort required to establish this context.)

Instead, because the question is too big to answer accurately or fully, most people find a more expedient way to answer. The shared and implicit social understanding of the situation is that the person will provide some answer, not necessarily a well-processed one. I think the same assumption is implicit in answering the Satisfaction with Life Scale. It is too demanding to follow the literal instructions of the question, so the respondent figures out an expedient answer.

But the expedient answer may not be accurate or may include much that is inaccurate. The constrained time of the data collection situation and the implicit message it carries for the respondent is, thus, part of the question. These factors are examples of context effects that have been well documented to influence responses to survey questions of well-being; for example, Schwarz and Strack (1999) note that individuals rarely retrieve all the information that may be relevant to a judgment asked for by survey questions about their well-being. They produce judgments based on currently available information. *Currently available* are pivotal words in the rushed minute of the survey situation.

Shortcuts in responding: considering what is socially desirable. When you are under pressure to complete a brief survey question, you look for shortcuts. You don't undertake a careful evaluation of the various influences on how you are feeling. You don't have time. You conduct a search process until you have enough information to form a judgment with sufficient subjective certainty (Schwarz & Strack, 1999; Bodenhausen & Wyer, 1985). In such truncated searches, irrelevant or inappropriate information may influence the answers one provides. This is the basis for the often-cited results of Schwarz and Clore's (1983) studies wherein sunny and rainy weather affected the mood and thus the responses participants gave to questions about their happiness and satisfaction with their lives as a whole.

The same principle is at work in study participants' responses to the SWLS, but due to a different influence. Their shortcuts rely on readily available folk theories of happiness, specifically, on theories that are salient to them.

Evidence in the interviews. Years ago, a leading business periodical profiled a Harvard graduate who became CEO of a recognized public company. The article depicted him as a captain of industry and concluded that he was a leader with daring, vision, and uncommon strength in directing his company. The magazine writer seemed to admire him. This participant had been interviewed by the Harvard study some time earlier, when he was already serving in a senior position in a publicly held corporation. During multiple meetings the participant conveyed that his work and his public reputation were a deep source of insecurity, which he focused on in the manner of a self-repair goal. It was his way of trying to cope with a longstanding emotional problem. The magazine writer had reduced him to a one-dimensional character almost to the point of caricature and had not considered—or likely even been aware of—the deeper and fuller picture of this man's life.

Much like this magazine article, the SWLS pulled for participants to draw on cultural ideas of how happy they are—or should be—in answering questions intended to capture how they actually felt about their lives. This encouraged the participant to look at himself as a stranger might see him and to use this perspective rather than a more subjective one to answer the question. The study participants' privilege—elite educational pedigree, high occupational status, and high net worth—was a readily available feature of their lives that could be summoned in a pinch to respond to survey questions about their happiness. Participants were well rehearsed and primed to take this perspective. They knew they embodied cultural ideals that indicated they should be happy. Participants defaulted into this habit of representing themselves at the beginning of the study's interviews.

Early on, when the research relationship was still one between strangers, participants frequently gave more favorable accounts of not only their careers but also their lives than they gave later in the interviews. This was truer of darker participants but applied to other participants to some degree as well. I understood this to be a normal social posture one might take when talking to a stranger. But the early posture was striking in contrast to the posture later in the interviews. It was as if the participant was initially portraying a truth about his life that was only loosely connected to the fuller and more complex personal disclosure that came later. For example, one participant (Jerome Vaughn) portrayed an exotic life of travel early in the interviews, which later in the interviews evolved into a narrative of aimless wandering and an attempt to escape pain. Another participant spoke of his great career accomplishments before revealing the psychiatric problems that his career triggered. In both cases, the conveyances of the participant eventually became more multidimensional and showed a more subjective vantage point on his life experiences. Early, accounts were more unidimensional and more positive—much like the expedient answer to the question "How are you?"—than they were later on.

Why SWLS Associates with Career Effects

As part of the shifting posture during interviews, participants presented their careers and career accomplishments as more central to their lives than they portrayed them later on in the interviews. Later in the interviews, when the conversation deepened, participants began to speak about the personal and less public aspects of their careers as well as their lives. It was not until these points in the interviews that a fuller picture emerged of the role career played in the quality of their lives, as well as a fuller picture of how happy the participants were. The divergence between happier and less happy participants showed itself more clearly when the interview reached this point. It was no longer a conversation between strangers, but rather a shared inquiry between confidants. There was more disclosure and more complexity.

Participants' initial default position in interviews is likely the one they adopted in responding to the SWLS. The questions of the measure and the impersonal context of survey administration asked them to speak to a stranger. This inquiry did not seek out a multidimensional and subjective consideration of their lives as the interviews did. This suggests a main reason why the SWLS shows an association with career effects (wealth, subjective career success, and career satisfaction) that the analyses of brightness and darkness do not. As they did at the outset of interviews, participants answering the SWLS likely conceived of their careers as more central to their lives and more favorable in impacting their life satisfaction than they came to convey in a more probing inquiry.[5] Culturally primed and available theories of their own presumed well-being—particularly those that conferred a more desirable assessment—were substituted as shortcuts in the pressured moment to answer the five items of the SWLS.

This chapter's critique of the SWLS finds fault with its design for presuming that cognitive judgments of one's life overall can be separated from affective and cultural influences on these judgments. The SWLS regards currently available information—without any probing or secondary analysis—as a good approximation of happiness, even though these unaccounted-for effects alter responses.

But the SWLS is a well-validated measure that captures a conception of happiness in wide use in research. There is much that could be critiqued in the other direction about the approach to happiness developed in this study. Some of the obvious criticisms:

- The interview situation elicits reflections and accounts of a life history in a way that does not mirror everyday life; few people have the chance to reflect exhaustively on their lives with another person.
- The influence of my psychological processes, as interviewer, on those of the participant pulled the discussion in certain directions and helped construct the narrative account.
- The grounded theoretical analysis and the assessment procedure it produced yielded a specific conception of the life history data that was not developed and tested in a literature on happiness or with other samples. This conception reflects my perspective and the perspectives of other members of the research team.
- It would also be possible to criticize the small interview sample and be concerned about generalizing from it.

In short, a main critique would be that this effort is shot through with idiosyncratic and specific features that make it biased and lead it to a particular conclusion that others might not have reached, one that might not apply well to other groups, even of similar populations.

But each of these criticisms could as easily be directed toward the SWLS, the survey situation in which it is administered, and the biases of the literature and research tradition in which the SWLS is embedded. In fact, that is what I have tried to show in this chapter. Although it seems to capture something valuable about the happiness of participants, how a person resolves the glass half full / half empty dilemma will determine whether the person notices the SWLS's deficits or its strengths relative to those of this study's measure. I ultimately tend toward the half empty because I believe that the SWLS does not show the important things that this study's qualitative approach and measure show. The SWLS and a study premised on survey measurement alone could not have captured participant well-being as richly and soundly or placed it in the larger context of a life and its development.

Diener, in a compendium of his life's scholarship on subjective well-being (SWB) (Diener, 2009a), gets close to articulating similar reasons for concern about the use of self-report measures, which include the SWLS. He cautions researchers against overreliance on these measures. "Clinical psychologists have long been wary of an uncritical acceptance of self-reports, and therefore have often sought additional information about their clients in behavioral measures, in nonverbal signs of emotion, and in the reports of significant others," he says. "It is time that SWB researchers adopt such a catholic approach to assessment. Where the measures converge, greater confidence can be placed in the results. If the measures diverge, the researcher can gain greater insight into how and why groups and individuals differ in SWB. Although additional measures can be expensive and time-consuming, their use seems imperative if we are to truly understand the SWB differences between groups" (Diener, 2009a, p. 54).

This study's qualitative assessment procedure, although serving a broader research agenda than strictly the study of subjective well-being, heeds Diener's call. It offers a viable alternative to understanding individuals and groups and their happiness.

CHAPTER 10

A Paradigm for Understanding Adult Life

The book's paradigm explaining particular lives—those who are prizewinners of competitive success in America—engages with happiness research well beyond a critique of the field's main technique for measuring happiness. By developing a new approach to the study of happiness using qualitative data, the book and the study on which it is based offer a deep account of participant happiness grounded in concepts beyond those previously used in the field and beyond those available to correlational self-report designs. The resulting paradigm offers a new understanding not only of participants' lives but, I argue, of adult life. Based on one of the rare longitudinal data sets in human development, the book's core findings mirror basic patterns found in happiness and personality research on general samples. This chapter shows how this book's paradigm helps to explain those patterns while simultaneously contributing a new understanding of adult development.

According to happiness and personality research on general samples, circumstances, a category including socioeconomic status, don't matter much to happiness; setpoint does, and to a lesser extent intentional activity. Most people show stability in personality and happiness in adulthood. Relationships and social investment are central factors. Change is less frequent in adulthood, and positive psychology, despite a flourishing interest in effective interventions that promote greater happiness, still regards hedonic adaptation as hard to overcome.

Patterns this book observes about a selective sample, which reveal previously unrecognized explanations for happiness and development, are strikingly similar to those observed in happiness and personality research on general samples, while using different concepts. Competitive success has little to do with participants' well-being. The identity story, brightness and darkness, and their drivers—two models of human development—show a dominant pattern of stability, and not even career experience as a whole supersedes family life and the social forces shaping how lives turn out.

The convergence of fundamental patterns in a specialized sample and general samples not only lends additional support to the book's paradigm but invites us to turn the lens in the other direction. The book's paradigm helps to illuminate lives broadly, not only in the selective sample studied.

Clinical life history interviews exposed a conception of the person—and, relatedly, happiness—in narrative identity, allowing portrayal in psychobiography. Narrative identity as a concept organizes experience, an integration imperceptible to conventional happiness research. This use of narrative data to observe and portray happiness weds strengths of clinical case descriptions and biography with systematic study of a sample representing a population. The book was able to reveal what happy and unhappy lives look like in their messy, multifaceted complexity.

The book shows why happiness is not best understood as a self-report in which much context is missing for the respondent in evaluating, construing, and communicating experience. The person-centered approach at the heart of this book shows what is at work: a multifaceted system saturated with affect interacting with the environment. Happiness observed in interviews is how one feels in relation to one's own unique, most central, long-term efforts to make one's life meaningful and significant. It is the central tendency of overall affect—of intrapsychic brightness rather than darkness—that permeates one's experience of these strivings and their results. Happy people experience fortification, connection, and enrichment; unhappy people experience depleting struggles, a sense of invalidation, and disconnection.

Observing happiness this way avoids undetected personality-culture interactions leading less happy people to inflate self-reports, skewing results. Core findings in this book would have been obscured or misstated had they relied only on survey self-reports.

Happiness is not genetically predetermined. If it were, then significant changers in this study, such as Hoyt, who traversed the breadth of the life course river, would be hard to explain. Genes don't change. Although mainstream happiness scholarship has come around to a weaker genetic argument, this book offers a more radical view of the potential for fundamental transformation.

Happiness *is* the product of development. Divergent from the correlational accounts informing main theories in happiness research, this book suggests that the stability observed in general samples is likely shaped by a formative worldview interacting with the environment, reinforcing itself directly and through mediating behaviors. New experiences become refracted into familiar understandings and feelings while guiding the individual to externalize and enact his or her assumptions in the reality he or she shares with others and society. In this understanding the environment is an integral actor in happiness. The book recognizes that these processes can be and are interrupted in change, and it specifies how. In both the model of relative stability and the model of significant change, social competence is prominent.

The finding in happiness research that the pursuit of materialistic and financial goals is associated with lower levels of happiness is explained differently in this book. Less happy people are predisposed to pursue materialistic and financial goals—more, on balance in their lives, than others—not because they are more materialistic and financially motivated but because they have less developed social investment.[1]

Happiness in this book's account thus comes to be understood in a new light—more than as merely an outcome variable to be explained by forces of hedonic adaptation (or by the environment or another construct) that may or may not overshadow the individual's will to bring about a desired life. It is understood also to be a reflection of that will, indeed, a deep-seated psychological drive that contours the individual's life trajectory. Society provides the opportunities for roles, relationships, and experiences in which to manifest this drive—whether for brighter or for darker—as a reality construed in experiences with others as one progresses through life.

This book's new explanation and understanding of happiness come with a host of tools produced in its investigation: an interview method, a procedure for assessing happiness in narrative, a method for displaying participant experience, and a host of constructs that can be compared and revised in further study.

For happiness research the book offers a person-centered paradigm that is humanistic and developmental. Happiness research recognizes similar patterns but does not contextualize them in any single life or cinch them together into a similar unified explanation of adult life.

THE PARADIGM'S ILLUMINATION OF ADULT LIFE FOR OTHER GROUPS

The book's paradigm helps explain why lives in demographic groups so different from the Harvard sample show similar patterns in happiness and personality research. Clinical experience and consultation with other experienced clinicians familiar with this research suggest how women's lives are illustrative. Consistent with patterns of general samples that include women, women's adult lives show the dynamics of person-environment interactions over time elucidated in this book, even while they may adhere to norms quite different from the Harvard sample.

Opportunities and resources on the social landscape—and norms for engaging this landscape—on which women's lives play out may diverge in important ways from those of male study participants. A study of women conducted in a manner comparable to the Harvard study may reveal many of the same sites of emotional investment as the study sample (marriage/partnership, health and mental health, family of origin in adulthood, and so on) but show different experience in them—with spouses and partners; with mothers, fathers, and siblings; and with health and mental health. Further, important domains, such as motherhood and intimate nonfamilial close relationships not central to the worldview and well-being of men, may emerge in studies of women. For women, the Remembered Early Life (REL) identity story would likely be shaped by a different landscape as well, entailing different concerns in women's formative identities.

Brightness and darkness in the lives of women would appear in the analysis of *their* life goals and domains, as occurred when analyzing the Harvard sample's particular experience using chapter 4's assessment procedure for clinical life history interviews carried out until saturation. If analyzed longitudinally, women's lives would likely show similar direct effects of the REL identity story on later identity stories, a key path of influence in this book's account of stable development.

At the same time, normative behavioral investments in family formation over the long sweep of adult life may help to distinguish happier and less happy women, as they do for the Harvard sample. These behavioral investments would likely serve to reinforce the REL identity story's impact on later identity stories—the second key path of influence in this book's account of stable development. But these behaviors for women may be different from marriage and parenting norms appearing in the Harvard sample (that is, married one or two times, currently married, living with partner; two or more children). For cohorts of women now in their twenties and thirties, more than for older cohorts (and more than for older cohorts of men), normative behaviors are more likely to be different and might incorporate family-like intimate and caregiving relationships outside of traditional nuclear family arrangements.

The REL identity story's long-term influence acting directly and indirectly through socioculturally distinctive norms helps account for stability in general samples similar to the Harvard cohort. Similarly, the disruption to these influences captured in the book's account of change would help explain the experience of a minority of women and individuals in other demographic groups observed in general samples to change.

Even for younger generations of women and cohorts of professional women whose investment in educational and career trajectories exceeds that of earlier generations, competitive success may not generate more change than it does for men, any more than it did for most participants in the Harvard sample for whom competitive success represented marked intergenerational gain in resources and status (see chapter 8). For some cohorts of women (or men) less invested in educational attainment and/or full-time paid work, competitive success would be even less of a consideration and consequence than it was in the Harvard sample.

Similar illumination of patterns of well-being and development shared by other groups in general samples would be possible using the paradigm developed in this book, by adapting it to reflect the unique sociocultural conditions of their life course experience. Closer study of minority groups or those from disadvantaged backgrounds would lead to a fuller understanding and quite possibly helpful revisions to the paradigm. I exercise caution in speculating about what might be found in such further study. Happiness research suggests that elements of this paradigm might be less applicable to individuals whose basic needs have not been met, yet the overshadowing of circumstances by personality influences on happiness in general samples (mirroring the experience of Harvard participants from disadvantaged backgrounds discussed in chapter 8) suggests that even for these individuals the book's understanding of happiness and development may largely apply.

ENVIRONMENTAL CONTINGENCY OF DEVELOPMENT

The general questions arise: Why don't general samples show more change, and might they in future generations, given the important role of environmental forces in the book's understanding of significant change? The landscape on which the lives of most Americans are being played out is less stable than the landscape on which the Harvard sample lived. Instability in social and historical conditions, including turbulent disruption, affect less advantaged groups more than the Harvard sample. Yet general samples generally do not show markedly more instability in personality and happiness than the Harvard sample. There is reason to believe these forces often do not penetrate key features of intrapsychic experience focal in this book's paradigm.

Compared with other groups, the Harvard sample lived under conditions of relative environmental stability (in occupation, family, community, and so on), relative control over their lives, and protective advantages against instability (such as financial resources, social network, and cultural capital). Their generation also enjoyed privilege. They grew up, entered adulthood, and played out their adult lives without disruption from war, social movement, and economic turbulence. They mostly avoided the Vietnam War, predated the civil rights campus unrest of the 1960s, and enjoyed a period of US economic growth during their adult working lives. These favorable conditions provided overlapping scaffolding against exogenous shocks that might have disrupted their preparations, plans, and opportunities.

Like others in society facing dynamic environments, however, study participants continuously coped with dynamism in the environment and in their life circumstances. They adjusted their behavior and even the apparent direction of their lives, but these adjustments did not often significantly shift the lens through which they viewed their lives. Starting a business after working many years for larger companies, being downsized, marriage, divorce, geographic relocation, and so on—that is, changing conditions that are both positive and negative—were understood as not fundamentally altering the expected trajectory of a participant's life. New circumstances and the new behaviors they required entailed simply adapting and functioning within a normal range of expected contingencies. Most participants' worldviews largely assimilated these changes, preserving a relatively stable trajectory of intrapsychic development, except of course in cases of significant change.

Neugarten (1996a) similarly observed that it is not dynamism per se but unexpected turns and timing in the expected course of life that creates problems or new directions for people.[2] She recognized that changed circumstances, although posing some challenge to the individual's coping, are part of the expected course of life and do not normally result in a change to it.

The triggers of significant change in the Harvard sample were often proximal influences in roles and relationships rather than broad, distal forces of social or economic change in the environment. Other groups experiencing more volatility in these macro-level contingencies may in fact show more significant change due to the effects of these contingencies on proximal opportunities and constraints in work, marriage/partnership, parenting, and so on. In these cases the book's model of change would help account for these forces interacting with the individual's intrapsychic system to produce change in worldview and well-being.

However, significant divergence from the Harvard sample's experience of relative intrapsychic stability does not seem highly probable—and not only because of evidence already cited from general samples. Changed conditions of the life course in most cases would be insufficient to penetrate the individual's highly resilient long-term worldview.

Much life course research (for example, Elder, 1999; Cohler, 2007, 2008, 2012) foregrounds a different issue and should not be confused with the argument I am making. It foregrounds the differential effect on cohorts of such macroenvironmental changes as war, depression, or norms of sexual and gender identity; it does not have this book's focus on the intrapsychic. The dynamically ordered system of the individual explained by this book's paradigm is highly adaptive and not usually altered by the normal range of contingencies encountered in adulthood. These contingencies include normative life stages and transitions described by Erikson and by Levinson, as discussed below. They also include social and historical change facing generation cohorts. Life course research on samples from earlier generations experiencing disruptive social change underlines the point.

A study of men from young adulthood to late midlife and early old age (Elder & Crosnoe, 2002) facing dramatic disruptions presented by exogenous forces during the life course shows earlier formative forces shaping well-being. These individuals, born between 1903 and 1920, members of the Terman Study of the Gifted, came into direct contact with World War II and major changes in American society and economy. Two-fifths served in the military and another one-fifth worked in the defense industry. Patterns observed in their intrapsychic experience resonate distinctly with Harvard study participants traveling brighter and darker currents of the life course river. Spanning a period of thirty-two years, from the time participants were twenty-six to thirty-five years old until late midlife, the study found:

> Negative feelings about self in young adulthood diminished the perceived gratification from life for these men in ways that often contradicted actual accomplishments. Some of these men had reached the pinnacle of their field in medicine, architecture, and engineering, but readily perceived "the things they did not achieve" and resented personal sacrifices along the way. By contrast, an early sense of well-being typically enabled less successful men to feel more fulfilled by their life course. As the Terman men entered their later years, the quality of their life and aging had more to do with early signs of mental health than with past career success and its affirmation. (pp. 173–74)

Even though the United States is witnessing dramatic change in the political culture and social and economic landscapes, if history and prior research are a guide, the book's paradigm seems likely to illuminate the adult life of young adults and future generations as they negotiate their landscapes of the life course.

A NEW PARADIGM IN ADULT DEVELOPMENT

This book's account of adult life diverges from established theories in adult development because it emerged from a study examining happiness in the context of development and because of its empirical approach and resources.

Theories put forth by Erik Erikson (1950), George Vaillant (2012), and Daniel Levinson (1978) are principally concerned with stages and transitions in adult life patterned by society. This focus leads these theories to foreground the dynamism of adult life—roles and tasks in family, work, and society— and corresponding psychological change. While stages and transitions have psychological impact, this book converges with happiness and personality research in finding that over the period of the life course that is this book's focus, they do not determine an individual's overall worldview or well-being.

Erikson's (1950) theory of lifespan development, one of the most influential psychoanalytic perspectives on development of the twentieth century, accounts for accretions and changes in the personality (ego) arising from the progression through incremental stages from birth through death, as the individual faces choices between successive polarities of positive and negative outcomes. In adulthood, the polarities are intimacy versus isolation, generativity versus stagnation, and ego integrity versus despair. (The task of identity formation versus role diffusion, technically speaking, is the first task of the young adult in contemporary society.) Erikson's theory and the Grant Study (Vaillant, 2012)—the most rigorous empirical longitudinal evaluation of Erikson's epigenetic theory from late adolescence onward—highlight the interaction between society and the individual in bringing these challenges (and their resolution) to the psychological foreground in a given stage of development. The individual is expected to assume new roles and functions and to mature, or adapt, thus realizing the positive or healthy resolution of the polarity.

Erikson's concept of identity (1950, 1956, 1959) is the site where the individual negotiates with himself and others (society)—and represents—the person he is. It is formed of his childhood identifications but is his unique creation, something new and integral to him. For Erikson the formation of identity, the fifth stage, is a specific achievement of adolescence, laying the groundwork·

for assumption of an occupational niche and entry into a relationship consti-
tuting intimacy. Even though Erikson understands identity to continue to be
negotiated in adulthood, his theory foregrounds other struggles in later stages.

In this book's paradigm, once identity is formed, by the time of late adolescence, it does not undergo revision as a normative lifelong process; nor do
other struggles take center stage in shaping worldview and well-being. Some
individuals change significantly, whereas most do not. The identity story for
most participants seems largely intact even as new psychosocial challenges are
negotiated. Hovanec and Martin, for example, both married and appeared in
some measure to fulfill the Eriksonian task of intimacy, but these circumstances
did not fundamentally change either man's preexisting worldview. In fact, each
man was attempting *through marriage* to carry out his values and goals, embedded in a stable worldview. The same was true through subsequent stages
and explains why participants' identity stories retained their stability over the
period encompassing three of Erikson's stages.

Although in this book the identity story is Erikson's concept of identity
operationalized in narrative—and intrapsychic brightness and intrapsychic
darkness distinctly resonate with Eriksonian themes of identity integration and
role diffusion—the book observes the individual interacting with the environment quite differently from Erikson's epigenetic theory.

It may be that the book's view of development, because of its focus on the
individual's intrapsychic experience, chronicles development in terms of only
one component construct in Erikson's larger theory—namely, the concept of
identity. Although concerned with social interactions and psychosocial behaviors, the book is more narrowly focused on the intrapsychic themes in the
identity story and the experience of identity integration, that is, brightness
and darkness, than Erikson's more encompassing conception of personality
as the accretion of ego capabilities. Nonetheless, the book raises an important
question: How fully is the psychology of the individual changed by Eriksonian
stages after the resolution of identity versus role diffusion?

Neither Erikson nor the Grant Study, in my reading, clearly answers the
question. Neither explores Eriksonian epigenetic theory using expansive longitudinal clinical interviews of the kind informing this book, which decidedly
demonstrate stability across stages. Erikson derived his theory from his pene-
trating clinical and societal observations rather than from systematic longitudinal interview data. The Grant Study does not have interview data comparable
to this book's and has not been concerned, given its behavioral focus, with the
insight such data might offer about the individual's worldview and its development (as explained in note 9 in chapter 1). Both Erikson and the Grant Study

were focused more on conceptualizing and chronicling the interplay between the development of personality and society. By contrast, this book begins with the person and his worldview in late adolescence and chronicles its development in two models not accounted for by societally patterned tasks.

Daniel Levinson's theory of adult development (Levinson, 1978) is another widely recognized and influential view, particularly among the public. It, too, is focused on stages and transitions of adulthood, but more than Erikson's theory, it is focused on task demands and has less to say explicitly about the individual's identity or worldview.

Levinson argues in favor of four normative stages of adult life, representing discontinuities or transitions in the individual's assemblage of roles, relationships, and commitments, which he calls "life structure" (Levinson, 1978, p. 41). These transitions represent changes of earlier life patterns of behavior, such as divorce and remarriage, in response to the changing tasks and demands of the new stage of life. Earlier patterns are renegotiated as efforts to realize greater inclusion of aspects of one's dreams and values in the life structure.

Levinson's theory is not focused on the worldview of the individual and its development as shown in this book; nor is it derived from longitudinal qualitative data capable of observing change and continuity in the individual's worldview. Levinson's interviews are extensive qualitative explorations (longer than the Harvard Student Study's); they are retrospective rather than prospective and come from a cross-sectional sample of forty men, between thirty-five and forty-five years old. These data span only a ten-year segment of the lifecycle. Levinson extrapolates to a theory of the life cycle occurring prior to and after the period he directly studies, based on these interviews.

Erikson's and Levinson's theories and the Grant Study have been pioneering influences in the understanding of the dynamism of adult life. This book suggests, however, that societally patterned stages and seasons of life are negotiated within the person's preexisting worldview rather than fundamentally altering it. Roles, relationships, developmental concerns, and tasks are changing on the surface, but beneath the surface, a formative lens filters and organizes the phenomenology of experience, central strivings, and life course behavior. The stages are not breaks with the past but, rather, largely extensions of it—except in less common instances when they contribute to significant change. Fundamental change, a real possibility in lives, is better explained by factors understood by this book, which I revisit in chapter 11.

Difference from McAdams's Life Story Model of Narrative Identity

McAdams's life story model of narrative identity (McAdams, 1985, 1993, 1996, 2008b), foundational to the narrative study of lives and to personality psychology, needs to be addressed. It has been particularly influential in bringing empirical rigor to the study of narrative identity scalable to samples, a commitment shared by this book. The life story, akin to the identity story, is understood as the site where the individual fashions a coherent and meaningful account of his life, understood as Eriksonian identity. But the life story approach conceptualizes important content differently from this book's clinical life history, diverges in operational approach, and has been deployed toward different goals from this book's concern with operationalizing happiness in narrative and observing its development.

The life story model of narrative identity views identity as a literary form—a story with setting, scene, character, plot, and theme—that is internalized and evolving, providing a measure of unity and purpose to the person's self-understanding (McAdams, 2008b). It answers questions of Eriksonian identity: "Who am I?" and "How do I fit into the adult world?" (McAdams, 2008c). Elicited through a structured interview protocol lasting two to three hours, it asks the individual for aspects of this form, including scenes, low points, high points, turning points, and other features (McAdams, 2008b). While eliciting emotional aspects of experience, the life story model is focused, relative to the study's clinical life history interview protocol, more on conscious and cognitive dimensions, and it is shorter.

Coding schemes capturing patterns in the life story (such as themes of redemption, contamination, intimacy, and power) help explain, and associate with, a broad array of concepts in personality psychology and lifespan developmental psychology (McAdams, 2001). This has helped to secure a central place for narrative identity in the field of personality psychology, alongside trait-centered and variable-centered conceptions of persons (McAdams, 1995; McAdams & Pals, 2006).

Although McAdams and others have investigated patterns in life story narratives that associate with external self-report measures of well-being (reviewed in Adler et al., 2016),[3] well-being has not been operationalized as a holistic construct inhering in life stories and observed longitudinally as part of an account of human development.

The adult clinical life history interviews reported in this book grow out of a *clinical* life history approach to the study of lives developed by Robert White (1952) not shared by the life story model. The approach was carried out longitudinally in a study observing happiness in narrative, linking it to narrative identity, and observing how they both develop across decades in adulthood.

Contrary to the life story approach, the clinical life history interviews described in this book do not ask the individual to follow a literary form or any particular form. They seek to elicit the individual's recounting of his life while providing as little structure as possible. Using clinical techniques (see online appendix 2), the interviews explore many areas and aspects of the individual's life, seeking the fullest possible understanding of how the individual sees his life, his history, and himself. They recognize affect associated with experiences as a marker of significance and thus incorporate an examination of the affective quality of experiences. Although the life story approach reveals motivational and unconscious processes, it gives these concerns a less central place, particularly in how these processes shape how the life history is recounted and presented. This book's clinical life history interviews are exhaustive, proceeding to the point of saturation, lasting on average seven to nine hours over multiple meetings with an adult. In addition to the aforementioned Eriksonian questions, the clinical life history interviews answer the questions "What are the most important experiences I have had?"; "How do I feel about them and my life overall?"; and "What concerns, criteria, and mental processes shape answers?"

The resulting account provides a portrait of how the individual constructs the most important experiences of his life using his own method of organization and structure. This is the identity story. The study's interview assessment procedure, presented in chapter 4, operationalizes well-being observed in this structure. It considers motivation, affect, cognition, and conscious and unconscious mental processes that organize a participant's feelings about himself and his life. While the construct correlates with other measures of well-being, it is a measure of well-being in its own right. It shows well-being to be located within narrative identity, and it shows both well-being and narrative identity to be shaped by forces of development.

This book's picture of adult life brings the experiencing human subject to the fore, showcasing forces that shape experience and placing the promise of the competitive journey in a new light.

CHAPTER 11

The Forces Shaping Our Well-Being

The promise that competitive success is a ticket to the good life, although persuasive to a large number of Americans, is a false promise. Only Americans who are struggling to meet basic needs or who are otherwise disadvantaged might enjoy substantially increased well-being from marked gains in status and wealth accrued through competitive success. Even for these Americans, it is likely that their children, more than themselves, would benefit—owing to more favorable early conditions as formative developmental trajectories take hold. For others (and even to a degree for these Americans), the pervasive discourse and cultural value system in the United States linking competitive success to happiness distracts from the deeper foundations of well-being brought forth in this book.

The success-happiness notion offers a limited conception of the person, largely overlooking an individual's development, the psychological system shaping his or her happiness, and the social foundation of this psychological system. It presumes a socioeconomic actor rather than a psychological actor who is capable of acting upon himself or herself to shape his or her socioeconomic circumstances and, in turn, his or her well-being. But this presumption is unlikely to be valid. My findings indicate that socioeconomic attainment almost certainly will not supplant the principal sources of well-being for most Americans.

The opposite assertion—that socioeconomic attainment *causes* unhappiness—also is unfounded. The failure to develop socially is what causes unhappiness. The Harvard sample includes many happy men, and many of them realized high levels of career success. The happiest men in the study had both rewarding family lives and careers. It was not either-or. They were able to uphold their interests in and commitments to their career—toward those they served, their colleagues, and community, as well as intellectual and spiritual matters—while doing the same across an array of dimensions important to them as husbands and fathers.

The saturated discourse presuming a connection between socioeconomic attainment and happiness reaches into the early years of life and may be adversely affecting children just as their life trajectories are taking shape. Anxiety about college admission contributes to an intense and early focus on scholastic and extracurricular achievement, especially in middle-class and upper-class families. Undergraduate education today, more so than when the study participants came of age, is widely seen as a gateway to the good life rooted in occupational attainment and as a bulwark against an economically insecure future.

Organizing childhood to revolve around this anxiety risks socializing these children into careerist values and practices at the expense of their social development. Scholastic and extracurricular excellence and admission to a selective undergraduate institution cannot replace the indispensable contribution of social competence to a happy life. The trajectories of the Harvard sample, among the most educationally and occupationally successful members of society, leave no doubt about the long reach of social competence into adulthood. If current and future generations of children are steered toward competitive success at the expense of developing social competence, they will likely experience lasting negative consequences.

Happiness research has helped to redress misinformation about the foundations of happiness by disseminating a more subject-centric view of the person, recognizing a limited role of material circumstance in human experience. It has begun to map out central factors contributing to happiness in general samples. This book helps to advance this effort by offering a fuller and more compelling picture of the experiencing human subject.

I am often asked how the insights of this book can be applied to individual lives: "What are the takeaways?" As basic research, this book suggests which priorities matter—social competence and the quality of adult family life, for example—and how they matter. It does not offer instruction on how to enact these priorities in the circumstances of an individual's life. But the book does nonetheless offer practical insights.

THE POSSIBILITY OF CHANGE

Change is the central concern of psychotherapists and clinicians of all persuasions and is also increasingly discussed by positive psychologists. This book shows that significant change in well-being, although uncommon, is possible in the natural course of adult life.

This book understands change in chronic well-being as a deeply transformative experience. More modest change may occur more frequently and may be how professionals and the public conceive of change. One consultant to the study noted, poignantly, that if the less happy participants had a life span of 150 years, dramatic transformation of the kind exhibited by Hoyt might be more common. If the Scale of Intrapsychic Brightness and Darkness included smaller units of measure and a larger sample, it might have found greater frequency of less transformative change.

This book finds that significant change is elusive in the near term but that some critical elements are likely to facilitate it in the long term. Hoyt and Vaughn illustrate that the process of significant change does not follow an easily discernible path or respond to deliberate decision making in the near term. Trial and error, sustained pursuit, and resilience of the tested spirit over the long term seem essential. Conversely, and sadly, the trials and tribulations of those who change to darker lives deplete their spirits over the long term. Not a single event or loss but repeated injuries led to Costa's significant feeling of defeat.

Change is not the product of short-term volition, interventions, or a clear plan for how the future will unfold or will be experienced. Hoyt and Vaughn found new elements in careers and family lives but did not recognize in advance that they were going to enjoy a sweeping change in their worldview and well-being.

Relationships, especially in adult family, appear as a key instrument of change. Hoyt, Vaughn, Russo, and others benefited from marriage or remarriage, relationships with children, and mentors at work. These relationships presented new possibilities beyond those previously imagined and beyond the previous reach of each man. Breaking the tether and distancing from a long-time relationship coloring an abiding worldview entails great loss. But the void can be filled by a new worldview. Relationships helped to shake up elements of the worldview, both distancing from old worldviews and filling the void by developing and validating a new one.

Poignant positive early life experiences with important others facilitated change. Hoyt's experience of his mother, or Vaughn's experience of his family before their immigration, had the potential to seed a new worldview. It is not clear whether less happy, relatively stable men, such as Martin or Fisher, lacked this past experience or did not respond to it.

This book's observations about change are not a prediction of when and in which lives it will occur. But they underscore it as a possibility and likely sources contributing to it.

PARADIGM FOR UNDERSTANDING SELF AND OTHER

A paradigm for understanding the experiencing self is perhaps this book's most important practical contribution. Recognizing ourselves in this new way, we can apply that same understanding to others. Happiness is not a formula or a quick fix. It is how one feels in relation to one's unique, most central, long-term efforts across adulthood to make one's life meaningful and significant. The experiencing subject is fuller and more complex and more unique than could be inferred from any list of standardized instructions. This book illustrates how to observe the experiencing subject and how to connect him or her to a rational way of seeing his or her development.

This paradigm became real for participants during the study's interviewing process. Many people, scholars and nonscholars alike, with whom I have shared this research have seemed intrigued but mystified by the study's exhaustive interviews. Similarly, many participants could not understand in advance how it was possible or necessary to spend so much time exploring their lives. But participants' later reaction ultimately bespeaks recognition of a different understanding.

As noted, the interviews explored two basic questions: "What are the most important experiences I have had?" and "How do I feel about them and my life overall?" Many adult participants, within an hour or two of beginning this exploration, recognized something profound was beginning to take shape. They would often sit up in their chairs, look at me more intently, and survey their experiences with more purpose in answering questions. Their alertness and energy showed a newfound depth of commitment to the inquiry.

By the end of the interviews most participants were viewing a picture of their lives that they had not fully seen before. Yet the experiences they spoke of were not new to them. Discrete experiences—from a memorable car ride with parents, to summer camp, to a spouse's bout of illness, to a child's problems in school, to the smell of dirt on a mountain bike trail—were already well known to participants, having been recounted in conversations and memory over the years. But suddenly these experiences fit into a holistic understanding that reframed their meaning. The familiar was no longer familiar. Participants themselves were no longer familiar but rather newly recognized actors making choices and inferring meaning. Their answers, it suddenly became clear, were addressing questions not only about the past but also about the present: "What am I up to in my life?" and "How do I feel about it?"

One participant said the conversations were the most important he had had in decades. Others said they were the most important they had had in years. Most participants, as the interviews were approaching saturation, seemed to feel, if not consciously recognize, the potential for personal transformation. Most agreed to an additional meeting or to spend more time if there were areas of their lives we had not covered, despite their unforgiving schedules as highly committed professionals with full personal lives. The large majority of participants enthusiastically requested the research findings, recognizing their potential relevance to the lives they were leading.

Clinical life history interviews have practical import for the interviewee because they bring awareness of himself as an experiencing subject. The clinical life history interview cuts to the heart of long-practiced assumptions and beliefs; these include one's central strivings as well as one's attributions to important situations and events, important others, ourselves, and the world at large. Although a seemingly mundane act of conversation between two people, the method allows the individual more fully—and I suggest more accurately—to apprehend basic commitments influencing the long-term trajectory of his or her life than is possible in most other conversations and in the course of everyday life. The exhaustive interview process offers experiential learning tailored to the personal reality of the individual.

If the mirror of the interviews—the mirror of greater self-understanding—were held up in extended conversations with Livingston, he might come to a lasting new view of his life. He might recognize that his difficulties did not arise principally from his career in finance but rather from the premature death of his father and his family's profound sense of loss and resulting dysfunction. His concern with being a provider and his sensitivity to the movements of the markets reflect this formative reality, intellectually visible to him at times as personal history but hidden from his immediate awareness in perceiving his life. Livingston, further, does not credit fully his marriage and children for their contributions in helping him avoid the slide into lower levels of chronic well-being. If he could see his assumptions and his commitments, and how they affect him, he could consider whether to reaffirm or to alter them. Change for Livingston would not occur quickly, as it did not in the lives of significant changers, but through a sustained inquiry of the kind undertaken in the study's interviews, it would become more of a real possibility.

Livingston might have pursued a different career, been less reactive to threatening conditions in his career, or not experienced his career as being central to his life, if he had seen these assumptions earlier in his life. Wealth and status might have been less important to him. Livingston might have found a mentor at work or might have related to his family differently, shaking up his worldview. The future, likewise, could entail choices and commitments moving him to a new position in the current of the life course river.

These speculative possibilities cannot predict how or even whether Livingston would change were the mirror of the study's interviews available to him on a sustained basis. He might elect to reaffirm his commitments. The mirror would nevertheless offer a rational understanding of how he came to experience his life as he does, an understanding more fully reflecting his development and how he currently experiences well-being.

Effective therapists seem to offer this kind of mirror, a space for reconsideration of one's commitments. But rather than focusing on solving problems, the study's interviews let participants guide the discussion to whatever affectively important experiences they had, positive or negative or both. Even participants struggling with mental health issues, by belonging to a study of a nonclinical population, were able to engage the exercise without the implicit focus on distress that is part of psychotherapy.

There was no indication that the college interviews changed the course of participants' lives; nor does it seem that the adult interviews would. The engagement would have to be more intensive and sustained for that to occur. Learning that occurred from being in the interviews offers the chance to recognize the basic insights of the study in our own lives: that our worldview is shaped by our experience of the past; that our feelings about our lives inhere in this worldview; and that this worldview, unless interrupted, fosters central behaviors and the future experience we can expect to have in our lives. What we do with this insight is up to us.

When the boxes rose from the Murray Center basement and I first beheld the pages they contained, I had no more of an idea what the future held for me than any of the men reporting to the study had their first semester of college. I knew the study offered the potential for a rare educational opportunity, but I had little idea how profound the work would be in informing my understanding of lives. William Hovanec, David Martin, and the other men of the study, over the years, were to become known to me in a way that few people are. Each time I entered the room to have a conversation with a participant about his life, I found myself inside a structure of thoughts and feelings and consciousness not of my own making. My own reality seemed to shift and I would begin to look at the world, and notice things, the way my interviewee did. Repeating this experience over and over again—more than 120 times for this study—drove home something I had felt in my training as a clinician and that now took on new meaning.

We rarely transcend the social ground that stands between us and others. Most people we know, we know as strangers. We meet them at work or on the street, in school or when traveling, when reading about them in newspapers, or when standing in a checkout line. I believe this observation is true for most people: the preponderance of other people we encounter in our lives are not known to us intimately. We don't know them the way we know spouses, romantic partners, children, other family members, and close friends. And sometimes even intimates are not known to us as fully as participants shared themselves with me in this study. Talking at length with forty-some thoughtful, intelligent, and experienced individuals offered a tremendous lesson in what is missing.

My experience conducting this research enlarged my understanding of other people. One research assistant echoed my sentiment when she said she cannot imagine what her life would have been like had she not had a chance to read the transcribed interviews with these men. It is not clear yet how it changed her life or how my experience with the study changed mine; only perspective over the long term will tell. But it is clear that it did, and that it taught me more than I could possibly have imagined. It has shown me myself in these men's lives and in what I found in them.

I hope this book repays in some degree the privilege these men offered me, by returning a faithful rendering to them and to interested others of what they conveyed and what I came to understand from them. Across the many parts of this book I have tried to impart a broad sensibility, an intuition and knowledge, about the internal worlds I came to know.

What I have written about participants obeys the same principles that I observed in their worldviews. Because of my being the ultimate arbiter of what went into these pages, and my role in conducting the study, I have become a central part of the study, its data, and its findings. It is a product of my own way of observing the world. I conceptualized the research question and the approach of the study; I conducted and participated in the adult interviews; each participant I wrote about, and each of the summations of the sample's characteristics, was available to me in my repertoire of knowing others.

I devoted considerable space to the psychobiographical sketches early in this book because I wanted to underscore that each participant inhabited his own universe with its own properties, even though I later observed shared patterns. I felt my perspective enriched and expanded by the perspectives of the research team, systematic analyses, and standards of careful reasoning and transparency. The college era of the study carries the imprint of Stanley King's insight and that of his colleagues. I hope that this book is well-enough informed by these other sources, and sufficiently resonant with the reader's own understandings, to be persuasive in its central claims. I also hope that participants find resonance, if not agreement, with what I came to understand about their lives. In the end, however, whatever its strengths and whatever efforts I have taken to broaden and vet my perspective, I have presented no more than a perspective. That, these men imprinted upon me, is both a wealth and a limitation.

ACKNOWLEDGMENTS

I have no hope of doing justice in thanking the people and institutions that helped me carry out this project.

I conducted the research and wrote this manuscript at the University of Chicago. Bert Cohler, Barbara Schneider, Linda Waite, Rick Shweder, and, more recently, Bill Goldstein provided a depth of commitment and insight beyond words. Bert's premature death continues to leave a gaping hole in my world. Marvin Zonis has also been an exceptional source of support and advice. The Center on Aging, the Center for Health & the Social Sciences, the Department of Comparative Human Development, and the Division of Social Sciences provided a rich intellectual community.

I also thank Dan McAdams, Robert Bellah, Norman Bradburn, George Vaillant, and Dan and Margie Offer for their advice. Robert Bellah's and Dan Offer's passing are a great loss.

Monica Higgins, an early collaborator and mentor at Harvard, led me to the Henry A. Murray Research Center and enthusiastically encouraged this project. A remarkable research archive at Harvard, the Murray Center provided data (McArthur & King, 1992; Osherson, 1992), permissions, and support for this work; Sonia Barbosa and Copeland Young (and, early on, Nicole Zarrett) were particularly helpful. Samuel Osherson permitted use of interview data in a follow-up. David Winter provided archival data. Stanley King, Charles McArthur, Charles Bidwell, Rebecca Vreeland, Harry Scarr, Bruce Finnie, Helen Tartakoff, M. Robert Gardner, and Elizabeth Keul assembled a remarkable college-era data set.

I received help in data collection, preparation, and analysis from many people and institutions. Peter Conlin and the Harvard Alumni Office provided background information. Paula Upman and Jane Schapka helped locate research participants. George Rumsey and Droz & Associates helped create the survey instrument. Catherine Humpherys and Zabrina Santiago helped manage the survey administration. Forest Gregg and Kyle Schmitt helped with early data preparation and analysis. The University of Chicago Survey Lab, led by Martha Van Haitsma, Kevin Ulrich, and previously David Chearo, cleaned and organized a high-quality data set; Hsi-Yen Chen championed these efforts. James Pustejovsky was an excellent statistical advisor.

A team of qualitative researchers brought Herculean devotion and great sensitivity to interview analyses: Catherine Humpherys (lead qualitative RA), Johanna Solomon (RA), Amy Fried-Eisenberg (RA), Scott Swan (RA), Greg Rizzolo (RA), and Janice Muhr (consultant). Janice provided critical insight into supervision and findings. Janet Dykstra transcribed the study's follow-up interviews with consistently high quality.

I am indebted to Linda Waite and Barbara Schneider, and the institutions that support them, for their generous financial support. Linda's financial support throughout and Barbara's during data collection and analysis as well as their counsel and friendship throughout were indispensable. Research and fellowship support was provided by the Center on Demography and the Economics of Aging at the National Opinion Research Center (NORC) and the University of Chicago, directed by Linda Waite (Grants P30 AG-12857-08, 5T32AG000243-20 and T32-AG00243 from the National Institute on Aging); Pilot Grant 5P30AG012857 was awarded to this project. Research support was provided by the Alfred P. Sloan Center on Parents, Children and Work at the University of Chicago and the National Opinion Research Center, codirected by Barbara Schneider and Linda Waite. Research and fellowship support was also provided by the Social Isolation, Loneliness, Health and Aging Process Project for which Linda J. Waite and Mary Elizabeth Hughes were coinvestigators (Grant P01 AG18911 from the National Institute on Aging) and for which John Cacioppo was principal investigator. Richard Suzman, former director of social and behavioral research at the National Institute on Aging, and Kathleen Parks, director of NORC's academic research centers, as well as research program associate directors Melissa Howe and Kelsey Bogue, also supported this work. The Harvard Student Study in the college era was supported by National Institute of Mental Health grant MH-09151.

My longtime intellectual collaborator and friend, Drew Guest, helped enormously from start to finish with this project. So did other friends and colleagues at various stages to whom I am deeply indebted: Nicole Gallicchio,

Omri Ben-Shahar, Bambi Chapin, Suzanne Pelka, Lainie Goldwert, Christine El Ouardani, Julia Mossbridge, Issam Aburaya, Will Bennis, Julia Cassaniti, Pinky Hota, Helene Cohen, Ashley Drake, Liz Fein, Brent Finger, Randy Horton, Eleonora Bartoli, and Shana Sandberg.

I am grateful for the clinical insight of Frank Summers, Don McDevitt, Leon Kaufmann, and Mark Reinecke, and especially to Frank for his unwavering support of this work. Molly Daniels and Sandi Wisenberg consulted on the writing of psychobiographical sketches. Molly's passing is a tremendous loss to me.

Christie Henry's editorial commitment to this project, Jackie Wehmueller's extraordinary developmental editing, and Paul Stepansky's devoted editorial guidance and friendship have been invaluable. I am indebted to Jim Anderson for his support of my work. I also thank anonymous readers for feedback that helped greatly in preparing the final manuscript.

I thank my brothers, sisters-in-law, and parents for their ongoing support and interest in my work. I could not have completed this project without the unending generosity, counsel, and good humor of my wife, Julie.

Lastly, I thank the participants of the Harvard Student Study. They persevered through one of the largest interviewing and surveying efforts of an entire sample that I am aware of. My debt of gratitude is large, and so, too, was Stan King's. I hope the seriousness with which their contributions have been preserved and utilized in this project will be accepted as a small token of my appreciation.

Although this project has benefited from an extraordinary endowment of advice, perspective, and support from individuals and institutions, I bear sole responsibility for its claims and findings.

APPENDIX 1: PRIMARY
PSYCHOBIOGRAPHICAL SKETCHES

Pseudonym	Chapter	Brief Description	Longitudinal Trajectory of Overall Affect
Vincent Costa	4	An athlete from a working-class family and drawn to the arts, Costa had difficulty entering the Harvard world socially and gaining traction in work and relationships as an adult. He exemplifies a trajectory of significant change from an evenly mixed affective profile in college to an overall dark affective profile in late midlife.	Significant Change: Evenly mixed → overall dark
Joseph Fisher	4	The child of immigrants, Fisher excelled academically at Harvard, became an academic with mixed career satisfaction, and struggled to form close relationships. He exemplifies a trajectory of relative affective stability, classified in college and late midlife as mixed dark.	Relative Stability: Mixed dark → mixed dark
William Hovanec	3	An athlete from a rural background, Hovanec came to Harvard with a vision for his life. He developed friends, earned respectable grades, excelled as an athlete, and surmounted Harvard's challenge to his vision. He became a business executive and ran his own business. His satisfaction as a parent helped ameliorate dissatisfactions in his career and marriage. Hovanec exemplifies a trajectory of relative stability in overall affect, classified as mixed bright in college and then overall bright in late midlife. (His trajectory is a version of relative stability called *affect elaboration*.)	Relative Stability: Mixed bright → overall bright

Pseudonym	Chapter	Brief Description	Longitudinal Trajectory of Overall Affect
Lawrence Hoyt	4	The son of a successful professional, Hoyt struggled with social disconnection, grades, and pressure from his father to pursue a similar professional career. Many years after college the death of Hoyt's relative helped to trigger Hoyt's dramatic trajectory of significant change to a brighter overall affect. He was classified as overall dark in college and overall bright in late midlife.	Significant Change: Overall dark → overall bright
David Martin	3	The son of a successful business executive, Martin excelled academically but experienced difficulty forming friendships and dating and had an emotional crisis at Harvard. He later became a business executive and started his own business, hoping to earn his father's respect. His estranged marriage without children and career anxiety mirrored his earlier difficulties. Martin exemplifies a trajectory of relative stability in overall affect, classified at separate times as overall dark.	Relative Stability: Overall dark → overall dark
Robert Payne	4	From an established family, Payne came to Harvard with a strong foundation of positive experiences and felt a calling to serve others. He found a suitable career direction several years after Harvard, married, and had children. His trajectory is a version of relative stability in overall affect called *affect elaboration*. He was classified as mixed bright in college and overall bright in late midlife.	Relative Stability: Mixed bright → overall bright
Louis Russo	4	From a working-class family and academically inclined, Russo was ambivalent about upward mobility. He had difficulty applying himself in college and stagnated in his career for an extended period. Over time Russo overcame his reticence and lack of resolve and secured a senior appointment at a well-respected academic institution. This and his family life contributed to Russo's significant change of modest degree and positive direction, the most common pattern of significant change in the sample.	Significant Change: Mixed dark → mixed bright

The study's data—in-person interviews and surveys—were collected from participants in college and again in their late fifties and early sixties. The study has two longitudinal samples: interview ($N = 37$) and survey ($N = 207$). The interview sample also participated in the survey study and is thus referred to as the *subsample* or the *interview sample*. The *survey sample* or the *full sample* refers to all survey participants, including those in the subsample.

The full sample was created from incoming Harvard College freshmen in 1960 and 1961. Twenty-five percent of the incoming class list for two entering classes (1964 and 1965) was selected at random. A small number of participants were added to increase the sample size for certain demographic groups.[1] The goal in adding students was to ensure the sample was representative of the Harvard experience (King, 1973).

A subsample of fifty students was drawn from this full sample, not randomly but by design to include the range of students at Harvard. The determining variables included type of secondary school (private and public schools, including a range of public school types); family socioeconomic status to include scholarship as well as legacy students and the range in between; Catholics, Jews, and Protestants in proportion to their estimated numbers at Harvard; blacks in proportion to their estimated numbers at Harvard; athletes; intellectuals; and commuters (King, 1973). The main practical effect of these selection decisions was to introduce more socioeconomic variation in the family backgrounds of the subsample than in the full sample.

The original study began with 667 students recruited at the start of college, but in carrying out the longitudinal study, I reduced this sample to 400 participants. I included all members of the class of 1964 plus members of the class of 1965 to whom projective tests (e.g., Thematic Apperception Test [Murray, 1943]) were also given.[2] I had both lists of participants' names, but not the names of the remaining members of the class of 1965. The restriction of the sample to this size helped manage the time and cost of the follow-up. It did not alter the sample characteristics that were determined by the initial selection. Thus, for purposes of the follow-up, the college-era survey study consisted of four hundred persons. The multiple entering classes and varying number of years to graduate among participants meant the study included participants from the graduating classes of 1963, 1964, 1965, and 1966.

The college study asked survey participants to complete an extraordinarily wide range of paper-and-pencil instruments during repeated visits to the testing center each year of college. The college testing protocol produced over ten thousand coded variables. Test fatigue affected participation rates and did so selectively for some instruments and not others. For the follow-up study, I selected parsimoniously among the college measures, considering the research questions as well as data quality and completeness. (See appendix 5 for variables and measures used.) The general college survey participation rate was 65% (261 of 400).

Of the fifty original interview participants, some dropped out of the study during the college era, some dropped out of Harvard, and some completed an insufficient number of interviews to be retained in the study. For the purposes of the follow-up study, 86% (43 of 50) of the college subsample completed the full battery of college interviews necessary to be included in the follow-up. Appendix 3 presents the roster of college interviews and interview topics.

In 2005 I administered a survey instrument by mail to the four hundred participants from the college-era of the study. I did so blind to who would later be excluded from longitudinal analyses for failing to meet standards of full college participation in the study. Measures from this survey used in this book's research are presented in appendix 5.

Of the four hundred potential adult survey participants, 6.3% (25 of 400) were confirmed to be deceased. Three were disabled and unable to complete the questionnaire. The number of deceased and disabled is likely higher but could not be confirmed. Eleven participants were unreachable. I extrapolate that one of these unreachable participants was deceased, although I expect the number is higher.[3]

The adult survey participation rate, based on all original participants, is 74% (294 of 400). Of the reachable, living, and able survey participants (361), the participation rate was 81% (294 of 361).[4] This is an indicator of the willing participation, and the retention, of participants who were contacted. It was not the study's purpose to investigate mortality as an outcome, and there is no reason to suspect that the basic issues of interest are affected by mortality.

In 2000 and 2001 I conducted pilot interviews of five of the original members of the interview sample in preparation for a full follow-up of the interview sample. From 2003 through 2006 I conducted in-person interviews with other willing original members of the subsample (McArthur & King, 1992). These interviews followed the protocol presented in online appendix 1 and the approach to clinical interviewing described in online appendix 2. A brief summary of interview topics is presented in appendix 3. My follow-up interviews (including administering the Thematic Apperception Test [Murray, 1943]) lasted an average of seven to nine hours per participant and were conducted in two to four meetings (a single meeting in the case of one participant) over a period of one or more weeks. I also reinterviewed three of the pilot participants to test whether my interviewing approach revealed similar patterns a second time, which it did, and to ensure consistency of these pilot participants' data with the other interview participants.

For the original interview sample, forty-nine participants were accounted for in the adult wave of the study.[5] Three were deceased; a fourth passed away during the study but had completed all interviews and a survey. One participated in the survey but not in the interviews. The adult interview participation rate, based on all original participants, is 82% (41 of 50). Of the reachable, living, and able interview participants (46), the adult interview participation rate was 89% (41 of 46).

LONGITUDINAL PARTICIPATION RATES

Participation rates in the longitudinal interview sample and the longitudinal survey sample are 80% and 57%, respectively, of the living, reachable, and able participants in the two samples, and 74% and 52%, respectively, of the participants originally selected for the study's samples. Some longitudinal participants were further excluded from specific quantitative analyses because they did not respond to select survey items.

Table A2.1 presents the participation rates for the two samples in each era and then longitudinally. It also reflects the range of participation in the study's main longitudinal statistical analyses, multivariate regressions presented in chapters 6, 8, and 9. Row *X* reports the interview sample's participation across time, and row *Y* reports the survey sample's participation across time. Note that

- The study's principal findings are based on qualitative analyses (grounded theoretical analyses and assessment of interviews) of the thirty-seven-member interview sample (row X, column 4).
- These analyses are replicated in regressions using coded interview and survey data (row X, column 5).
- Further replication analyses use the longitudinal survey sample with complete item-level response records (row Y, column 5).
- Additional nonlongitudinal analyses are performed on samples in one era of the study (both rows X and Y, columns 1 and 2).

TABLE A2.1. Participation Rates for Interview, Survey, and Mixed-Method Samples

		(0)	(1)	(2)	(3)	(4)	(5)
(X)	The Interview Sample	Original Interview Sample	Completed College Interviews	Completed Adult Interviews	Completed Interviews in Either Era	Longitudinal Interview Sample	Longitudinal Interview Sample with Full Item-Level Participation in the Survey Study[a]
Original interview sample (*N* = 50)	*N*	50	43	41	47	37	28–36
	%	100%	86%	82%	94%	74%	56%–72%
Reachable, living, and able interview sample for follow-up (*N* = 46)	%			89%		80%	61%–78%

		(0)	(1)	(2)	(3)	(4)	(5)
(Y)	The Survey Sample	Original Survey Sample	Completed College Surveys	Completed Adult Survey	Completed Surveys in Either Era	Longitudinal Survey Sample	Longitudinal Survey Sample with Full Item-Level Participation[b]
Original survey sample (*N* = 400)	*N*	400	261	294	348	207	187–208
	%	100%	65%	74%	87%	52%	47%–52%
Reachable, living, and able survey sample for follow-up (*N* = 361)	%			81%		57%	52%–58%

Note: Regressions used all available cases, which varied depending on the completeness of sample participation. Analyses of variables used in main longitudinal analyses, including standard controls, compared the longitudinal sample to nonrespondents in each era and determined that nonresponse did not introduce systematic bias into the longitudinal sample.

[a] Longitudinal interview sample members were included in longitudinal subsample regression analyses only if they responded to all survey questions used as variables.

[b] Longitudinal survey members were included in longitudinal regression analyses only if they responded to all survey questions used as variables.

Text Box A3.1. Summary

College Interviews (1960–1965): Approximately 15 clinical interviews and 2 Thematic Apperception Tests for 43 members of a 50-person subsample (McArthur & King, 1992; Murray, 1943).

Late Midlife Interviews (2003–2006; pilot interviews, 2000–2001): An average of 7 to 9 hours of clinical life history interviews and 1 Thematic Apperception Test conducted over 2 to 4 meetings (1 participant: 1 meeting) within a period of 1 or more weeks for 41 members of the surviving 46-person subsample.

CLINICAL INTERVIEWING

Numerous features distinguish the approach to clinical interviewing used in this study. See online appendix 2.

COLLEGE INTERVIEWS

Most interviews were conducted by Stanley H. King and most tests administered by Charles C. McArthur with Charles E. Bidwell, Bruce Finnie, and others contributing. Interviews and interview topics include

Freshman year

- three social history interviews emphasizing activities, interests, appraisal of teachers, reaction to courses, division of time, characteristics of peer group, and perception of the values and norms of Harvard;
- one family history interview emphasizing family structure and relations, developmental history of the student, early memories, significant experience outside the family, and other important previous life experiences;
- one Harvard Day interview providing description in great detail of one day at Harvard, involving descriptions of feelings about people and events as well as activity;
- one career goals and plans interview emphasizing the reasons for career choice or choices under consideration and the reasons for rejecting certain career lines;
- one Thematic Apperception Test in which the participant tells stories about social situations depicted in cards shown to him. These stories are treated as an extension of the interview rather than formally coded.

Sophomore year

- one beginning sophomore interview exploring summer experiences, relationships with parents and others in the family, reactions to the beginning of the second year at Harvard, and plans for the year;
- one Harvard Day interview;
- one ending sophomore interview assessing the student's school year in terms of reactions to courses and other events at Harvard, his peer-group relationships, feelings about himself and about important issues of the day, and his plans for the summer.

Junior year

- same interview schedule as sophomore year.

Senior year

- one beginning senior year interview;
- one ending senior year interview—emphasizing the student's assessment of his experience at Harvard and his senior year, his plans for occupation, and life goals;
- one Thematic Apperception Test.

LATE MIDLIFE INTERVIEWS

All interviews and tests were conducted by me. See online appendix 1 for interview protocol. Interview topics include

- educational history focusing on choices, performance, experiences, and satisfaction with each program attended;
- career socialization, history, success, and satisfaction;
- retirement plans and goals;
- family structure and roles, including a history of marriages and partnerships, parenting roles, relationships with children, children's health and adjustment;
- adult relationships with parents and siblings, family, health and occupation circumstances of parents and siblings in adult life;
- early life history of family, school, community, friendships, interests, and influences;
- religious beliefs, practices, and religious involvement;
- adult friendships, community involvement, leisure activities, and other social ties;
- financial circumstances and goals;
- health circumstances and behaviors;
- mental health problems, substance abuse problems, interventions, and outcomes;
- changes in personality and life circumstances since college;
- evaluation of domains of life and life overall;
- repetition of the Thematic Apperception Test given in college.

The study's overall approach to analyzing collected data emphasizes the use of accepted practices and procedures and the transparency of interpretations and inferences.

The three principal kinds of analyses conducted by the study are grounded theory (Glaser & Strauss, 1967; Charmaz, 2003), independent coding of interviews, and multivariate linear regressions. A fourth kind—psychobiographical description—is used to illustrate the study's findings in the lives of exemplars rather than to generate findings.

A progression of analytic steps generated the study's findings and the main components of the book's argument.

First, I used a grounded theoretical approach to derive the analytic framework for capturing intrapsychic brightness and darkness, the study's central construct in life histories. Grounded theory builds a map of concepts and the relationships between them from the ground up, one participant at a time. By adding new cases and data incrementally and revising the conceptual map to account for all cases, the research team eventually reached a stable analytic picture. Specifically, the process began when a central tendency of affect appeared in a subset of transcribed interviews to two observers (the lead qualitative coder and I) but required a series of decisions to classify the component constructs and their relationships to this central tendency and to reach agreement on an overall classification. Chapter 4 explains the procedure and its development and characteristics.

Second, the study team assessed brightness and darkness in life histories in each era, utilizing the newly developed procedure.

Third, drawing upon these completed analyses, I qualitatively observed two models of development, one for stability (chapter 5) and one for change (chapter 7). Multiple analyses informed the models. Upon completing the analysis of a college participant's interviews, coders met in case conference to compare ratings and then assessed whether the individual had changed longitudinally. They based their knowledge of the adult case on the assessments previously completed by another team of raters. In a later analysis, each of two coders classified the longitudinal patterns they observed for half the sample, including stability and change and factors responsible. I performed the same analysis for the entire sample. These analyses were then compared and integrated into a systematic picture of the factors responsible in each model.

Fourth, I used multivariate linear regressions (and other statistical techniques) to retest a simplified version of the qualitatively observed model of stable development (chapter 6).

Fifth, in post hoc analyses I used a grounded approach to explore additional questions of interest about the whole sample (chapter 8), several of which I then also examined statistically: socioeconomic attainment has no effect on happiness; family life, not career, determines brightness and darkness; and psychiatric difficulties preceding career explain career failure.

Sixth, I compared a conventional measure of happiness with coded brightness and darkness using statistical and grounded theoretical analyses to explain differences (chapter 9).

Seventh, I developed a psychobiographical method for representing the sample, described in online appendix 3. This entailed selection of cases to represent the variety of well-being and developmental trajectories in the sample and secondary dimensions, such as family background and profession, using all prior analyses plus additional qualitative and statistical analyses. It also entailed the development of a standard method of portraying histories for consistency across cases presented in this book.

TABLE A5.1

Variables and Measures	Time of Capture	Values and Range	Source
Model of Stable Development			
Adult brightness and darkness	Adult interviews	1 to 7: most dark, dark, mixed tendency toward dark, evenly mixed, mixed tendency toward bright, bright, most bright	Adult Scale of Intrapsychic Brightness and Darkness coded measure. See chapter 4 for development of this measure.
Collēge brightness and darkness	College interviews	2 to 5: dark, mixed tendency toward dark, evenly mixed, mixed tendency toward bright	College Scale of Intrapsychic Brightness and Darkness coded measure. See chapter 4 for development of this measure.
Remembered Early Life (REL) Affect Scale	Junior and senior year paper-and-pencil instruments	1 to 3	Combines three measures in archival data set See appendix 7 for development of this measure.

Variables and Measures	Time of Capture	Values and Range	Source

Model of Stable Development (continued)

Variables and Measures	Time of Capture	Values and Range	Source
Behavioral achievements	Adult written survey	Yes, no	Combines three psychosocial attainments in marriage/partnership, parenting, and work into a binary variable denoting fulfillment of these normative behaviors or not. See figure 6.2.

Standard Controls

Variables and Measures	Time of Capture	Values and Range	Source
Father's education	Adult written survey	Less than college degree, college degree, master's or higher degree	Health and Retirement Study (Juster & Suzman, 1995)
Comes from the eastern US	Adult written survey	Yes, no	Harvard Student Study
Adult self-reported overall health	Adult written survey	Poor to excellent	Health and Retirement Study (2004); Juster & Suzman (1995); Wallace & Herzog (1995)

Alternative Explanations

Variables and Measures	Time of Capture	Values and Range	Source
Think of self as religious person?	Adult written survey	No, not at all; yes, somewhat; yes, very	Personal conversation (Waite, 2005)
Identifies as Protestant	Freshman year paper-and-pencil instrument	Yes, no	Harvard Student Study
No religious identification	Freshman year paper-and-pencil instrument	Yes, no	Harvard Student Study

Objective Career Success

Variables and Measures	Time of Capture	Values and Range	Source
General Social Survey 1989 occupational prestige	Adult written survey	11 to 90	Measure of occupational prestige comes from the General Social Survey (NORC 1989, GSS appendix G; Nakao & Treas, 1990; Nakao et al., 1990) and is assigned on the basis of 3-digit occupational codes in Census

Variables and Measures	Time of Capture	Values and Range	Source
Objective Career Success (continued)			
			1980 Industry and Occupation Classification System. (NORC, 2010, GSS appendix F). Census codes are determined using responses to questions about nature of work role, responsibilities, and employer. The University of Wisconsin Survey Center, a specialized coding center, assigned codes in the 3-digit Census 1990 Industry and Occupation Classification System. These codes were converted to 1980 Census classifications and then to 1989 prestige scores. (These census classifications differ immaterially.) Dr. Joseph Schwartz, Department of Psychiatry and Behavioral Science, SUNY Stony Brook, assigned prestige scores.
Household net worth	Adult written survey	9 categories (in dollars): negative / 0–100K / 100–400K / 400K–1M / 1–2M / 2–4M / 4–10M / 10–25M / >25M	Item modified from Health and Retirement Study (Juster & Suzman, 1995)
College-Era Brightness and Darkness			
College brightness and darkness	College interviews	2 to 5: dark, mixed tendency toward dark, evenly mixed, mixed tendency toward bright	College Scale of Intrapsychic Brightness and Darkness coded measure. See chapter 4 for development of this measure.
Intelligence			
SAT score	Freshman year, archival data set	430 to 800, rounded to two digits	Scholastic Aptitude Test for college admission score provided to Harvard Student Study by Harvard College

Variables and Measures	Time of Capture	Values and Range	Source
Intelligence (continued)			
Junior year academic class rank	Junior year, archival data set	Groups 1–6 and unsatisfactory	Rank determined by Harvard College using its classification system, provided to Harvard Student Study
Personality Traits in College			
Neuroticism	Junior year paper-and-pencil instrument	0 to 87	Archival data set, 87 MMPI items used to calculate scale developed by Johnson et al. (1984)
Extraversion	Junior year paper-and-pencil instrument	0 to 69	Archival data set, MMPI Si scale (69 items) developed by Drake (1946)
Deferred gratification (conscientiousness)	Senior year paper-and-pencil instrument	0 to 16	16-item Choice Behavior Questionnaire. Deferred gratification is a construct of 5-factor model personality trait of conscientiousness (John & Srivastava, 1999).
Mental Health Problems			
Received psychiatric help during college, on campus or off campus	Senior year, archival data set	Yes, no	Binary variable recoded as endorsement if respondent reported (senior year) that during college he was a patient at the University Health Services psychiatric clinic or that he consulted a psychiatrist, psychologist, or counselor for help with emotional problems. Questions developed for the Harvard Student Study.
Psychiatric usage since 18 years old: 7+ months of medication, therapy, counseling, or self-help group	Adult written survey	Yes, no	Binary variable recoded as 7+ months of psychiatric usage specified as the length of time ("never," "less than one month," "two to six months," "seven months to one year," "over a year but less than two," "two to five years," "over five years") for any of the following: took prescribed medication; saw a psychiatrist, psychologist, social worker, marriage therapist, or another

Variables and Measures	Time of Capture	Values and Range	Source
Mental Health Problems (continued)			
			professional counselor; attended a self-help group; saw a minister, priest, rabbi, or other spiritual advisor for counseling. Question developed for Harvard Student Study.
Other Domain Measures			
Subjective career success	Adult written survey	1 to 10: least success to most successful	"On a scale of 1 to 10, how would you rate your career success compared to that of others by the standards in your field?" Question developed for Harvard Student Study.
Career satisfaction	Adult written survey	1 to 5: very dissatisfied to very satisfied	"How satisfied or dissatisfied are you with the career you have had?" Modified version of domain satisfaction questions in Health and Retirement Study (1992c), Codebook (HRS 1), Section E, questions V2608 through V2617 (Juster & Suzman, 1995; Wallace & Herzog, 1995)
Family life satisfaction	Adult written survey	1 to 5: very dissatisfied to very satisfied	"How satisfied or dissatisfied are you with your family life?" Health and Retirement Study (1992a), Codebook (HRS 1), Section E, question V2616 (Juster & Suzman, 1995; Wallace & Herzog, 1995)
Career failure	Adult written survey	Yes, no	Career failure combines measures from survey responses and is defined as any of these three conditions being true: unemployed or disabled; household net worth is negative or less than $100K; occupational prestige is in bottom 15% of same-age male national population based on the 2004 General Social Survey (Smith et al., 1972–2016). See chapter 8 for rationale for creation of this measure.

Variables and Measures	Time of Capture	Values and Range	Source
Associations with Adult Brightness and Darkness			
General Measures of Life and Self Satisfaction			
Satisfaction with Life Scale (SWLS)	Adult written survey	5 to 35	5-item Likert scale measuring subjective well-being (Diener et al., 1985b; Pavot & Diener, 1993)
Satisfaction with life as a whole	Adult written survey	1 to 5: very dis-satisfied to very satisfied	"How satisfied or dissatisfied are you with your life as a whole?" Health and Retirement Study, 1992b, Codebook (HRS 1), Section E, question V2617 (Juster & Suzman, 1995; Wallace & Herzog, 1995)
Rosenberg Self-Esteem Scale	Adult written survey	10 to 40	10-item Likert scale (Rosenberg, 1965)
CES-Depression Scale	Adult written survey	0 to 8	8-item short version of CES-D, a measure of depressive symptoms (Radloff, 1977)
Affect Balance Scale	Adult written survey	0 to 10	10-item scale measuring affect balance in the "past few weeks" (Bradburn, 1969)
Disavowal of Negative Affect			
Disavowal of distress, mistrust, social anxiety, and emotional dysregulation (MMPI K scale)	Adult written survey	0 to 4	4-factor scale measuring defensiveness and socially desirable presentation. The heaviest-loading items for each factor on a 4-factor model of the MMPI K scale were used. The factor analysis, provided by Roger Greene, Pacific Graduate School of Psychology, Palo Alto, CA, March 21, 2005, in a personal communication, was carried out by Stuart Greenberg on a normal population. Each factor was weighted equally and summed into a scale (Meehl & Hathaway, 1946, reprinted in Dahlstrom & Dahlstrom, 1980; Hathaway & McKinley, 1951)

Variables and Measures	Time of Capture	Values and Range	Source

Associations with College Brightness and Darkness

General Measures of Mood and Felt Efficacy

"While I have my ups and downs, my predominant feeling is a happy one."	Senior year paper-and-pencil instrument	1 to 7: "I disagree very much" to "I agree very much"	Responses were recoded into categories of strong, ambiguous, and negative endorsement
"I usually have the feeling that I am working successfully toward my life goals."	Senior year paper-and-pencil instrument	1 to 7: "I disagree very much" to "I agree very much"	Responses were recoded into categories of strong, ambiguous, and negative endorsement
"I have had (or would like to have) some form of psychotherapy or psychoanalysis."	Senior year paper-and-pencil instrument	1 to 7: "I disagree very much" to "I agree very much"	Responses were recoded into categories of strong, ambiguous, and negative endorsement

Self-esteem

Individual Rating Scale self-esteem ratings	Senior year paper-and-pencil instrument	25 to 200	Archival data set. 25 items. Self-ratings along 25 trait dimensions. Respondent ranks self in eighths in relation to a target group, in this case, other members of respondent's rooming group. Dimensions include intelligence, emotional maturity, general culture, social poise, physical attractiveness, neatness, sociability, generosity, manners, cheerfulness, consistency, sincerity, initiative, trustfulness, flexibility, sportsmanship, individuality, self-understanding, interest in opposite sex, dependability, understanding of others, self-acceptance, popularity, prestige, overall adjustment (Brownfain, 1952)

Variables and Measures	Time of Capture	Values and Range	Source
Disavowal of Negative Affect			
Disavowal of distress, mistrust, social anxiety, and emotional dysregulation (MMPI K scale)	Junior year paper-and-pencil instrument	0 to 30	30-item measure of defensiveness and socially desirable presentation, which is part of the Minnesota Multiphasic Personality Inventory (Meehl & Hathaway, 1946, reprinted in Dahlstrom & Dahlstrom, 1980; Hathaway & McKinley, 1951)
Other Measures			
Total household inheritance	Adult written survey	5 categories (in %): none / 25 or less / 26 to 50 / 51 to 75 / 76 or more	"If you or your wife or partner received an inheritance, trust funds, large gifts, or financial transfers *as a child or as an adult*, what percentage of your household's net worth would you estimate comes from these funds and transfers?" Question developed for the Harvard Student Study.

TABLE A6.1

Reported parental behavior	Parents as a unit	Health of parents

- Rejecting
- Loving
- Neglecting
- Overprotective
- Overseductive
- Encourage autonomy/self-esteem
- Role-reversing
- Pressure to achieve—punitive or supportive
	- Perceived stability and quality
	  of parental relationship
	  (problems vs. good marriage)
	- Conflict or harmony, especially
	  over children?
	- Gender roles of parents
	- First marriage vs. remarriage
	- Single parent
		- Death
		- Debilitating illness
		- Good health?
		- Lack of energy

Parent-child relationship	Feelings about self in parent-child relationship

- Love and affection vs. rejecting
- Attentive vs. neglecting
- Put in effort vs. not
- Understanding—confided in parent, hid
  things, felt aloof from
- Generous vs. punitive or depleting
- Discipline: rules and punishment
- Consistent, strict
- Seen as helpful vs. harmful
- Disciplinary styles and practices perceived
  as fair, good vs. unfair, bad, overprotective
- Source of wisdom and advice
- Sense of safety and security
- Activities / time spent together
	- Image of self as successful
	- Unconscious self-contempt
	- Open rejection of self
	- Self-idealization
	- Degree of similarity between described and ideal self
	- Initiative
	- Autonomy

Family structure and related aspects	Family environment
- Who lives in the home—parents, siblings, extended family, caregiver, others? - Who lives nearby and has regular contact—grandparents, aunts, uncles, extended family-like relations? - Is there frequent moving? - Is either parent, or participant, an immigrant? Does either parent not speak English as native tongue? - Religion - Parents are married? - Any major physical or mental illnesses (including additions or seeing a therapist) with the participant or others in the family? - Has there been a death in the family?	- Warmth or support - Coldness or conflict in family - Sense of family stability or instability

- Siblings
   - Number of siblings
   - Older vs. younger siblings vs. only child?
   - Who's living at home?
   - Sibling rivalry
   - Lack of mutual activities and interaction
   - Companionship
   - Close in age
   - Distant in age
   - Siblings as role model or follower
   - Sibling problems or set high standards
   - Illness or death of siblings	

Influences of Extended Family and Others

Are there grandparents, aunts, uncles, cousins, caregivers, others?
- Involvement
- Role models or mentors
- Sources of support–emotional, financial, advice, etc.
- Sources of refuge / additional venue outside of home
- Provide sense of a larger world
- Is there a caregiver or nonnuclear family member at home?
- Death or debilitating illness

Culture and Family Background	Class background	Geography	Neighborhood/town
- Any features that shape family's social world - Immigration or language issues (for self or parents or both) - Ethnicity - Religious values, affiliation, and practices	- Father's occupation and education, and history of these - Father's employment adds or detracts - Poverty or wealth stand out - Mother's occupation and education - Public vs. private vs. prep (boarding) school	- Rural vs. urban - State or country of origin - Did he go away to boarding school?	- Places of importance - Friends and other children - Physical features (rural, urban, suburban) - Socioeconomic community characteristics

School	Social involvements	Hobbies/interests	Self-image and feelings about self not captured elsewhere
- How hard or easy - Academic performance - Boarding vs. private vs. public vs. other - Sense of community? - Friendships? - Teachers, role models, mentors - Stimulates interest or engages? - Sports - Extracurricular activities	- Amount and satisfaction with -Dating -Individual friends (other than siblings) -Friendships -Groups of friends -Social acceptance and involvement	- Reading - Sports - Outdoor activities - Camp - Church - Boy Scouts - Formal social involvements besides school (and family)	- Initiative - Autonomy - Successful - Dislikes, disrespects, or rejects aspects of self - Idealizes aspects of self - Sees self as intelligent - Able or unable to achieve goals - Believes liked by others

The goal of the Remembered Early Life Affect Scale was to leverage the college survey data set to capture individual differences in the affect of college-era Remembered Early Life (REL) first observed in grounded analysis of the college interviews. I was interested not in the many aspects of REL experience showing up in the interviews (see appendix 6) but rather in an affectively broad measure focusing on REL in home and family and with parents. These two innermost concentric circles or sites of affectively significant REL experiences (see figure 5.2) account for a major share of the variation in REL Affect.

In creating the measure, I reviewed the archival survey data set, made theoretical decisions about what items to include, standardized and combined them into a scale, imputed missing values, and carried out select post hoc analyses as a check on certain steps.

Written survey questions administered in the junior and senior years of college best fit the construct, which I conceptualize as a relatively stable underlying trait.

The three measures I chose to combine into the REL Affect Scale are

1. "My home life was always happy." (Likert question administered senior year.) Response choices: "I disagree very much," "I disagree pretty much," "I disagree a little," "I can't say," "I agree a little," "I agree pretty much," "I agree very much."
2. "On the whole I am satisfied with the way my parents have brought me up." (Likert question administered senior year.) Same response choices as for question 1.

3. MMPI Family Conflict subscale (Jenkins 1958; Dahlstrom et al., 1972, 1975) composed of twenty-two yes-no items (administered junior year):

   1) My father was a good man.
   2) I loved my father.
   3) My mother was a good woman.
   4) I loved my mother.
   5) I have been quite independent and free from family rule.
   6) I have never been made especially nervous over trouble that any members of my family have gotten into.
   7) At times I have very much wanted to leave home.
   8) My parents have often objected to the kind of people I went around with.
   9) At times I have very much wanted to leave home.
   10) The things that some of my family have done have frightened me.
   11) My mother or father often made me obey even when I thought that it was unreasonable.
   12) The man who had most to do with me when I was a child (such as my father, stepfather, etc.) was very strict with me.
   13) I have very few quarrels with members of my family.
   14) I believe that my home life is as pleasant as that of most people I know.
   15) My relatives are nearly all in sympathy with me.
   16) The members of my family and my close relatives get along quite well.
   17) My family does not like the work I have chosen (or the work I intend to choose for my life work).
   18) There is very little love and companionship in my family as compared to other homes.
   19) Some of my family have habits that bother and annoy me very much.
   20) My parents and family find more fault with me than they should.
   21) I have reason for feeling jealous of one or more members of my family.
   22) My people treat me more like a child than a grown-up.

I carried out a principal components factor analysis of the MMPI subscale items. Ten of the twenty-two items are worded to ask about present rather than past experiences with family, but it does not appear that there is a factor structure related to the time orientation of the items. I used all available cases in the longitudinal survey sample ($N = 207$) for this analysis.

I standardized the three measures based on all available cases and categorized the Likert question responses based on semantic meaning into positive, middle, and negative groups. A negative response was defined as disagreeing with (or not endorsing) the positive descriptor in the question stem and included "I disagree very much," "I disagree pretty much," "I disagree a little," or "I can't say." A positive response endorsed the positively worded stem and included "I agree pretty much" or "I agree very much." A middle response, "I agree a little," endorsed the question with notable reservation. Positive, middle, and negative responses for the home life question accounted for 39%, 19%, and 42%, respectively, of 189 respondents. For the parental upbringing question these categories accounted for 70%, 12%, and 18%, respectively, of 185 respondents.

For the MMPI measure, I categorized responses from 195 respondents using the top and bottom quartiles, with these distributions resulting for family conflict subscale: low, 32%; middle, 45%; high, 23%.

The three measures capture theoretically different but broad aspects of the innermost concentric circles. I combined them into a scale giving equal weight to these three aspects. The negative measure of family conflict is reverse coded. The scale averages the three measures and has a range of 1 to 3.

To retain the largest possible longitudinal sample, when value was missing for one of the two Likert scales senior year, I drew on the junior year response for the same question. This added twelve responses for the home life question and thirteen responses for the parental upbringing question.

I imputed an REL Affect Scale value if at least one of the underlying three responses was available for a participant. This second imputation strategy added twenty and three longitudinal cases for the full sample and subsample, respectively.

The REL Affect Scale distribution for the longitudinal survey sample (N = 207) is shown in figure A7.1.

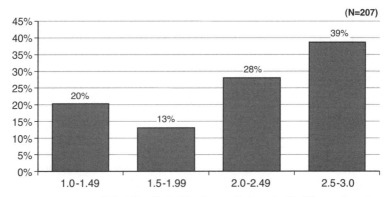

FIGURE A7.1. REL Affect Scale Distribution for Longitudinal Survey Sample

NOTES

1. Selection criteria and attrition generated the longitudinal sample of 207 participants examined in this book, as explained in appendix 2.

2. Harvard College was an all-male institution at the time the study began and did not accept women.

3. McArthur's directorship lasted from 1954 to 1972, George Vaillant's from 1972 to 2004 (Vaillant, 2012).

4. Other members of the original research team included Charles E. Bidwell, Rebecca S. Vreeland, Harry Scarr, Bruce Finnie, Helen H. Tartakoff, M. Robert Gardner, and executive secretary Elizabeth Keul. Dana L. Farnsworth, director of the University Health Services, was close to the study as well.

5. This may reflect in part a lack of receptivity to the study's approach, namely, the movement in psychology from the end of World War II to the 1980s away from holistic conceptions of the person to more structured forms of assessment and more focus on component constructs (Barenbaum & Winter, 2008).

6. Samuel Osherson selected a subsample of 50 from a group of 370 survey respondents in a study of human development focusing on work and intimacy in midlife (Osherson, 1980, 1986, 1992; Osherson & Dill, 1983).

7. Henry Murray served as director of the Harvard Psychological Clinic (starting in 1928) and later as a central figure in the Department of Social Relations at Harvard (Harvard Department of Psychology website). Erik Erikson (formerly Erik Homberger) and Robert White were collaborators of Henry Murray's at the Harvard Psychological Clinic and contributing authors to Murray's inaugural treatise on the study of lives, *Explorations in Personality* (Murray, 1938). Erikson and White published significant works throughout their careers in the study of lives (Erikson, 1950, 1958, 1968, 1969; White, 1952).

8. The life course paradigm is distinct from a lifecycle paradigm. The latter is concerned with sequencing of roles and stages of development and does not attend to variation patterned

by cultural, social, and historical realities of a person's life (Giele & Elder, 1998). Erikson's (1950) and Levinson's (1978) theories fall into a lifecycle paradigm because they principally focus on a series of incremental stages, giving less attention to the cultural, social, and historical conditions of the era that give rise to these stages.

9. The Grant Study, also called the Harvard Study of Adult Development, follows a cohort of Harvard College students from college to old age and death. This cohort is roughly a generation older (classes of 1939 to 1944) than participants in the Harvard Student Study.

Vaillant, the study's director from 1972 to 2004 (e.g., Vaillant, 1974, 1975, 1976, 1977, 1990, 2002, 2012; Vaillant & Vaillant, 1990), has pursued multiple lines of inquiry in behavioral health (e.g., mental health, alcoholism); physical health (e.g., absence of disabling disease, longevity); and psychosocial health (e.g., functioning in work, family, and leisure). One central line of inquiry has been to examine support for and to refine Erik Erikson's (1950) epigenetic theory of development (discussed in chapter 10). This agenda differs from the Harvard Student Study's interest in understanding and explaining the rich subjective world and well-being of the individual through his narrative.

Vaillant notes that the Grant Study gives privilege to behavior: "What people say doesn't mean much. It's what they do that predicts the future" (Vaillant, 2012, p. 353). The Grant Study uses frequent questionnaires throughout adulthood and infrequent psychiatric interviews that focus mostly on behavioral functioning and health. Behaviors are taken as revealing the internal workings of the mind, both the resolution of Erikson's stages and how individuals experience and resolve distress. For example, in testing whether a participant has been successful in achieving a given Eriksonian stage, the study assesses a list of behavioral markers; in one instance, ten years or more of marriage without separation is an item on the checklist of behaviors meaning intimacy rather than isolation. In explaining such success (or failure) in achieving an Eriksonian stage, Vaillant classifies defenses, following Anna Freud (but refining the classification further), as more mature or less mature. For example, the use of humor is a more mature psychological operation for resolving distress than is passive-aggression. The more mature the defenses, the better the person is understood to be able to handle the increasingly demanding tasks of Erikson's advancing stages. The Harvard Student Study, as I show in this book, does not make inferences about a participant's psychology or happiness based on reported behaviors or within a predetermined conceptual scheme—of psychological defenses or otherwise.

Grant Study interviews with its adult participants, reflecting that study's agenda, are shorter than the Harvard Student Study's. Two interviews with each participant lasting roughly two hours each were carried out a decade or more apart over the period from age forty-five to age eighty. Unlike the Harvard Student Study, analyses of interview content rely on notes written by interviewers rather than on verbatim transcriptions. They were not machine recorded (Vaillant, 2012).

10. Consistent with my own review of the literature, McAdams (1994) noted some time ago (prior to the follow-up of the Harvard Student Study) that systematic long-term longitudinal life story data, including Robert White–style clinical life history data, for samples are "virtually nonexistent" (p. 308).

CHAPTER TWO

1. Early in the project, while evaluating the archival data set, I read several of the college cases, but with one exception I read them superficially, and I did not encounter the adult until several years later.

2. For sociologists in particular I point out that the circumstances, objective events, and life situations portrayed within the psychobiographical sketches are by design treated as part of the individual's subjective experience. This book follows a psychological discipline in recognizing the subjective prism through which individuals experience even apparently objective events, roles, and facts conveyed in clinical life histories.

3. To be more precise, I had made this observation using grounded theory and then reached a similar conclusion in a later analysis utilizing the technique of independent observer assessments described in chapter 4.

4. Online appendix 3 describes how I selected Martin and Hovanec and others to represent the sample and how I crafted their psychobiographical sketches.

CHAPTER THREE

1. Life goals are central strivings that encompass a participant's efforts across multiple areas or domains of his life, such as work and marriage. They show where a participant's attention and energies have been devoted in his life. They also serve as his personal standards for evaluating how things have turned out.

2. Two of the three members of the study team who assessed Caulder's adult history reached this conclusion, whereas one saw him as less hopeful. I wrote the sketch of Caulder to reflect the perspective of the two observers, to illustrate the concept, but in the study's official assessment, the three observers' perspectives were "averaged." I explain the use of averaging in the next chapter when presenting the study's numeric assessment procedure.

3. Serving a secondary purpose, Fisher's example adds cultural and socioeconomic variety to the picture of the sample presented in this book. Despite dramatically different backgrounds, Fisher and Costa in college show common themes linked to the study's central construct, intrapsychic brightness and darkness, further illustrating the construct's relevance to the varied lives. Online appendix 3 explains how I selected exemplars and used psychobiographical method to represent the sample.

4. There is reason to attribute a large share of Costa's difficulties to his class background. He had fewer resources than Fisher to help him navigate the educational, social, and career landscape opened to him by going to Harvard. Being admitted to Harvard may have been a burden rather than an opportunity, because it complicated his choices and placed him between two worlds. But while this comparison between Costa and Fisher may hold true, many other participants (such as Louis Russo, who appears later in this chapter) from similarly disadvantaged backgrounds negotiated the transition into adult life and the traverse across the adult years more successfully than Costa. Costa's control over and individual influence on the trajectory of his life should not be missed, any more than it should be overweighted. Whatever the role of class background versus individual agency, Costa's example illustrates marked change in a participant's central affective tendency over time.

5. I also considered two other possible factors in affect elaboration from college to late mid-life: artifacts of the study's data collection circumstances across the two eras of the study, and the strong effect of the Harvard College environment.

First, artifacts of data collection circumstances. As an interviewer, I was a generation younger than adult participants and had less life experience and was less established in a career. In anthropological terms, I was studying "up," which gave me greater permission to ask challenging questions and be less cautious in interviewing than did Stanley King's positioning relative to participants. An adult, parent, and Harvard faculty member studying students, he related to a more vulnerable population. His caution and care for their well-being came through clearly in the interviews and may explain a less probing style. Other college-era interviewers were similarly positioned relative to participants.

Further, Stanley King and the college interviewers were not as focused on observing affective tendencies as I was in interviewing adult participants, even if participants might have been as emotionally varied in college. The college study focused on aspects of personality, only one aspect of which included affect and mood (King, 1973) although it produced useful archival material about affective tendencies that I later used in my follow-up.

Emotional display in face-to-face encounter provides much information that cannot be captured in a written record. College interviewees may have appeared more affectively vivid were the study team to have observed them in person side by side with their adult selves rather than in archival data.

Second, how did the environment of Harvard College influence the affect display of the college participants? Many participants experienced their Harvard years as an exceptional time in life. Chapter 8 describes features of a demanding culture emphasizing individualism and achievement. A strong situation in the sociological sense, the Harvard environment may have washed out more vivid displays of individual differences among the sample's affective tendencies, although as illustrated already in case histories, differences in these tendencies were still readily recognizable.

After weighing these considerations, I concluded that the sample's affect elaboration in adulthood was primarily the result of age and vantage point on the life course, as described by Erikson (1950, 1982).

6. Costa technically does not move "across" the center of the current, since he starts in college at the center of the current. But he does not begin in the darker channel of the current, and he moves a significant distance from where he started into this channel and displays a new balance of affect.

7. The study's concept of change differs from normative developmental changes described by the lifecycle theories of Erikson (1950), Vaillant (1977), and Levinson (1978). It also differs from generation-cohort changes in social and historical conditions of the life course observed by Elder (Giele & Elder, 1998; Elder et al., 2003). These other theories profile changing conditions that serve as a backdrop against which individual trajectories of brightness and darkness appear as change or stability in this study, as will be discussed further in chapter 10.

CHAPTER FOUR

1. Without a sound procedure, concepts of interest would not have been clearly recognizable to observers in the data. In order to complete an assessment, they would have had to go outside of its instructions and apply their own criteria, making agreement very difficult. Independent observers, in effect, would no longer be carrying out the same procedure.

2. Grant Study interviewers recorded "longhand notes" (Vaillant, 2012, p. 374) during semistructured interviews, probing further when a question elicited a problem in a man's life. Portions of these notes were coded.

3. An informal experiment confirmed the need for the study's systematic, saturated interviews and their use in full to carry out the assessment. I tried applying the assessment procedure to the lives of individuals whom I know well but did not interview and found critical insight missing.

4. This study's assessment procedure diverges conceptually from Bradburn's (1969) Affect Balance Scale (ABS). It recognizes happiness holistically as a person-level system with a central tendency operating across time, whereas ABS surveys recent affective experience using ten close-ended questions. Bradburn found positive and negative affect to be separate factors but then synthesized them into a single affect balance measure. This study observes greater linkage. The summed-up affect balance—or intrapsychic brightness or darkness, in this study's lexicon—is a single force in a participant's life, even as it reflects constituent positive and negative parts.

5. I requested that all assessments include an evaluation of the career and marriage/romantic relationships domains, whether or not coders determined them to be important to overall affect.

6. The concept of life goals used in this study has common features with Klinger's current concerns (e.g., guides a person's thoughts, emotional reactions, and behaviors), Little's personal projects (e.g., organizes a person's behavior), and Emmons's personal strivings (e.g., coherent, superordinate patterns of goals strivings) (Emmons, 1999). I do not use any of these constructs because life goals in this study indicate the individual's strivings and values applied to multiple life course domains over a long period. This is a more specific (and somewhat different) concept of motive than any of these more inclusive concepts. Further, life goals are observed differently, appearing in clinical life histories rather than being explicitly requested through listing an individual's concerns, project, or goals (Emmons, 1999). This study's method does not rely on a conscious reporting of life goals.

7. Short interviews and coding strategies that sample portions of interviews can lead to inaccurate conclusions in analyzing the construct in question because it is not possible to understand the participant's experience in parts of it without understanding his experience of his life overall. These shortcuts are taken in much social science research. For example, in coding defenses, the Grant Study selected episodes in the life history to code rather than coding the entire life history. Life history data were not systematically collected to the point of saturation (nor were interviews machine recorded and transcribed [Valliant, 2012]), which means that episodes were selected without knowledge of the entire life history (Vaillant, 1977). The coded episodes cannot be assumed to reveal these psychological processes in the participant's life overall. Random or unsystematic sampling of parts from a larger whole makes it difficult to draw

inferences about the whole. The overall life history, rather than parts of it, is the most salient field for observing a participant's life experience.

8. The average number of ratings per case was 2.5 (Shrout & Fleiss, 1979).

9. The Affect Balance Scale asks about general experiences of positive and negative affect felt in the recent past "During the past few weeks did you ever feel . . ." "bored" or "on top of the world?," for example. It consists of ten yes-no questions, summed into a scale of endorsed positive minus negative items (Bradburn, 1969).

10. Larsen et al. (1985) reported that the ABS performs more poorly than several other measures of subjective well-being. They suggest that perhaps there are too few questions, in light of the narrowness of most items (e.g., "Upset because someone criticized you").

11. The K scale measures defensiveness or overly favorable self-presentation and is used to adjust the clinical scales of the MMPI to be more accurate (reprinted in Dahlstrom & Dahlstrom, 1980).

12. We used a standard of forced agreement for a second reason as well. We did not want to average college ratings, because the narrower range of the scale meant there were already fewer distinctions, and the averages would have been harder to interpret meaningfully. Forced agreement allowed us to rate all cases as a meaningful integer on our scale.

CHAPTER FIVE

1. I compare this book's construct, *identity story*, with the *life story model of identity* (McAdams, 1985, 1993, 1996, 2001, 2008b) in chapter 10. They both capture Erikson's concept of identity (Erikson, 1950, 1956, 1959) in narrative form but differ in substantial ways.

2. This claim is in conversation with an extensive discussion in psychology about whether remembered autobiographical experiences are veridical. McAdams (2001) provides a review of the nuanced positions in this debate, ranging from a constructivist and reconstructivist view at one extreme—that memories reflect current circumstances and concerns—to the other extreme, that memories are reliable accounts of past experiences.

What is novel in the present research is the depth of the longitudinal evidence separated by many decades for observing the stability of remembered experiences in shaping narrative autobiographical accounts. I am not arguing in favor of the veridical and reliable nature of autobiographical memory. Rather, I see it as a psychological factor that, once formed, is a force in its own right. The REL identity story seems largely formed by the time participants arrive at Harvard and the study. It is already a vital factor in shaping how they see their lives and the world during college, and it continues to be later. In this sense I follow McAdams, who draws on Singer's (1995; Singer & Salovey, 1993) notion of self-defining memories, recognizing the centrality of such memories to current narrative accounts of one's life history.

This study's data reveal a more stable quality to the recollected past and the identity story than the evolving self-understanding that McAdams (2001) observes in the life story. (See chapter 10 for a comparison of the two approaches.) This difference may be attributable to the more central place given to affective patterns in the identity story; these may be more stable than cognitive constructions. It also may be attributable to more extensive interviewing carried out in this research. The participant's perspective is probed to the point of saturation, where the participant's own conception of his account feels stable and complete to him and to the interviewer.

3. Funding, time constraints, and other reasons indicated against a separate coding effort for this construct.

4. This observation emphasizes the primacy of the past in shaping narrative identity in the present, rather than a commonly advanced perspective emphasizing the conditions of the present in shaping narrative recollections of the past. I also assume that some aspects of the college and adult experience shape participants' recollections of the past. I do not have data during the earlier years (prior to participants' arrival at Harvard) about the facts and experiences of the REL as they occurred. I emphasize the primacy of the past, however, because the REL accounts are anchored in the facts and circumstances of social contexts prior to Harvard. The central affective tendencies of these accounts appear to be relatively stable during the college years and in adulthood, in spite of current concerns and circumstances. This leads me to infer that there is some "there" there, although I am not concerned with the veridicality of these accounts or whether they are purely accounts of the past. I treat the REL as a fact in its own right, one that helps explain the relatively stable pattern of affect from college to late midlife.

5. Chapter 3 discusses this difference in elaboration and the reasons for a narrower affective range captured by the college Scale of Intrapsychic Brightness and Darkness.

6. I use concentric circles as an expedient way to suggest a diagram of these sites of early experience in participants' Remembered Early Life identity stories, but at the cost of some accuracy. Concentric circles suggest that the innermost sites are part of outer sites; this is true in some measure, as parents and family provide interpretive lenses for experiences occurring in other, more distal and encompassing, circles, like community and school. Families transmit values and influences from society and culture to the developing child. But another diagrammatic representation might be more accurate, as inner circles contain forces of their own exerting a direct influence. (This model of REL experiences has much in common with Bronfenbrenner's [1994] ecological models of human development but was developed independently within this study's analysis of its data.)

7. The norms for this Harvard group are unlikely to be the same for other groups or birth cohorts in American society. However, the general argument I am making here—that early psychological dispositions interact with behavioral norms over the adult life course—as I argue in chapter 10, also helps illumine the development of other groups as well.

8. I am not making an argument for social conformity but rather describing an empirical finding. It is a significant association, not a definition of well-being. There are exceptions in the sample, wherein participants on the brighter current of the river did not invest in and sustain a marriage or partnership, children, or a career. Conversely, some participants in the darker current seemed stably invested in all of these realms.

9. For example, research suggests an association between marriage and subjective well-being, but the effect sizes are small (Diener & McGavran, 2008). Being in an unhappy marriage may associate with lower subjective well-being than not being married. Men without children are apparently less lonely and less depressed than fathers with poor relationships with their children but more lonely and more depressed than fathers with good relationships with their children (Diener & McGavran, 2008).

10. Later in this chapter I refer to these strategies for living as orientations embedded in identity stories. The two concepts are essentially the same thing, except strategies for living refer to how participants engage with their lives, whereas orientations emphasize the identity story as the source of these strategies.

11. Social competence is a widely used and researched concept in developmental scholarship. Following Waters and Sroufe (1983), I approach it as a broad developmental construct in the realm of social behavior, referring to the individual's "ability to generate and coordinate flexible, adaptive responses to demands and to generate and capitalize on opportunities in the environment" (p. 79). Rather than attempting to lay out a broad theory, my usage refers to aspects of competence in social behavior that distinguish brighter and darker participants.

CHAPTER SIX

1. I will argue in chapter 8 that the most important behavioral dividing line between brighter and darker participants is stable family formation. It becomes visible only after considering stable participants and changers side by side, as I do in chapters 7 and 8.

2. To maximize the number of cases, I use the longitudinal survey sample to present normative behaviors. Pearson Chi-squared tests show no significant differences between the longitudinal interview sample and the remaining participants in the longitudinal survey sample in how frequently they fulfilled each of the three behaviors individually as well as together. The longitudinal interview sample's ($N = 37$) frequencies for these behaviors are: marriage/partnership: 68%; parenting: 68%; work: 65%; all three together: 38%.

3. I use a measure of father's education administered in the adult era of the study, although it applies to the college era, to maximize complete longitudinal cases. This measure associates, for all available longitudinal cases, with a measure of father's education in the archival data set. Few fathers changed the level of their educational attainment after their sons graduated from college.

4. I use a question asking for the city and state, or country, where the respondent spent most of his youth, administered in the adult era of the study, to maximize complete longitudinal cases.

CHAPTER SEVEN

1. Rich case histories have often been used to develop theory in human development and have been the basis of several seminal theories. Robert White in *Lives in Progress* (1975) describes aspects of personality development based on three lives. In *Childhood and Society*, Erik Erikson (1950) describes the Eight Stages of Man based on clinical case experience. In *The Seasons of a Man's Life*, Daniel Levinson (1978) proposes a theory of adult development based on a sample of forty men. In her book *In a Different Voice*, Carol Gilligan (1982) proposes a theory of female moral development based on a sample of twenty-five women.

2. My usage of *identification* is similar to the psychoanalytic conception of identification, a generic term that refers to all the mental processes by which an individual becomes like another in one or several aspects. But I use *identification* more broadly to refer to any important aspects of the human or social environment that the individual incorporates into his personality or, in this study's conception, the identity story. These do not depend specifically on these aspects being part of another person (Moore & Fine, 1990).

3. This model of significant change does not address the role of psychotherapy (or other interventions) because the study lacks the empirical resources (for example, a well-defined group of patients, standard treatment, and control conditions across cases) to weigh in responsibly on this issue. Some participants received psychotherapy, psychopharmacology, and in some instances psychoanalysis. If these interventions played a role in change, they would have contributed to factors 2, 3, and 4 in the model.

4. Freud's "compulsion to repeat" shares similar characteristics to the vicious cycle of the self-repair goal that I describe but offers a far more elaborate account of the motivation and experience, understood within his psychoanalytic metapsychology (S. Freud, 1954; Russell, 2006).

5. Intrapsychic brightness and darkness is a trait-like construct of personality. White's comments addressed the whole personality, but they are equally correct in describing the parts of personality focal in this research.

CHAPTER EIGHT

1. The research team's assessments of adult participants' life histories confirm this finding initially observed in grounded theoretical analysis.

2. For the three participants, I do not want to overstate the case by suggesting that socio-economic attainment in their careers singularly made them happy. Their identity stories were notably enhanced toward greater brightness by experiences in family life, either in families they created or in their families of origin. Russo, for example, was deeply affected by his wife's help in opening him up to new experiences and emotions as a spouse and parent that he had not felt before. The CEO found great satisfaction in his relationships at work and in improved relationships with a sibling and a parent. Further, these relationships meant that others shared in the experience of socioeconomic attainment in careers and overall positive affect in career and infused it with meaning. Socioeconomic attainment thus did not exist in a social vacuum; participants' personal and relational lives affected it.

3. A small number do this by choice; they are a different breed, to whom this analysis does not apply.

4. Domain satisfaction questions are presented in this list: a. your health and physical condition; b. your financial situation; c. your friendships; d. your community life; e. your religious or spiritual life; f. your marriage or marriage-like partnership; g. being single; h. your family life; i. your current job; j. being unemployed, disabled, or otherwise seeking work; k. being retired; l. the career you have had; m. your life as a whole. Items f. through k. include "Not applicable" as an answer choice.

CHAPTER NINE

1. I list explanatory and control variables on the tables of regression results. For a fuller explanation of the procedure and the variables, see chapter 6.

2. The identity story (introduced in chapter 5) is a multifaceted construct that includes a component approximating self-esteem as well as life satisfaction, whereas the SWLS focuses on life satisfaction, although the SWLS has been found to correlate with self-esteem. In an inter-

national sample of students (N = 12,600), it correlated at .47 (Diener, 2009a) and among this study's interview subsample (N = 38) and longitudinal survey sample (N = 204), it correlates at .78*** and .62***, respectively.

3. As discussed in chapter 4, I considered and rejected these two measures (among others) in lieu of deriving a measure of happiness from interviews.

4. Several participants protested or refused the questions of the scale. Some selected multiple response choices for an item. In response to the fifth question of the scale, for example, one participant wrote "neither" (agree nor disagree) and "don't know." Another wrote: "ridiculous question (sorry, nothing personal, just my feeling)."

5. In some exceptional cases, a participant initially presented himself in interviews as darker than he appeared later, when a fuller picture of his life had emerged. An overweighting of his career experience led him to a darker frame for his life because his career had been a difficult experience.

CHAPTER TEN

1. Theories to explain why materialistic and financial goals are associated with lower levels of happiness (Kasser, 2002; Nickerson et al., 2003; Headey, 2008; Van Boven, 2005) remain unclear (Solberg et al., 2004; Diener & Seligman, 2004). It may be that the Harvard sample shows less variation in how vigorously they pursue materialistic and financial goals and happiness than general samples, thus obscuring the effect on happiness found in general samples. However, it is likely that cross-sectional self-report designs used in happiness research are unable to detect the hidden effect of social investment on materialistic and financial goals observed in this book. One main line of happiness research assumes that self-reported goals are actual goals (Kasser, 2002); similar to chapter 9's discussion of the Satisfaction with Life Scale, there is reason to doubt that respondents can size up and report accurately the goals that they are committed to.

2. Neugarten (1996b) believed that by adolescence most people develop an expected life cycle. (She borrowed this idea from Robert Butler [1963].) People evaluate their lives in relation to their current place in the expected course of life, where they believe they should be at this time, based on social input. (This expected course of life is specific to a cohort and its norms.)

3. McAdams and others have investigated, for example, these themes that associate with external self-report measures of subjective well-being and psychological well-being: redemption and contamination (McAdams et al., 2001, 2004), personal growth (Bauer & McAdams, 2004), narrative growth goals (Bauer & McAdams, 2010), and emotional tone (McAdams et al., 2001).

APPENDIX 2

1. I estimate that less than 10% of the full sample was added after the random selection. I do not have precise data on this issue. The added groups include African Americans, the top five and bottom five students in each class based on predicted academic rank, and all participants in Project Talent, a national educational program offering educational opportunities to talented youth.

2. I do not use these participants' projective tests in research reported in this book.

3. I assume the same proportion of deceased (6.3% of 11) among the unreachable as among

the confirmed, although it is likely some participants were not reachable because they were no longer alive.

4. Previously, I administered a pilot version of the survey instrument to roughly thirty members of the subsample. I used pilot survey responses for four subsample participants who did not respond to the 2005 survey.

5. Includes participants who had contact with the original study team and excludes one unknown and lost to the college study before it began (King, 1973).

REFERENCES

Adler, J. M., Lodi-Smith, J., Philippe, F. L., & Houle, I. (2016). The incremental validity of narrative identity in predicting well-being: A review of the field and recommendations for the future. *Personality and Social Psychology Review, 20*(2), 142–175.

Barenbaum, N. B., & Winter, D. G. (2008). History of modern personality theory and research. In O. P. John, R. W. Robins & L. A. Pervin (Eds.), *Handbook of personality: Theory and measurement* (3rd ed., pp. 3–26). New York: Guilford Press.

Barron, F. (1953). An ego-strength scale which predicts response to psychotherapy. *Journal of Consulting Psychology, 5,* 327–333.

Bauer, J. J., & McAdams, D. P. (2004). Personal growth in adults' stories of life transitions. *Journal of Personality, 72,* 573–602.

Bauer, J. J., & McAdams, D. P. (2010). Eudaimonic growth: Narrative growth goals predict increases in ego development and subjective well-being 3 years later. *Developmental Psychology, 46*(4), 761–772.

Block, J. (1965). *The challenge of response sets*. New York: Appleton-Century-Crofts.

Bodenhausen, G. V., & Wyer, R. S. (1985). Effects of stereotypes on decision making and information-processing strategies. *Journal of Personality and Social Psychology, 48*(2), 267–82.

Bradburn, N. M. (1969). *The structure of psychological well-being*. Chicago: Aldine.

Brickman, P., & Campbell, D. T. (1971). Hedonic relativism and planning the good society. In M. H. Appley (Ed.), *Adaptation level theory: A symposium* (pp. 287–302). New York: Academic Press.

Brickman, P., Coates, D., & Janoff-Bulman, R. (1978). Lottery winners and accident victims: Is happiness relative? *Journal of Personality and Social Psychology, 36,* 917–927.

Bronfenbrenner, U. (1994). Ecological models of human development. In *International Encyclopedia of Education* (Vol. 3, 2nd Ed). Oxford: Elsevier. Reprinted in: Gauvain, M. & Cole, M. (Eds.), *Readings on the development of children,* (2nd ed., pp. 37–42). New York: Freeman.

Brown, A. (2014). Public and private college grads rank about equally in life satisfaction. Retrieved from http://www.pewsocialtrends.org/2014/02/11/the-rising-cost-of-not-going-to-college/

Brownfain, J. (1952). Stability of the self-concept as a dimension of personality. *Journal of Abnormal Social Psychology, 47*, 597–606.

Bruner, J. S. (1990). *Acts of meaning.* Cambridge, MA: Harvard University Press.

Burgard, S., Stewart, J., & Schwartz, J. (n.d.). Occupational status. Retrieved from http://www.macses.ucsf.edu/research/socialenviron/occupation.php

Butler, R. (1963). The life review: An interpretation of reminiscence in the aged. *Psychiatry, 26*, 65–76.

Carstensen, L., & Cone, J. (1983). Social desirability and the measurement of psychological well-being in elderly persons. *Journal of Gerontology, 38*(6), 713–715.

Caspi, A., & Roberts, B. W. (1999). Personality continuity and change across the life course. In L. A. Pervin & O. P. John (Eds.), *Handbook of personality: Theory and research* (2nd ed., pp. 300–326). New York: Guilford Press.

Charmaz, K. (2003). Grounded theory. In J. A. Smith (Ed.), *Qualitative psychology: a practical guide to research methods* (pp. 81–110). London: Sage Publications.

Cohler, B. (1982). Personal narrative and life course. In P. Baltes & O. G. Brim Jr. (Eds.), *Life span development and behavior* (Vol. 4, pp. 205–241). New York: Academic Press.

Cohler, B. (2007). *Writing desire: Sixty years of gay autobiography.* Madison: University of Wisconsin Press.

Cohler, B. (2008). Two lives two times: Life-writing after Shoah. *Narrative Inquiry, 18*, 1–28.

Cohler, B. (2012). Confronting destruction: Social context and life-story in the diaries of two adolescents in Eastern European ghettos during the Shoah. *American Journal of Orthopsychiatry, 82*(2), 220–230.

Costa, P. T., & McCrae, R. R. (1992). *Revised NEO Personality Inventory (NEO-PI-R) and NEO Five-Factor Inventory (NEO-FFI) professional manual.* Odessa, FL: Psychological Assessment Resources, Inc.

Crowne, D. P., & Marlowe, D. (1960). A new scale of social desirability independent of psycopathy. *Journal of Consulting Psychology, 24*, 349–354.

Dahlstrom, W. G., & Dahlstrom, L. E. (1980). *Basic readings on the MMPI: A new selection on personality measurement.* Minneapolis: University of Minnesota Press.

Dahlstrom, W. G., Welsh, G. S., & Dahlstrom, L. E. (1972). *An MMPI handbook: A guide to use in clinical practice and research.* Minneapolis: University of Minnesota Press.

Dahlstrom, W. G., Welsh, G. S., & Dahlstrom, L. E. (1975). *An MMPI handbook: Research applications.* Minneapolis: University of Minnesota Press.

Diener, E. (1984). Subjective well-being. *Psychological Bulletin, 95*, 542–575.

Diener, E. (2000). Subjective well-being: The science of happiness and a proposal for a national index. *American Psychologist, 55*(1), 34–43.

Diener, E. (2009a). Assessing subjective well-being: Progress and opportunities. In E. Diener & E. Diener (Ed.), *Assessing well-being, Vol. 3, The collected works of Ed Diener* (Social Indicators Research Series) (p. 26). Dordrecht, the Netherlands: Springer.

Diener, E. (2009b). *The Satisfaction with Life Scale.* Retrieved from http://internal.psychology.illinois.edu/~ediener/SWLS.html

Diener, E., Emmons, R. A., Larsen, R. J., & Griffin, S. (1985). The satisfaction with life scale. *Journal of Personality Assessment, 49*(1), 71–75.

Diener, E., Heintzelman, S. J., Kushlev, K., Tay, L., Wirtz, D., Lutes, L. D., & Oishi, S. (2017). Findings all psychologists should know from the new science on subjective well-being. *Canadian Psychology / Psychologie canadienne, 58*(2), 87–104.

Diener, E., Horwitz, J., & Emmons, R. (1985). Happiness of the very wealthy. *Social Indicators Research, 16*, 263–274.

Diener, E., Kahneman, D., Arora, R., Harter, J., & Tov, W. (2009). Income's differential influence on judgments of life versus affective well-being. In E. Diener & E. Diener (Ed.), *Assessing well-being: The collected works of Ed Diener* (Social Indicators Research Series) (pp. 233–245). New York: Springer Science + Business Media.

Diener, E., Lucas, R. E., & Scollon, C. N. (2006). Beyond the hedonic treadmill: Revising the adaptation theory of well-being. *American Psychologist, 61*(4), 305–314.

Diener, E., Oishi, S., & Lucas, R. E. (2003). Personality, culture, and subjective well-being: Emotional and cognitive evaluations of life. *Annual Review of Psychology, 54*, 403–425.

Diener, E., & Seligman, M. E. (2004). Beyond money. Toward an economy of well-being. *Psychological Science in the Public Interest, 5*, 1–31.

Diener, E., & Suh, E. M. (1999). National differences in subjective well-being. In D. Kahneman, E. Diener & N. Schwarz (Eds.), *Well-being: The foundations of hedonic psychology* (pp. 434–450). New York: Russell Sage Foundation.

Diener, E., Suh, E. M., Lucas, R. E., & Smith, H. E. (1999). Subjective well-being: Three decades of progress. *Psychological Bulletin, 125*(2), 276–302.

Diener, M. L., & McGavran, M. B. (2008). What makes people happy? A developmental approach to the literature on family relationships and well-being. In M. Eid & R. J. Larsen (Eds.), *The science of subjective well-being* (pp. 347–375). New York: Guilford Press.

Drake, L. E. (1946). A social I.E. scale for the Minnesota Multiphasic Personality Inventory. *Journal of Applied Psychology, 30*, 51–54.

Elder, G. H., Jr. (1998). The life course as developmental theory. *Child Development, 69*(1), 1–12.

Elder, G. H., Jr. (1999). *Children of the Great Depression*. Boulder, CO: Westview Press.

Elder, G. H., Jr., & Crosnoe, R. (2002). The influence of early behavior patterns on later life. In L. Pulkkinen & A. Caspi (Eds.), *Paths to successful development: Personality in the life course* (pp. 157–176). New York: Cambridge University Press.

Elder, G. H., Jr., Kirkpatrick Johnson, M., & Crosnoe, R. (2003). The emergence and development of life course theory. In J. T. Mortimer & M. J. Shanahan (Eds.), *Handbook of the life course* (pp. 3–19). New York: Kluwer Academic/Plenum.

Emmons, R. (1999). Motives and goals. In R. Hogan, J. Johnson, & S. R. Briggs (Eds.), *Handbook of personality psychology* (pp. 485–512). San Diego, CA: Academic Press.

Erikson, E. H. (1950). *Childhood and society*. New York: Norton.

Erikson, E. H. (1956). The problem of ego identity. *Journal of the American Psychoanalytic Association, 4*, 53–121.

Erikson, E. H. (1958). *Young man Luther: A study in psychoanalysis and history*. New York: Norton.

Erikson, E. H. (1959). Identity and the life cycle: Selected papers. *Psychological Issues, 1*, 50–100.

Erikson, E. H. (1968). *Youth and crisis.* New York: Norton.

Erikson, E. H. (1969). *Gandhi's truth: On the origins of militant nonviolence.* New York: Norton.

Erikson, E. H. (1982). *The life cycle completed.* New York: Norton.

Fastame, M. C., & Penna, M. P. (2012). Does social desirability confound the assessment of self-reported measures of well-being and metacognitive efficiency in young and older adults? *Clinical Gerontologist, 35*(3), 239–256.

Fine, A., & Kotelchuk, M. (2010). *Rethinking MCH: The life course model as an organizing framework* [Concept paper]. US Department of Health and Human Services, Health Resources and Services Administration, Maternal and Child Health Bureau. Retrieved from http://mchb.hrsa.gov/lifecourse

Foley Center Website. (n.d.). *Foley Longitudinal Study of Adult Development description.* Retrieved from http://www.sesp.northwestern.edu/foley/research/flsa/

Frederick, S., & Loewenstein, G. (1999). Hedonic adaptation. In D. Kahneman, E. Diener, & N. Schwartz (Eds.), *Well-being: The foundations of hedonic psychology* (pp. 302–329). New York: Russell Sage Foundation.

Freud, A. (1937). *The ego and the mechanisms of defense.* London: Hogarth Press and Institute of Psycho-Analysis.

Freud, S. (1954). Beyond the pleasure principle (1920). In J. Strachey (Ed.), *Complete psychological works* (Standard Edition) (J. Strachey, Trans., Vol. 3). London: Hogarth Press.

Geertz, C. (1973). Thick description: Toward an interpretive theory of culture. In *The interpretation of cultures: Selected essays* (pp. 3–30). New York: Basic Books.

George, C., Kaplan, N., & Main, M. (1984, 1985, 1996). *Adult attachment interview* (3rd ed.).University of California, Berkeley, Department of Psychology.

Giele, J. Z., & Elder, G. H. (Eds.). (1998). *Methods of life course research: Qualitative and quantitative approaches.* Thousand Oaks, CA: Sage.

Gilligan, C. (1982). *In a different voice: Psychological theory and women's development.* Cambridge, MA: Harvard University Press.

Glaser, B. G., & Strauss, A. (1967). *The discovery of grounded theory: Strategies for qualitative research.* Chicago: Aldine.

Grossman, I., Na, J., Varnum, M. E., Kitayama, S., & Nisbett, R. E. (2013). A route to well-being: Intelligence versus wise-reasoning. *Journal of Experimental Psychology General, 142*(3), 944–53.

Haan, N. (1977). *Coping and defending: Processes of self-environment organization.* New York: Academic Press.

Harvard Department of Psychology website. (n.d.). Retrieved from https://psychology.fas.harvard.edu/people/henry-murrayHathaway, S. R., & McKinley, J. C. (1951). *The Minnesota Multiphasic Personality Inventory manual.* New York: Psychological Corporation.

Haybron, D. (2011). Happiness. In E. Zalta (Ed.), *The Stanford encyclopedia of philosophy.* Retrieved from http://plato.stanford.edu/archives/fall2011/entries/happiness

Headey, B. (2008). Life goals matter to happiness: A revision of set-point theory. *Social Indicators Research, 86*, 213–231.

Health and Retirement Study (1992a). *Health and Retirement Study codebook, 1992 (HRS 1), Section E, question V2616*. (n.d.). Retrieved from http://hrsonline.isr.umich.edu/modules/meta/1992/core/codebook/09_e.htm

Health and Retirement Study (1992b). *Health and Retirement Study codebook, 1992 (HRS 1), Section E, question V2617*. (n.d.). Retrieved from http://hrsonline.isr.umich.edu/modules/meta/1992/core/codebook/09_e.htm

Health and Retirement Study (1992c). *Health and Retirement Study codebook, 1992 (HRS 1), Section E, questions V2608 through V2617*. (n.d.). Retrieved from http://hrsonline.isr.umich.edu/modules/meta/1992/core/codebook/09_e.htm

Health and Retirement Study (2004). *Health and Retirement Study codebook, 2004 HRS Core, Section C, question JC001*. (n.d.). Retrieved from http://hrsonline.isr.umich.edu/modules/meta/2004/core/codebook/h04c_ri.htm

Heath, D. (1974). Developmental continuity or crisis? [Review of the book *Five lives at Harvard: Personality change during college*, by S. H. King.] *Contemporary Psychology: APA Review of Books, 19*(10), 696–697.

Holahan, C. K., Sears, R. R., & Cronbach, L. J. (1995). *The gifted group in later maturity*. Stanford, CA: Stanford University Press.

Jahoda, M. (1958). *Current concepts of positive mental health*. New York: Basic Books.

Jenkins, C. D. (1958). *A judgmental scale of family conflict*. Unpublished materials, Boston University.

John, O. P., & Srivastava, S. (1999). The big-five trait taxonomy: History, measurement, and theoretical perspectives. In L. A. Pervin & O. P. John (Eds.), *Handbook of personality: Theory and research* (Vol. 2, pp. 102–138). New York: Guilford Press.

Johnson, J. H., Null, C., Butcher, J. N., & Johnson, K. N. (1984). Replicated item level factor analysis of the full MMPI. *Journal of Personality and Social Psychology, 47*(1), 105–114.

Johnson, T., & Fendrich, M. (2002). A validation of the Crowne-Marlowe Social Desirability scale. *57th Annual Meeting of the American Association for Public Opinion Research*, St. Pete Beach, FL. Retrieved from http://www.srl.uic.edu/publist/Conference/crownemarlowe.pdf

Josselson, R. (1993). A narrative introduction. In R. Josselson & A. Lieblich (Eds.), *The narrative study of lives* (pp. ix–xv). London: Sage.

Juster, F. T., & Suzman, R. (1995). An overview of the Health and Retirement study. *Journal of Human Resources, 30 (Suppl.)*, S7–S56.

Kahneman, D., & Deaton, A. (2010). High income improves evaluation of life but not emotional well-being. *Proceedings of the National Academy of Sciences, 107*(38), 16489–16493.

Kahneman, D., Diener, E., & Schwarz, N. (Eds.). (1999). *Well-being: The foundations of hedonic psychology*. New York: Russell Sage Foundation.

Kaplan, H. I., & Sadock, B. J. (1998). *Synopsis of psychiatry: Behavioral sciences, clinical psychiatry* (8th ed.). Baltimore: Lippincott, Williams, & Wilkins.

Kashdan, T. B., Biswas-Diener, R., & King, L. A. (2008). Reconsidering happiness: the costs of distinguishing between hedonics and eudaimonia. *Journal of Positive Psychology, 3*(4), 219–233.

Kasser, T. (2002). *The high price of materialism*. Cambridge, MA: MIT Press.

Keul, L. (2004, June 14). Personal conversation.

King, S. H. (1973). *Five lives at Harvard: Personality change during college.* Cambridge, MA: Harvard University Press.

Kozma, A., & Stones, M. J. (1987). Social desirability in measures of subjective well-being: a systematic evaluation. *Journal of Gerontology, 42*(1), 56–59.

Larsen, R. J., Diener, E., & Emmons, R. A. (1985). An evaluation of subjective well-being measures. *Social Indicators Research, 17,* 1–18.

Lawton, M. P. (1972). The dimensions of morale. In D. Kent, R. Kastenbaum, & S. Sherwood (Eds.), *Research, planning and action for the elderly* (pp. 144–165). New York: Behavioral Publications.

Lawton, M. P. (1975). The Philadelphia Geriatric Center Morale scale: A revision. *Journal of Gerontology, 30*(1), 85–89.

Levinson, D. J. (1978). *The seasons of a man's life.* New York: Knopf.

Libran, E. (2006). Personality dimensions and subjective well-being. *Spanish Journal of Psychology, 9*(1), 38–44.

Lucas, R. E. (2008). Personality and subjective well-being. In J. Larsen & M. Eid (Eds.), *The science of subjective well-being* (pp. 171–194). New York: Guilford Press.

Lucas, R. E., Clark, A. E., Georgellis, Y., & Diener, E. (2003). Reexamining adaptation and the set point model of happiness: Reactions to changes in marital status. *Journal of Personality and Social Psychology, 84,* 527–539.

Lucas, R. E., & Diener, E. (2015). Personality and subjective well-being: Current issues and controversies. In M. Mikulincer, P. R. Shaver, M. L. Cooper, & R. J. Larsen (Eds.), *APA handbook of personality and social psychology, Vol. 4. Personality processes and individual differences* (pp. 577–599). Washington, DC: American Psychological Association.

Lykken, D. T. (1999). *Happiness: What studies on twins show us about nature, nurture, and the happiness set-point.* New York: Golden Books.

Lykken, D. T., & Tellegen, A. (1996). Happiness is a stochastic phenomenon. *Psychological Science, 7*(3), 186–189.

Lyubomirsky, S. (2001). Why are some people happier than others? The role of cognitive and motivational processes in well-being. *American Psychologist, 56,* 239–249.

Lyubomirsky, S. (2007). *The how of happiness: A new approach to getting the life you want.* New York: Penguin Press.

McAdams, D. P. (1985). *Power, intimacy, and the life story: inquiries into identity.* New York: Guilford Press.

McAdams, D. P. (1992). The five-factor model in personality: A critical appraisal. *Journal of Personality, 60*(2), 329–361.

McAdams, D. P. (1993). *The stories we live by: Personal myths and the making of the self.* New York: Morrow.

McAdams, D. P. (1994). Can personality change? Levels of stability and growth in personality across the lifespan. In T. Heatherton & J. Weinberger (Eds.), *Can personality change?* (pp. 299–313). Washington, DC: American Psychological Association Press.

McAdams, D. P. (1995). What do we know when we know a person? *Journal of Personality, 63*(3), 365–396.

McAdams, D. P. (1996). Personality, modernity, and the storied self: A contemporary framework for studying persons. *Psychological Inquiry, 7,* 295–321.

McAdams, D. P. (2001). The psychology of life stories. *Review of General Psychology, 5*, 100–122.

McAdams, D. P. (2008a). Foreword. In H. A. Murray, *Explorations in personality* (70th Anniversary Edition (reissue of 1938 Edition), pp. viii–xxxv). New York: Oxford University Press.

McAdams, D. P. (2008b). *The life story interview.* Retrieved from http://www.sesp.northwestern.edu/foley/instruments/interview/

McAdams, D. P. (2008c). Personal narratives and the life story. In O. P. John, R. W. Robins, & L. A. Pervin (Eds.), *Handbook of personality: Theory and research* (3rd ed., pp. 241–261). New York: Guilford Press.

McAdams, D. P., & Pals, J. L. (2006). A new big five: Fundamental principles for an integrative science of personality. *American Psychologist, 61*(3), 204–217.

McAdams, D. P., & Pals, J. L. (2007). The role of theory in personality research. In R. Robins, C. Fraley & R. Krueger (Eds.), *Handbook of research methods in personality psychology* (pp. 3–20). New York: Guilford Press.

McAdams, D. P., Anyidoho, N. A., Brown, C., Huang, Y. T., Kaplan, B., & Machado, M. A. (2004). Traits and stories: Links between dispositional and narrative features of personality. *Journal of Personality, 72*, 761–784.

McAdams, D. P., Bauer, J. J., Sakaeda, A., Anyidoho, N. A., Machado, M. A., . . . Magrino, K. (2006). Continuity and change in the life story: A longitudinal study of autobiographical memories in emerging adulthood. *Journal of Personality, 74*, 1371–1400.

McAdams, D. P., Reynolds, J., Lewis, M., Patten, A., & Bowman, P. J. (2001). When bad things turn good and good things turn bad: Sequences of redemption and contamination in life narrative, and their relation to psychosocial adaptation in midlife and in students. *Personality and Social Psychology Bulletin, 27*, 208–230.

McArthur, C. C., & King, S. H. (1992). *Harvard Student Study, 1960–1964.* Henry A. Murray Research Archives, Institute for Quantitative Social Science, Harvard University.

McCrae, R. R. (1986). Well-being scales do not measure social desirability. *Journal of Gerontology, 41*, 390–392.

McCrae, R. R., & Costa, P. T. (1983). Social desirability scales: More substance than style. *Journal of Consulting and Clinical Psychology, 51*, 882–888.

McCrae, R. R., & Costa, P. T. (1987). Validation of the five-factor model of personality across instruments and observers. *Journal of Personality and Social Psychology, 52*, 81–90.

McCrae, R. R., & Costa, P. T. (1997). Personality trait structure as a human universal. *American Psychologist, 52*, 509–516.

McCrae, R. & Costa, P. (1999). The five-factor theory of personality. In L. Pervin & O. John (Eds.), *Handbook of personality: Theory and research* (2nd ed., pp. 139–153). New York: Guilford.

McCrae, R., & Costa, P. (2002). *Personality in adulthood: A five-factor theory perspective* (2nd ed.). New York: Guilford.

Meehl, P. E., & Hathaway, S. R. (1946). The K factor as a suppressor variable in the MMPI. *Journal of Applied Psychology, 30*, 525–564.

Moore, B. E. & Fine, B. D. (1990). *Psychoanalytic terms and concepts.* New Haven, CT: Yale University Press.

Murray, H. A. (1938). *Explorations in personality: A clinical and experimental study of fifty men of college age.* New York: Oxford University Press.

Murray, H. A. (1943). *Thematic Apperception Test: TAT.* Cambridge, MA: Harvard University Press.

Nakao, K. & Treas, J. (1990). *Computing 1989 occupational prestige scores* [GSS Methodological Report No. 70]. Chicago: National Opinion Research Center.

Nakao, K., Hodge, R. W., & Treas, J. (1990). *On revising prestige scores for all occupations.* [GSS Methodological Report No. 69]. Chicago: National Opinion Research Center.

NORC (National Opinion Research Center). (1989). GSS Codebook, Appendix G: Prestige Scores and Socioeconomic Index (SEI) Distributions. Retrieved from http://publicdata .norc.org/GSS/DOCUMENTS/BOOK/GSS_Codebook_AppendixG.pdf

NORC (National Opinion Research Center). (2010). GSS codebook, appendix F: Distributions. Occupational classification. Retrieved from http://publicdata.norc.org/GSS /DOCUMENTS/BOOK/GSS_Codebook_AppendixF.pdf

Neugarten, B. L. (1996a). Personality and the aging process. In B. L. Neugarten & D. A. Neugarten (Eds.), *The meanings of age: Selected papers of Bernice L. Neugarten* (pp. 270–80). Chicago: University of Chicago Press.

Neugarten, B. L. (1996b). The changing meanings of age. In B. L. Neugarten & D. A. Neugarten (Eds.), *The meanings of age: Selected papers of Bernice L. Neugarten* (pp. 72–77). Chicago: University of Chicago Press.

Neugarten, B. L., Havighurst, R. J., & Tobin, S. S. (1961). The measurement of life satisfaction. *Journal of Gerontology, 16*(2), 134–143.

Nickerson, C., Schwarz, N., Diener, E., & Kahneman, D. (2003). Zeroing in on the dark side of the American dream: A closer look at the negative consequences of the goal for financial success. *Psychological Science, 14,* 531–536.

Ogilvie, D. M. (2004). *Fantasies of flight.* New York: Oxford University Press.

Osherson, S. D. (1980). *Holding on or letting go: Men and career change at midlife.* New York: Free Press.

Osherson, S. D. (1986). *Finding our fathers: The unfinished business of manhood.* New York: Free Press.

Osherson, S. D. (1992). *Patterns of Midlife Career Development Project, 1977–1980.* Henry A. Murray Research Archives, Institute for Quantitative Social Science, Harvard University.

Osherson, S. D., & Dill, D. (1983). Varying work and family choices: Their impact on men's work satisfaction. *Journal of Marriage and the Family, 45*(2), 339–346.

Paulhus, D. L. (1984). Two-component models of socially desirable responding. *Journal of Personality and Social Psychology, 46,* 598–609.

Paulhus, D. L. (1991). Measurement and control of response bias. In J. P. Robinson, P. R. Shaver, & L. S. Wrightsman (Eds.), *Measures of personality and social psychological attitudes* (pp. 17–59). San Diego: Academic Press, 1991.

Pavot, W., & Diener, E. (1993). Review of the Satisfaction with Life Scale. *Psychological Assessment, 5,* 164–172.

Pavot, W., & Diener, E. (2011). Personality and happiness: Predicting the experience of subjective well-being. In T. Chamorro-Premuzic, S. von Stumm, & A. Furnham (Eds.),

The Wiley Blackwell handbook of individual differences (pp. 699–717). Oxford: Wiley Blackwell, 2015.

Pavot, W., & Diener, E. (2013). Happiness experienced: The science of subjective well-being. In S. A. David, I. Boniwell, & A. C. Ayers (Eds.), *The Oxford handbook of happiness* (pp. 134–151). New York: Oxford University Press.

Peterson, W. A., & Mangen, D. J. (1982). *Research instruments in social gerontology, Vol. 1, Clinical and Social Psychology*. Minneapolis: University of Minnesota Press.

Ponocny, I., Weismayer, C., Stross, B., & Dressler, S. G. (2016). Are most people happy? Exploring the meaning of subjective well-being ratings. *Journal of Happiness Studies, 17*(6), 2635–2653.

Radloff, L. S. (1977). The CES-D scale: A self-report depression scale for research in the general population. *Applied Psychological Measurement, 1*, 385–401.

Ray, J., & Kafka, S. (2014). Life in college matters for life after college. Retrieved from http://www.gallup.com/poll/168848/life-college-matters-lifecollege.aspx

Roberts, B. (2003). Personality trait development in adulthood. In J. T. Mortimer & M. J. Shanahan (Eds.), *Handbook of the life course* (pp. 579–598). New York: Kluwer Academic / Plenum Publishers.

Rosenberg, M. (1965). *Society and the adolescent self-image*. Princeton, NJ: Princeton University Press.

Røysamb, E., Harris, J. R., Magnus, P., Vittersø, J., & Tambs, K. (2002). Subjective well-being: Sex-specific effects of genetic and environmental factors. *Personality and Individual Differences, 32*(2), 211–223.

Russell, P. L. (2006). Trauma, repetition and affect. *Contemporary Psychoanalysis, 42*, 601–620.

Ryff, C. (1989). Happiness is everything, or is it? Explorations on the meaning of psychological well-being. *Journal of Personality and Social Psychology, 57*, 1069–1081.

Ryff, C. D., & Keyes, C. L. (1995). The structure of psychological well-being revisited. *Journal of Personality and Social Psychology, 69*, 719–727.

Sarbin, T. R. (Ed.). (1986). *Narrative psychology: The storied nature of human conduct*. New York: Praeger.

Schafer, R. (1994). *Retelling a life: Narration and dialogue in psychoanalysis*. New York: Basic Books.

Schwartz, J. (1996). Current conceptual models and considerations from a behavioral medicine perspective. *Journal of Occupational Health Psychology, 1*, 287–310.

Schwarz, N., & Clore, G. L. (1983). Mood, misattribution, and judgments of well-being: Informative and directive functions of affective states. *Journal of Personality and Social Psychology, 45*, 513–523.

Schwarz, N. & Strack, F. (1999). Reports of subjective well-being: Judgmental processes and their methodological implications. In E. Kahneman, E. Diener, & N. Schwarz (Eds.), *Well-being: The foundations of hedonic psychology* (pp. 61–84). New York: Russell Sage Foundation.

Seligman, M. E. (2011). *Flourish: A visionary new understanding of happiness and well-being*. New York: Free Press.

Singer, J. A. (1995). Seeing one's self: Locating narrative memory in a framework of personality. *Journal of Personality, 63*, 429–457.

Singer, J. A., & Salovey, P. (1993). *The remembered self.* New York: Free Press.

Shrout, P. E., & Fleiss, J. L. (1979). Intraclass correlations: Uses in assessing rater reliability. *Psychological Bulletin, 86*(2), 420–428.

Smith, Tom W., Marsden, P., Hout, M., & Kim, J. General Social Surveys (1972–2016) [machine-readable data file]. Principal Investigator, Tom W. Smith; Co-Principal Investigator, Peter V. Marsden; Co-Principal Investigator, Michael Hout; Sponsored by National Science Foundation. NORC ed. Chicago: NORC at the University of Chicago [producer and distributor]. Data retrieved from the GSS Data Explorer website at gssdataexplorer .norc.org.

Solberg, E. G., Diener, E., & Robinson, M. D. (2004). Why are materialists less satisfied? In T. Kasser & A. D. Kanner (Eds.), *Psychology and consumer culture: the struggle for a good life in a materialistic world.* (pp. 29–48). Washington, DC: American Psychological Association.

Steel, P., Schmidt, J., & Shultz, J. (2008). Refining the relationship between personality and subjective well-being. *Psychological Bulletin, 134*(1), 138–161.

Stubbe, J. H., Posthuma, D., Boomsma, D. I., & De Geus, E. J. C. (2005). Heritability of life satisfaction in adults: A twin-family study. *Psychological Medicine, 35*(11), 1581–1588.

Tellegen, A., Lykken, D. T., Bouchard, T. J., Wilcox, K., Segal, N., & Rich, S. (1988). Personality similarity in twins reared apart and together. *Journal of Personality and Social Psychology, 54*, 1031–1039.

Vaillant, G. E. (1974). Natural history of male psychological health, II: Some antecedents of healthy adult adjustment. *Archives of General Psychiatry, 31*, 15–22.

Vaillant, G. E. (1975). Natural history of male psychological health, III: Empirical dimensions of mental health. *Archives of General Psychology, 32*, 420–426.

Vaillant, G. E. (1976). Natural history of male psychological health, V: The relationship of choice of ego mechanisms of self-defense to adult adjustment. *Archives of General Psychology, 33*, 535–545.

Vaillant, G. E. (1977). *Adaptation to life.* Cambridge, MA: Harvard University Press.

Vaillant, G. E. (1990). Avoiding negative life outcomes: Evidence from a forty-five year study. In P. B. Baltes & M. M. Baltes (Eds.), *Successful aging: Perspectives from the behavioral sciences* (pp. 332–358). Cambridge: Cambridge University Press.

Vaillant, G. E. (1994). Ego mechanisms of defense and personality psychopathy. *Journal of Abnormal Psychology, 103*, 44–50.

Vaillant, G. E. (2002). *Aging well: Surprising guideposts to a happier life from the landmark Harvard study of adult development.* Boston: Little, Brown.

Vaillant, G. E. (2012). *Triumphs of experience: The men of the Harvard Grant study.* Cambridge, MA: Belknap Press of the Harvard University Press.

Vaillant, G. E., Bond, M., & Vaillant, C. O. (1986). An empirically validated hierarchy of defense mechanisms. *Archives of General Psychiatry, 73*, 786–794.

Vaillant, G. E., & Vaillant, C. O. (1990). Natural study of male psychological health, XII: A 45-year study of predictors of successful aging at age 65. *American Journal of Psychiatry, 147*(1), 31–37.

Van Boven, L. (2005). Experientialism, materialism, and the pursuit of happiness. *Review of General Psychology, 9*(2), 132–142.

Van Manen, M. (1990). *Researching lived experience: Human science for an action sensitive pedagogy.* Albany: State University of New York Press.

Waite, L. (2005, March). Personal conversation.

Wallace, R. B., & Herzog, A. R. (1995). Overview of the health measures in the Health and Retirement Study. *Journal of Human Resources, 30* [Special Issue on the Health and Retirement Study: Data quality and early results], S84–S107.

Waters, E., & Sroufe, L. A. (1983). Social competence as a developmental construct. *Developmental Review, 3*(1), 79–97.

Westen, D. (1998). The scientific legacy of Sigmund Freud: Toward a psychodynamically informed psychological science. *Psychological Bulletin, 124*(3), 333–371.

White, R. W. (1952). *Lives in progress: A study of the natural growth of personality* (1st ed.). New York: Dryden Press.

White, R. W. (1975). *Lives in progress: a study of the natural growth of personality* (3rd ed.). New York: Holt, Rinehart & Winston.

Whiteley, J. M. (1976). [Review of the book *Five lives at Harvard: Personality change during college*, by Stanley H. King]. *American Journal of Psychiatry, 133*, 3.

Yap, S. C. Y., Anusic, I., & Lucas, R. E. (2014). Does happiness change? Evidence from longitudinal studies. In K. M. Sheldon & R. E. Lucas (Eds.), *Stability of happiness: Theories and evidence on whether happiness can change* (pp. 127–145). San Diego: Elsevier Academic Press.

83; as exemplar of intrapsychic darkness, 15, 18–27, 29, 31, 39–41, 66–71, 74, 90–91, 93, 94, 97–98, 103, 107–9, 111–13, 147, 162, 188, 207, 214, 224, 251n4; as exemplar of stability, 15, 18–27, 28–29, 39–41, 47, 73, 74, 87, 90–91, 93, 94, 97–98, 103, 107–9, 111–13, 214, 224, 251n4; leakage in clinical life history interviews, 21, 59, 67, 69–70, 72, 75–76, 81, 188–89, 192–98; and self-repair, 72–73, 75–76, 103–8, 112–14

McAdams, D. P., 209–10, 219, 250n10, 254n2, 258n3. *See also* life story: and model of identity (McAdams's model)

McArthur, Charles C., ix, 9, 219, 227, 230, 249n3

measures. *See* variables and measures

mental health, 9, 26, 51, 57, 74, 76, 82, 171–72, 185, 202, 205, 216, 232, 238–39, 244, 250n9; and career failure, 164–68; psychiatric intervention and, 123–28, 179–80, 238

Minnesota Multiphasic Personality Inventory (MMPI): Family Conflict subscale, 247–48; K scale, 80, 81, 85, 122, 191, 238, 240, 242, 254n11; Neuroticism scale, 122, 238; Si scale, 122, 238

models of development. *See* change, longitudinal trajectory of; human development; stability, longitudinal trajectory of

Murray, Henry A., 10, 11, 249n7

Murray Research Center. *See* Henry A. Murray Research Center

narrative identity. *See* identity: narrative

narrative study of lives. *See* study of lives (research tradition)

Neugarten, B. L., 25, 52, 190, 204, 258n2

neuroticism (personality trait), 5, 118, 122, 125, 126, 128, 130–34, 238. *See also* five-factor model of personality

Osherson, Samuel D., 9, 219, 249n6

Payne, Robert, participant (pseudonym): and adult rating of intrapsychic brightness and

darkness, 77; and college rating of intrapsychic brightness and darkness, 83; as exemplar of affect elaboration, 29, 43–45; as exemplar of intrapsychic brightness, 29, 41, 43–45, 56, 71, 87, 109–10, 112–13, 114–15, 162, 224; as exemplar of stability, 29, 47, 87, 109–10, 112–13, 114–15, 224

personality psychology, xv, 10–11, 209. *See also* study of lives (research tradition)

personality traits, 2, 118, 122, 124–28, 130–34, 179–80; in college, 238. *See also* five-factor model of personality; *and specific trait(s)*

professional success. *See* career success

psychiatric illness. *See* mental health

psychobiographical sketches: summary of, 223–24; use of, xiv, 23, 25, 55, 74, 81, 85, 90, 93, 102–3, 147, 200, 218, 233–34, 251n2, 251n3, 251n4. *See also* Costa, Vincent, participant (pseudonym); Fisher, Joseph, participant (pseudonym); Hovanec, William, participant (pseudonym); Hoyt, Lawrence, participant (pseudonym); Martin, David, participant (pseudonym); Payne, Robert, participant (pseudonym); Russo, Louis, participant (pseudonym)

psychological well-being, 51, 258n3. *See also* happiness, scientific study of

REL. *See* Remembered Early Life (REL)

relative stability. *See* stability, longitudinal trajectory of

Remembered Early Life (REL): aspects appearing in interviews, 243–45, 254n2, 255n6; and development, 89, 93–99, 102–15, 116–20, 122, 124–34, 138–42, 146–49, 153–54, 156, 161, 202, 255n4; and identity story, 89, 93–99, 102–15, 116–17, 124, 146–49, 153, 178, 202–3, 254n2, 255n6; social sites of (concentric circles), 96–98, 147, 245–48, 255n6. *See also* Remembered Early Life (REL) Affect; Remembered Early Life (REL) Affect Scale

Remembered Early Life (REL) Affect, 116–18, 120, 124–34, 169, 170, 176–77, 179, 180,